ABOUT THE AUTHOR

Kye Printup

Katherine Gustafson is an award-winning writer, journalist, and editor whose articles, essays, and stories have been published in numerous print and online media, including *The Christian Science Monitor, Slate,* and *The Best Women's Travel Writing*. She has written about sustainable food for *Yes!* magazine, *The Huffington Post, Civil Eats,* Change.org, and *Tonic*. She lives with her husband in the Washington, D.C., area. Visit her on the Web at www.katherine gustafston.com.

CHANGE
COMES TO
DINNER

How Vertical Farmers, Urban Growers,
and Other Innovators Are Revolutionizing
How America Eats

KATHERINE GUSTAFSON

St. Martin's Griffin
New York

www.stmartins.com

Design by Steven Seighman

ISBN 978-0-312-57737-7 (trade paperback)
ISBN 978-1-4668-0241-4 (e-book)

First Edition: May 2012

10 9 8 7 6 5 4 3 2 1

For Aaron

CONTENTS

INTRODUCTION

Our Country Deserves Better Than Cheetos

IT ALL STARTED WITH BEANS.

That may seem like an unsexy way to begin (why not, you might ask, start with a pork tenderloin or a piece of chocolate cake?), but the beans I'm talking about are no ordinary beans.

Soaked overnight and simmered for four hours with star anise, a bay leaf, and a cinnamon stick, then flavored with a shake of salt and a dash of pepper, they are like nothing you've ever tasted. These beans are to the standard canned burrito-filler what steak is to Spam. Not since Jack and his stalk has a lowly legume made someone so quickly sit up and take notice.

While in my case there were no golden eggs involved, there nonetheless seemed to be something magical going on. How else could a food that I had always thought of as a necessary but uninspiring foundation for five-layer dip suddenly transform itself into something so utterly delicious you could eat it on its own for dinner? Not only that, but these beans had a name straight out of a fairy tale: Good Mother Stallard. Wasn't that the name of the old woman who lived in the shoe?

The Good Mother Stallard beans—their taste and their name and their amazing ability to completely satisfy my appetite—came to me like a revelation. That is, after they came to me dried from Napa, California, a one-pound bag of purple-and-white pebbles shipped in a cardboard box from a company called Rancho Gordo New World Specialty Food.

I had ordered them after reading about the company in *The Washington Post,* where food columnist Kim O'Donnel had written, "I urge bean lovers across America to explore the world of heirloom beans—older, wiser, and brimming with personality." While I was no bean lover—or so I thought—I was curious. How could a bean be construed to have the characteristics of my grandmother? And speaking of grandmothers, what in the world was an heirloom bean?

I pictured a bean-shaped locket hanging around my neck on a chain. Or a tarnished, old ring topped by a bean instead of a precious stone. The idea struck me as a doorway into a foreign world.

I grew up in a household where, as the saying goes, we ate to live, not lived to eat. We did not regard food as something that deserved over-much attention or effort. We ate home-cooked meals that always included vegetables of some kind, so we were a far cry from the modern fast-food-munching families bemoaned so extensively in today's media. But just the same, it never occurred to us to object to the tastelessness of the canned beans and out-of-season hothouse tomatoes we ate or to wonder how and at what cost they had been created. My main food-related concern as a child, as I remember, was how many helpings of ice cream I could finagle out of the babysitter.

It was the '80s and the '90s. My mother, charged with food preparation for the household, was an on-the-fly chef whose meals tended toward the simple meat-potatoes-veg trios of American tradition. She had little patience for elaborate recipes and unusual methods. While she did occasionally use a pressure cooker—the steaming climax of which would send me skittering away from the stove in thrilled terror as a child—and, impressively, made her own tortillas with a proper tortilla press when it was taco night, she did not embrace the finicky routines of our electric bread maker, which sat unused in the closet under the stairs for years, or our shelf full of cookbooks, which went by and large overlooked in favor of more . . . shall we say, "impressionistic" methods.

Cooking was not, she believed, something that should take up any more time than it absolutely had to. She had grown up in an era in which food had come to be ruled by convenience. Post-war homemakers like her mother saw high-priced modern developments—store-bought canned vegetables, frozen dinners, packaged snack foods—as not only labor-saving conveniences in the years after victory gardens had demanded much time and effort, but also the height of modernity and cosmopolitanism. *The Can-Opener Cookbook* became a bestseller upon publication in 1952, and the first electric can opener burst onto the U.S. market in 1956. My mother's youth coincided with the heyday of tuna casserole, canned soup, and TV dinners. Hers was a world of Chef Boyardee, Rice-A-Roni, Cheez Whiz, and Chex Mix.

It is no wonder, then, that at the dinner table of my childhood our salads were composed of crisp white wings of iceberg lettuce, our bread was Wonder Bread with the texture of a napkin, and our mashed potatoes were sometimes made from powdered mixes. To a child of midtwentieth-century America, this was simply standard fare.

My mother, I should note, who now in retirement regularly cooks Afghani *pulao* and whips up lentil soups from scratch, strenuously denies being so convenience-oriented as to stoop to powdered potatoes. However, I believe she doth protest too much. A conversation with her on this topic went like this:

Me: Is it true that you used to make our mashed potatoes from a powdered mix?

Her: Absolutely not! I *hated* that stuff! I always made them from scratch! It was my mother who loved that stuff.

Me: Really? Because I totally remember that. Are you sure?

Her (sheepishly, laughing): Well, no.

I don't mean to imply that my mother was not working hard or that she did not produce tasty and nutritious meals for her family. We had meats and fishes; we had vegetables and fruits; we even had real mashed potatoes on many occasions. She was a dogged producer in the kitchen, turning out meal after meal, night after night, and we always sat down to family dinner, sometimes even with candles burning.

But the point is that I grew up with the foodways that had been passed down to my parents, which were the ways of the industrialized world. People of their generation likely had family members—grandparents perhaps—who were involved in agriculture, so that farming was not a forbiddingly foreign concept, yet they grew up by and large as the guinea pigs of new, industrial food production methods. Their children—me, my siblings, and our peers, one more generation removed from farms and fields—were solidly ensnared in the corporate net. I am, I would venture to say, part of the first American generation whose entire experience of food has been mediated by the industrially supplied grocery store.

As a child, I had little idea where much of my food came from, and no one ever told me I should. I was amazed to discover that nuts sprout from trees, melons grow along the ground, raisins are dried grapes, and anybody can make pie crust in his or her own kitchen. As an adult, learning how to make bread by hand was an accomplishment that felt like breaking some kind of time-space continuum. For centuries, all over the world, people had been baking bread from scratch with little fanfare, as if the mysterious and complex process of kneading and rising and baking were not a potent and miraculous form of magic. It seemed hard to believe.

I was, apparently, more or less an ignoramus about food, and with that background to rely on, it was no wonder that I had no idea what the puzzling word "heirloom" referred to in relation to beans. A little research taught me that one of the impacts of our industrially mediated lives is that the number of plant and animal species under cultivation has been steadily dwindling for decades. As our country's patchwork of small and medium-sized farms has consolidated into larger and larger enterprises, each designed to produce one or just a few commodities, it has become inefficient to nurture a wide variety of crops and livestock.

Commercial agribusiness favors those few varieties of fruits, vegetables, and grains that can produce high yields, grow quickly, resist pests, and be transported without bruising, even if it means sacrificing taste, quality, nutrition, and diversity. In fact diversity is something most large commercial farms seem to have never heard of; they tend to grow vast fields of a single crop year after year, relying on chemical inputs, new hybrid varieties, and extremely mechanized production to keep up yields and discourage pests and disease in the increasingly degraded soils. The few varieties of crops that can thrive in such environments get the seal of approval from our commercial farming system.

But the biggest winners of all in the cultivation sweepstakes are those crops that can be used to create higher-value products such as meat and processed snack foods. Corn and soy, each occupying about 73 million acres of U.S. cropland, are the reigning monarchs of this upside down world in which the vast majority of the crops we grow are not meant for direct human consumption. This is a trend that started in—you guessed it—the 1950s, when my mother's generation was happily sitting down to frosted meatloaf made with cornflakes, ketchup, and canned tomato soup. From there, it's just a hop, skip, and a jump to Cheez Whiz and Chex Mix.

In 2000, U.S. farms produced 10 billion bushels of the world's total 23 billion bushels of corn, and 80 percent of that U.S. share went to feed domestic and overseas livestock, poultry, and fish. Tons more went to construct our processed snack foods, supply our soda machines with high-fructose corn syrup, and supplement our gasoline with ethanol. Our soybean production, meanwhile, accounting for more than half of the world's soy, also contributes to animal feed and produces soybean oil, which is used in food manufacturing and cooking, but also in such unlikely products as anticorrosion agents and waterproof cement. All the high-profit uses for these crops, combined with the completely incomprehensible government subsidization of their large-scale production, mean that these crops are flat-out taking over like some kind of invading army. On much of our country's farmland, the motto seems to be, "Grow corn and soy or go home."

In this monoculture-based, corn-and-soy-loving environment, many crops of all kinds are ignored and thereby sent spiraling rapidly toward endangerment and eventual extinction. Throughout history humans have eaten several thousand plant species, but today around the world we depend heavily on only 150 species, get 90 percent of our food from a mere 15 of them—rice, wheat, corn, sorghum, millet, rye, barley, cassava, sweet potato, potato, coconut, banana, common bean, soybean, and peanut—and obtain over half our calories and protein from just three: rice, corn, and wheat. Approximately 75 percent of the genetic diversity in the world's agricultural crop supply has disappeared since the beginning of the last century.

The terms "heirloom" and, alternately, "heritage" refer to species that have fallen out of widespread cultivation after having long served as tried-and-true standbys of the agricultural landscape. While there is no standard definition of "heirloom," there is general consensus that these seeds are open-pollinated, which means that they reproduce via natural processes and the seeds can be saved for use the following year. Many of the species we eat today are instead hybrid species produced through controlled cross-pollination, which requires human intervention and often prevents plants from reproducing new versions with the same characteristics. Farmers must purchase new seed every season to get the same results. This is a fact that came as a puzzling surprise to me, considering I've never grown so much as a tomato.

In this brave new agricultural world, hybrids bred to enable efficient and profitable industrial agriculture triumph (as do the seed companies that make them, but that's a story for another time). Meanwhile, species not deemed worthy of commercial cultivation, many of them heirlooms, struggle to retain a foothold on existence in small family farms and backyard kitchen gardens—and, it turns out, bean companies—around the country.

Our tendency to winnow the bounty of our agricultural universe down to a nub seems monumentally sad. We live in this vast and fascinating world but instead of celebrating it, we squash it under the enormous wheels of our industrial pesticide-spraying machines. And beyond that, it's dangerous. Genetic diversity among crops is essential to food security, since indigenous species adapted to certain landscapes are better able to resist disease, reproduce well, and withstand harsh conditions and poor-quality soils. Farmers who import seeds and breeds not as well adapted to their areas depend on more external inputs like fertilizers, pesticides, and irrigation, which limit their self-reliance and the fertility of their fields.

While it's not wise to grow things where they aren't supposed to be, it's also foolhardy to narrow down the number of species we're cultivating in any one place. As the Irish potato famine of the 1840s demonstrated, monoculture is an unbelievably stupid idea. One in eight Irish people died when the single species of potato they depended on, known as the "lumper," developed a rot that turned them all to slime. If the potato fields had contained even a modicum of diversity—with some "plumpers" or "slumpers," say, mixed in—the disaster would not have been nearly so extreme.

So Rancho Gordo New World Specialty Food not only is growing the most delicious beans you'll ever eat, but is also increasing the food security of the American agricultural system. How many small businesses can say that? Started in 2001 by entrepreneur Steve Sando, the company focuses primarily on heirloom beans native to the Americas. Steve roams extensively through the markets of Central and South America searching for species he has never encountered before. The list of varieties he sells reads like the playbill of a strange carnival: Eye of the Goat, Vaquero, Yellow Indian Woman, Black Calypso, Sangre de Toro.

My discovery of Rancho Gordo inspired conflicting feelings. I alternated between despair that our food system has become so out of whack as to send anything as delicious as the Good Mother Stallard bean hurtling toward oblivion, and inspiration at the fact that somebody somewhere had taken it upon himself to stop that from happening.

Here was one brave soul standing up in his own small way for the rights of discerning eaters everywhere. Here was one individual who had declared, right in the glaring face of the all-powerful industrial monoliths that rule the way we eat, that there is value in diversity, that age-old species are worth saving and eating, that people deserve more than the tasteless schlock their corporate overlords deign to provide.

Here was a food visionary.

Closing my lips around a divine forkful of Rancho Gordo beans,

I felt a strange upwelling in my heart, a pale emotion trembling in the face of my natural pessimism: hope. If people like Steve Sando are out there, designing innovative business plans and launching exciting projects to reinvigorate the better angels of our food universe, maybe there's hope for us yet.

Hope is essential because the loss of biological diversity Rancho Gordo works against is but a garnish on top of a smorgasbord of woes served up by the industrial production system that supplies the vast majority of food in the United States. The already-terrible, ever-worsening litany of concerns about that system includes the following alarming items—by no means an exhaustive list—each a rolling disaster in itself.

We have fewer and fewer farms and farmers. In the last two decades, the number of farms in the United States has declined by 63 percent while the average farm has gotten 67 percent larger, meaning more vast fields of one crop requiring more petrochemical pesticides and fertilizers, more erosion, and an increasingly anonymous and opaque food system. Residential and commercial development is rapidly overtaking farmland close to cities, which disadvantages small farms and ensures that food must be trucked long distances. Meanwhile, 40 percent of U.S. farmers are age fifty-five or older, and over 90 percent of them have to take off-farm income to make ends meet or secure health insurance. (Compare the latter figure to the 54 percent of farmers who pursued off-farm income in 1970 and the 30 percent who did in 1930.) While the number of small farms is growing, there are not enough young farmers to replace our aging agriculturalists.

Chemical pesticides and GMOs are everywhere. Chemical pesticides, which impact human nervous and endocrine systems, irritate skin and eyes, and likely increase risk of cancer, have collected in measurable amounts in water supplies around the world. According to data collected by the U.S. Department of Agriculture (USDA), pesticide use has increased by 383 million pounds since genetically modified organisms' (GMOs) commercial introduction thirteen years ago. Still, an estimated 70 to 75 percent of the processed foods in U.S. grocery stores contain GMOs, despite not being labeled as such, even though there remains no scientific consensus on whether these are safe for human consumption.

The food we make is killing us. In 2009, the USDA issued almost sixty recalls of contaminated foods, and cases of people being sickened by pathogen-laced meats and vegetables are regularly in the news. The megafarms on which we produce most of our meat keep animals in unsanitary, overcrowded conditions that make the animals ill, which raises the likelihood of meat contamination. An estimated 70 percent of the antibiotics administered in the United States go to animals on industrial farms to make them grow faster and prevent sickness. Such long-term, low-dose use of antibiotics in food animals inspires the emergence of drug-resistant bacteria that threaten human health. And, eating a diet high in processed foods, 67 percent of Americans age twenty or over are overweight or obese, as are 25 percent of children nineteen and under.

The dispiriting reality of the industrial food system has been well documented in scores of recent books, such as *The Omnivore's Dilemma* and *Fast Food Nation,* as well as in movies like *Food, Inc., Supersize Me,* and *King Corn.* The majority of these will make you want to chuck it all and open a bag of Cheetos on the principle that we're all doomed anyway, so you might as well enjoy your last few years with the taste of cheesy-atomic-orange delight on your tongue. (Secret, shameful fact about the author: irredeemable love for the Cheeto. Oh, the nuclear orange vibrancy; the solid, unnatural crunch; the cheesetastic, salt-lick taste! I maintain that I am an innocent victim of their insidious charms: researchers have now proven that such processed foods are addictive, just like cocaine and songs by Beyonce.)

As the grim reality of the industrial food system comes into focus, desperation and then depression set in among concerned denizens of our fair country. As a friend told me during a conversation about the topic, a frustrated pinch in her voice, "I'm so tired of doomsday accounts of how the world is coming to an end."

And as I started a gig as a writer on sustainable food for an activism website called Change.org, I could see what she meant. My first winter as a sustainable food blogger had me writing about childhood obesity and *E. coli*–laced beef and the Gulf of Mexico's dead zone the size of Rhode Island caused by petrochemical fertilizers running off our monstrous farms. My notes were riddled with soul-crushing words like "desertification," "contaminated groundwater," and "type 2 diabetes." With every new piece I wrote on GMOs taking over the world or pesticides infesting our strawberries or family farms falling prey to the gobbling maw of large scale operations, I felt my soul curl tighter and tighter into a fetal ball. My mind had started to turn the same bleak gray as the dull winter sky hovering outside the window.

But as I wrote, with the inspiration provided by Steve Sando at Rancho Gordo in mind, I kept a searching eye for the people who dared to strike out on their own to build a new vision of an alternative food universe. And all winter, one by one, the stories of these stalwart individuals working to create new options popped up in my writing like crocuses in a desiccated field. The more I looked, the more of them I found. As it turns out, they are everywhere, doing all manner of quirky and remarkable things. All around us, this country is in the midst of a transformation characterized by a swelling wave of inspiring, hopeful action to address how we grow, process, distribute, and eat our food.

In Virginia, an entrepreneur sells the products of local farms to city dwellers in an old school bus-cum-roving produce market. In Iowa, an extension agent helps retiring farmers pass their farms down to younger ones. In Missouri, an organization doubles the value of food stamps used at farmers' markets. In Arizona, a company develops a high-yield, low-risk method of growing food in shipping containers. In Washington State, a cooperative uses a mobile slaughterhouse to give small farmers access to needed facilities. And everywhere in between, other innovative enterprises, projects, and organizations are planting the seeds of a new agricultural reality, a vision based on old truths that might just save our country from itself.

There they were, the hopeful tales that those sensitive souls like my long-suffering friend crave. Their existence—indeed, their prevalence—was a breathtaking relief to me. If my readers wanted hope—if *I* needed hope—then hope was what I would supply. The clouds of winter cleared as I made a decision: I would go visit these brave, inspiring people and see for myself what we have to be glad about. I would choose a representative handful of these efforts and bring their stories to the people of this great country who are thirsting for good news. I had long known I wasn't cut out to be a muckraking journalist. Instead, I decided, I would go hoperaking. And with that, a springtime chorus of birds burst into song.

My hoperaking journey around the country took me to fifteen states and the District of Columbia, an absurd marathon filled with wheat fields, urban gardens, desert greenhouses, university cafeterias, hay bales, cherry tomatoes, and slaughtered lambs. In the next chapters I will drag you with me through every muddy field and bustling farmers' market to show you exactly what we have to be hopeful for and also to shed some small light on what a more sustainable U.S. food system might look like.

Whether you're looking for hope because you are an anticorporate crusader or an environmental watchdog or just a devotee of good food, let's agree to start this journey with the simple premise that our country deserves better than Cheetos, no matter how maddeningly delicious they are.

PART 1

LOCAL IS AS LOCAL DOES

CHAPTER 1

School Bus Farm Market

An unusual small business brings farm-fresh to the city

MY HOPERAKING JOURNEY BEGAN, like so many voyages of discovery do, on an old yellow school bus. This bus was not full of children, though, but food—tomatoes, potatoes, lettuce, apple cider, milk, ribs, chicken, barbeque sauce—all of it from farms within 150 miles of the Richmond street corner where I filled up my shopping basket in this unlikely vehicle.

Up by the steering wheel, Mark Lilly presided over the bus with a proprietary air, greeting people as they came aboard to browse in the apple barrels, wooden shelves, and freezers he had installed, showing kids the baby chicks he was keeping in a cage out on the sidewalk. The products I picked out to purchase—a tub of frozen pit-cooked barbeque made by a Mennonite family, a whole chicken from the famous Polyface Farm, a glass bottle of yogurt topped with blackberry jam—were things that I had spent ten hours driving all over the Virginia countryside with Mark to pick up a few days before. I couldn't wait to see how they tasted.

A visit with a local-food entrepreneur like Mark was, I felt, the logical place to start my journey; the commitment to eating locally is the sacred cow of the sustainable food movement. There seems to be a general—though sometimes only vaguely justified—consensus that sourcing as much of our food as possible from within a short driving distance of our houses is one of the most important things we can do to right the sinking ship of the U.S. food system.

I wondered if this was true. Is relocalizing our food economy the answer to our woes? It seemed improbable to me that small farmers selling at urban markets—the image almost universally associated with the idea of "eating local"—could be the much sought-after solution to all the complicated problems of our industrially dominated food system. Aren't these local farms just too small and too few and too apt to be growing things like garlic scapes and ramps, which—let's be honest—sound more like pieces of equipment found in a skateboard park than food?

The most familiar argument for locavorism arises from an objection to the massive distances that the vast majority of food eaten in the United States travels before it reaches dinner plates. The figure fifteen hundred miles is thrown around a lot, and while that number—calculated by the Leopold Center for Sustainable Agriculture—is only kind of true and then only if you live in Chicago, the exact number doesn't really matter; the sticking point is that we eat many things that have flown on airplanes from other hemispheres or been trucked across continents (or back and forth between states in a pointless bureaucratic shuffle) to get to us.

The ghastly carbon footprint of all that global food shipping is the more commonly reiterated reason to eat more locally. The environmental impact of getting an apple from five miles away, the logic goes, must surely be less than that of shipping your fruit in from New Zealand. Unfortunately for the locavores, the ecological argument for eating locally doesn't always stand up well to scrutiny. An apple in a load of millions shipped cross-country in an efficient eighteen-wheeler might well account for fewer carbon emissions than an apple in a single bushel driven thirty miles to a farmers' market in an old diesel farm truck. And that comparison doesn't account for the carbon dioxide expended by the shoppers getting to and from the place of purchase—a figure that might be lower for those who shop at grocery stores where only one trip is necessary than for those who take separate trips to farmers' markets, specialty shops, and other stores to put the week's menu together.

Making local and regional food distribution systems more robust and efficient would change the environmental calculus considerably. But as things stand now, other reasons for eating locally turn out to be far more compelling. What people want by and large, it seems to me, is to live in communities that are thriving, where they can find the means to be happy and healthy. What better way to make sure our communities thrive than by locating a chunk of the most important businesses of our lives—the work of feeding ourselves—close to our cities and in our own neighborhoods? Bolstering local food economies means creating and keeping local jobs, maintaining food producers' interest in and responsiveness to the needs and wants of the community (including the need for safe and healthy food), ensuring greater freshness, and providing local consumers with more instead of fewer options regarding where, when, and how to buy their food.

I still had my doubts about whether all those little guys farming their hearts out on their one-, five-, and twenty-acre parcels and dragging their wares to the farmers' market every week could feed our country effectively, but logic had it that they were doing vital work to keep our country from inexorably being taken over part and parcel by corporate food concerns. Local-food entrepreneurs were on the front lines, bringing us all hope. And hope is what I was after. In trying to find some small answer to the question, "What would a better food system look like?" I clearly needed to see "local food" in action. If what I found didn't appear to be the final, glorious solution to our food dilemmas, perhaps I could gain some hints about what such a solution might be.

So one April evening I headed south from my home in Washington, DC, to Richmond, the capital of Virginia, where Mark is making a go of it with his school bus-cum-roving farmers' market, an unusual business venture he calls Farm to Family. His bus route follows a schedule, but he uses his BlackBerry to remind his thousands of Facebook and Twitter fans of his location and to update them about any change of plans, which happen occasionally due to parking problems, absence of shoppers, or previously unscheduled visits.

When I inquired whether I might see his operation, Mark had kindly invited me to stay at his house for the night so I could come on his purchasing rounds at local farms early the following day. That's how I found myself sitting at a dining room table in a cozy house somewhere in Richmond eating a bowl of yogurt crisscrossed with a drizzle of maple syrup, products Mark buys from local farmers and sells on his bus.

"This is the best stuff you've ever tasted," Mark said, pointing at my bowl. Something about his friendly, low-key demeanor, shaved head, and sun-reddened cheeks reminded me obscurely of a firefighter. His wife Suzi, a warm woman in a teal "eat local" T-shirt and reddish hair twisted up in a clip, chatted with me about her job in the alternative healing and body care section of Ellwood Thompson's, a unique Richmond grocery store focused on local food. Not long after my visit, she would begin working full-time with mark on Farm to Family.

"The Fs should be green, darker green. Don't you think?" Mark interrupted, leaning over and showing Suzi a picture on his BlackBerry—the drafts of a Farm to Family logo sent by his designer.

"It's a little busy," she said. "You have to picture it on everything."

He brooded on this for a few moments then stalked away from the table, leaving Suzi to install me in a sweet-smelling, crimson guest room with an antique bedstead, a shelf of Buddhist relics, and a tinkling wind chime made of slices of pink stone.

The next morning as we sped down the highway toward the Shenandoah Valley in his truck, dragging a trailer equipped with six giant plastic coolers, Mark told me how he got the idea for the bus venture after experiencing a political awakening about issues of industrial food during a master's program in disaster science and emergency management. A research project about California's San Joaquin Valley for a class called Hazards and Threats to the Future led him into a sobering investigation of soil salination, monocultures, water shortages, labor issues, and petroleum's role in an area that grows almost 13 percent of the country's produce.

"It is really bad, what is going on out there," he said, propping his arm on the steering wheel. "If that system fails, that's going to have a major, major impact on the country." The idea for the bus venture started simmering in the back of his mind, but he would never have gone ahead if he hadn't lost his job working in food service at a university. By then he had already bought the old bus from Craigslist on a hunch.

All around us, spring had burst upon the countryside, the pink cotton candy fluff of redbud trees lacing the edges of the roadway. It was an unusually hot day for April; the temperature reading in the corner of the rearview mirror was climbing past eighty. The truck's AC was on the fritz.

"It all boils down to money," he went on. "What corporations do is they want to make as much money as they can and exploit anything in their path to get that done. These lobbyists and players in Washington—the government makes laws to benefit them, not to benefit the people." For a guy engaged in such a creative and optimistic business endeavor, he exuded a surprisingly intense sense of outrage.

We trundled off the highway onto a country road slicing through green hills and pulled into the parking lot of a McDonald's, of all places, where a white-bearded Mennonite farmer in a straw hat and his blue-skirted wife in a pale kerchief were waiting incongruously for us next to their truck and trailer.

This was Mike and Diana Puffenbarger, a thirty-years-married couple who run a farm, a barbeque business, and a hunting and fishing guide service. Mike's family has been producing maple syrup for five generations, and he himself has been at it for at least three decades. Their 4×4 sported a window sticker saying "TRUTH WILL SET YOU FREE, JOHN 8:32" alongside another emblazoned with a picture of a howling coyote in crosshairs surrounded by the motto "HUNT HARD, SHOOT STRAIGHT, KILL CLEAN, APOLOGIZE TO NO ONE."

As they helped load tubs of their pit-cooked barbeque and bottles of their syrup into Mark's truck, I asked Mike about their biggest challenge as small farmers.

"The government," he responded without a pause. "They're letting in all this junk from China. But *we* try to do something, they hammer us. We've been butchering meat for years from our farm and we've never had a recall. What's that tell you?" The Puffenbargers take their animals destined for sale as meat to a slaughterhouse as required by the USDA, the closest one being in Harrisonburg, eighty miles from their farm in Bolar, Virginia. They prefer to butcher at home the meat they eat themselves.

Mike's comment highlighted one of the many reasons local-food advocates cite for buying closer to home. The country's industrial food chain has been busy building itself an abysmal record on food safety. The USDA website posts hundreds of recalls of food products every year, the majority of them for posing a "possible health risk." The word *salmonella* makes a distressingly regular appearance on this list, as do *E. coli* and *Listeria,* a dangerous bacterium. One compelling reason to buy your food—especially your meat—from smaller-scale farmers who are involved in your community instead of from corporations whose operations are opaque, remote, and likely too massive to be handled safely is that smaller, closer-to-home producers are more likely to have both the ability and the motivation to make sure their products aren't tainted.

Back on the road, the pungent odor of manure wafting in the window and the temperature in the truck climbing toward incendiary, Mark told me he had been totally unprepared for what he was getting into when he started the bus business. His original idea was to go into food deserts—urban areas where residents don't have access to stores that carry fresh food—and sell his local meat and produce to these underserved communities. He got registered to accept food stamps and parked in poor neighborhoods, waiting for the rush of customers. But the people there looked at him like he was crazy and continued to spend their money in the corner store, where fresh vegetables are usually absent in favor of fried chicken, chips, and soda.

"I got blindsided. I was really naïve," he said. "A for-profit business has no incentive to go into a food desert and set up shop. If you're a for-profit business and you're bringing in high-quality stuff, it costs. I would be out of business if I were to just go into low-income areas." Mark was referencing one of the most prominent critiques of the locavore ethos: the cost of food from nearby small farms is almost always substantially higher than the products of industrial production you can buy in the average supermarket or at the corner store. Critics accuse the eat-local movement of promoting two separate food systems: one that's supplied with healthy, "happy" food for all the people who can afford it, and another stocked with ecologically damaging, pesticide laden, processed junk for everyone else.

But when you're trying to start a business like Mark Lilly, you don't have the time or money to fix the world's problems. You find the customers who can help you succeed. So, while still doing some work in low-income communities, including occasionally giving away free food (efforts for which he has received high-profile publicity, including a three-page spread in *People* magazine), he has focused mostly on parts of town where people have a little extra money to spend and are attuned to the politics of local food. He runs his own version of a community-supported agriculture (CSA) program, which he calls a USA for "urban-supported agriculture," that has people pay ahead of time for a season's worth of biweekly boxes of fresh food. He also delivers milk to people's doors early in the morning, just like guys used to do back in my grandmother's time.

"I'm giving people a way to opt out of the current system," he proudly told me as we rattled up a long, dirt drive into the cluttered parking area of Mountain View Dairy Farm. Proprietor Christie Huger, dressed for the heat in a white T-shirt, athletic shorts, and sandals, greeted us as Mark backed the truck up to the loading area by a dilapidated trailer office. They consulted for a few moments by a set of glass-fronted refrigerators before starting to load jars of blackberry yogurt and glass bottles of milk into the coolers in Mark's trailer.

Christie's tousled hair and tired smile suggested that it had already been a long day despite it not yet being noon. She used to be an art teacher, she told me, but she quit teaching two years ago to attend full-time to the farm. I asked her if it's been a hard transition, and she answered unhesitatingly: "If I went back to teaching it'd be easier. When you get up at four-thirty and then force yourself to come inside at eight at night to feed your kids dinner, it's hard." I wondered aloud if she planned to go back to teaching, and her answer was again immediate: no way.

I followed Christie's daughter Isabelle, an energetic girl in a peach tank top and a bowl haircut, toward a pen by the house where a tiny lamb was bleating manically. She grabbed a baby bottle full of water and kneeled down beside the animal.

"Do you want to be a farmer when you grow up?" I asked, thinking about that statistic I had recently come across: the average age of farmers in the United States is fifty-five and rising. We badly need kids to take an interest in this kind of life.

"I already am," she said matter-of-factly, squinting up at me in the sunshine. "I'm a sheep farmer. Because we have this little baby sheep."

My heart melted, and I realized that this moment, as much as the fresh, delicious milk itself, was what the consumers on Mark's bus are buying. From Mennonite farmers to milk in glass bottles to the old yellow school bus, Mark's business plays on city dwellers' sense of nostalgia for what they see as a safe, picturesque, and pastoral yesteryear. A common theme in the movement to reinvigorate local food systems is the idea of a David-and-Goliath battle between corporate overlords and the small family farmer, with the corporation representing the evils of mechanized, overcrowded, stifling, isolating modern life and the little guy laying claim to a virtuous existence of nature, space, freedom, and community. Not to mention little baby sheep.

I mentioned this observation to Mark as we got back on the road heading to our next stop. On the bus, he told me, visitors often revel in memories of other types of roving food vendors that populated their long-ago childhoods. Customers reminisce about the guys who used to come by their urban neighborhoods in trucks or with handcarts yelling "Fresh fish!" or "Watermelon!"

"Back in the day, there was the milkman and the meat delivery guy," Mark said. "You knew them. They came to your house. It was interactive. You chatted with them. That's what I try to do. I'm interactive. I chat with people."

Mark tries, in short, to give his customers "an experience." He brings baby animals for children to hold. He talks to customers about what they can do with what he sells—how to cook a spaghetti squash, for instance, or which kind of barbeque sauce will go best on pulled pork. At the time of our journey, his bus was plastered with hand-lettered signs proclaiming a variety of riling slogans, such as "EAT AT HOME, COOK, HAVE FUN!" and "DON'T RELY ON A FAILING, HIGHLY PROCESSED UNSUSTAINABLE TOXIC FOOD SYSTEM! GROW AND PRESERVE YOUR OWN FOOD NOW!"

When he invites customers onto his bus, he's asking them not only to step inside the vehicle, but also to move into another way of looking at our world of food. The way he thinks of it, coming onto his bus is the next best thing to experiencing the bracing goodness of the farm itself. "I'm packaging a farm onto a school bus," he said, "and bringing it to them."

Supporters of local food and small farms will be the first to insist vociferously that they are not in the business of rehashing some long-ago bucolic utopia, but that they're building new networks of small enterprises that draw on some of the best lessons we've collectively learned in the past. But even so, the idea that we are suffering from modern ills because we have somehow gotten away from a good life of fresh air and honest manual work nonetheless animates a sizable amount of interest in local food. And people are willing to pay extra to have a vision of a return to that idealized time served up with their kale and kohlrabi. It's a powerful narrative. Regardless that I don't in any way believe that poverty equals virtue and toil under the hot sun cleanses the soul, I felt for a moment, as I thought about that lamb suckling enthusiastically at the bottle offered by the little girl, the tragedy of my concrete-bound city life that does not include this type of countrified charm.

But life is, of course, more complicated than all of these visions and dichotomies can encompass. Even the man who spends his days driving from quaint farm to adorable homestead buying up yogurt in jars and field-raised poultry is as frenzied a denizen of the modern-day rat race as I've ever seen. Mark's BlackBerry was never far from his hand, even while driving his truck and trailer, and he lamented that he had been up working until three the night before. He radiated a contained but manic energy, the kind that wouldn't allow for any slowdown for a lunchtime picnic of the local foods we had collected. Instead, we got Subway sandwiches from a gas station and ate them in the car.

Usually, Mark insisted, he and Suzi eat almost exclusively the products they sell on the bus, which seems like it would be more chal-lenging because of the time it takes to prepare fresh, whole foods than because of any lack of availability or variety, even in the winter. He listed off the things he might be carrying on a typical day in February: "Hydroponic lettuce, tomatoes, eggs, bacon, sausage, barbeque, pota-toes, apples, butternut squash, chestnuts, collard greens, kale, onions, sweet potatoes, apples, milk, cheese, butter, yogurt, spaghetti squash. I have people who bake pies and breads and cookies for me. I've got maple syrup, apple butter, apple cider, peach cider . . ."

We pulled into a long straight drive labeled with a sign for the famous Polyface Farm, owned by Joel Salatin, whose innovative farming practices have captured the imagination of sustainable food advocates. Salatin insists that growing food should replenish natural resources instead of depleting them, improving the health of the animals, the people, and the soil instead of degrading it. He's become an outspoken advocate for the development of laws that would enable the success of our country's small farmers and has been catapulted to niche stardom by his appearances in both Michael Pollan's seminal work *The Omnivore's Dilemma* and in the Academy Award–nominated documentary *Food, Inc.*

As Mark disappeared into a walk-in freezer to pick up his order of meat, a family from Wisconsin come to witness "that famous farm" for themselves was piling out of a minivan and ogling the chicken houses. The scene might not have lived up to their pastoral imaginings: the part of Polyface a casual visitor sees is chaotic and down-at-the-heels like any farm. Used-up equipment is stacked here and there, vehicles are parked every which way, and a worn, white farmhouse squats unpretentiously in the yard. The famous farmer was nowhere to be seen, but his son Daniel and some farmhands were lingering over by the barn, swatting at bees with shovels and laughing at one another's antics. "They bore into the wood," said Daniel, chuckling, his teeth blindingly white in the sunshine. "It's not good." With his handsome, tanned face and his straw cowboy hat, he could have been a Western movie star.

"We put our first batch of roasters out on the field today," he told Mark. The Salatins have popularized the use of the chicken tractor, a wheeled coop with a mesh bottom moved from place to place, which allows the birds to fertilize the fields and get their nourishment from the grass, worms, and bugs. Raising poultry this way is more ecologically friendly and conducive to maintaining a thriving, diverse farm than the usual method of providing poultry feed and letting the birds' nitrogen-rich waste go to . . . well, waste.

If only all people could have access to and afford the wonderful food produced by places like Polyface. But even this most prominent of small farms provides an instructive example of the difficulty of reaching that noble goal. While Polyface does supply pork to two Chipotle Mexican Grill fast-food restaurants, the project took almost a year and a half of negotiations and logistical arrangements to succeed, and it required Salatin to double or even triple his production, a feat few small farms can manage. With more than 950 Chipotle locations across the country, Salatin's contribution is a drop in the bucket, and the majority of products from small producers remain the province of affluent individual buyers and high-end restaurants.

By two p.m., the temperature in the truck was up to eighty-six degrees, and we'd been on the road for seven hours. We still had several stops to go.

"These days are long and hard," Mark groaned as we pulled into Riverside Plant, a Mennonite-owned plant business positioned in several spacious greenhouses across a gravel drive from a neat white house. Plain garments ordered by size flapped on a clothesline in the side yard. "I'm burning out right now," Mark continued. "I have nothing outside this business. I don't socialize. I don't sleep. It's brutal."

His laments, however, were mitigated by the pride of success. After just nine months, his business—launched with four thousand dollars of his savings—had started making a profit, and interest in his bus was growing. The business could easily expand if only he had the financing and infrastructure to make that happen. "I could have a fleet of these just in Richmond," he said. "I could create hundreds of jobs."

The idea of bolstering a local economy, of course, is another ex-cellent argument advanced by boosters of local eating. Local-food production can be a key pillar of a community's economy: produc-ing, distributing, and selling food in a local area requires a local workforce, and the fact that everyone needs food no matter the state of the nation's economy means that such jobs aren't likely to dry up with every downturn.

Farm to Family isn't creating any jobs yet, however. Mark's just one guy with a gas-guzzling truck and a trailer roaming the Virginia countryside, transporting the goods in and out of his central ware-house, an old flower shop on a run-down commercial strip outside Richmond, which, shortly after my visit, he turned into a nonroving local-foods shop.

And while the concept of a mobile supermarket is innovative and the nostalgia-inducing school bus is a good marketing hook, the idea of any city's main alternative to the Safeway being a fleet of old school buses kitted out with burlap and smelling of onions left me slightly deflated. Although a good example of a hopeful enterprise, Mark's venture seemed a somewhat cumbersome way to inject local food into the cityscape. I was interested in what a more sustainable food system might look like, and the project of driving all day in a hot truck to pick up a box of potatoes here, a cooler of yogurt there didn't strike me as all that sustainable, especially considering the guy behind the wheel was so tired he seemed fit to collapse at any moment.

A company like Mark's—especially once expanded and able to run efficiently at a larger scale—can play an important role as part of a network of businesses and nonprofits offering a variety of alter-natives, the presence of which alone makes for a more sustainable local community. But I could see that if I was going to showcase all that is hopeful in local food and discover its potential, I would need to find a more expansive example. What I needed to find next was a place where a proper network of locally oriented endeavors was starting to form a veritable alternative economy of local food.

CHAPTER 2

Locavore Montana

A local-food economy grows in Big Sky country

I FOUND THE ENERGETIC—if fledgling—local-food economy I was looking for in Montana, a state with sky so wide it feels like the edge of the world. As you speed the endless highways, a film of smashed bugs collecting on your windshield, you prepare to hurtle at any moment off some unseen edge and fly into oblivion. In the Flathead Valley north of Missoula, where I arrived in a tiny rental car with a list of questions and the amazement of an East Coast city kid loosed into openness, the nearby Mission Mountains that bit into the sky with shining white teeth were all that seemed to keep the valley floor below pinned to the firmament.

Bright and early on a shining day in June, I drove down Main Street in Ronan, a town of around seventeen hundred with one traffic light, a few gas stations, a Subway sandwich shop, and a pizza place. At the Ronan Café midway down the wide alley of drowsy, low-slung shops, Mennonite young women were slinging giant helpings of biscuits and gravy amid cutesy wooden bric-a-brac. Outside, an old man administered water to the flowerpots adorning his shop, and up the street, a small theater advertised an Adam Sandler movie.

Other than those few signs of life, the town seemed to have settled in for a long sleep.

Across from the theater, I found what I had come to see: a sage green building labeled MISSION MOUNTAIN MARKET, home of the Lake County Community Development Corporation (CDC) and its Mission Mountain Food Enterprise Center, a nonprofit with the basic interior décor to prove it. The center was founded in 1998 as a community-based food-processing center dedicated to helping would-be food entrepreneurs launch their products and businesses. The things people make here run the gamut from bison jerky to cherry jam to catnip. Processing raw ingredients into "value-added" products allows food purveyors to increase their profit margins and for small farmers to make ends meet by creating and selling higher-priced goods such as artisan cheeses, sauces, and jams. The Food Enterprise Center also offers education and training, like concept-to-consumer courses, and assists in the development of cooperatives of various kinds.

My host, Karl Sutton, the food, agriculture, and cooperative de-velopment project coordinator and a woodsy-looking young guy in a beige striped shirt and a full beard, gave me the grand tour of the fa-cility. He guided me through a maze of rooms furnished with slum-bering machines, flipping on lights as he went. The original concept was for this to be a community kitchen, he said, but the plan ex-panded to include a magnificent hodgepodge of useful machinery more suited to proper commercial production: mixers, bread proof-ers, stoves, meat slicers, tea-bag makers, packagers, smokers, mari-naters, cherry pitters, vats, vacuum sealers, freezers, coolers, washers, storage rooms, a loading dock, and a mobile poultry slaughterhouse. In every room, metal forms huddled under protective plastic cover-ings, their cranks and knobs and gears bristling under the fluorescent lights. It was an army of useful equipment available to anyone for a fee.

"In Montana fifty years ago I think we produced ninety percent of our own food," Karl told me. "We had community-based food-processing facilities. We had wheat facilities where we could clean wheat. We had slaughter facilities so that people were eating their own beef. Now we're a commodity state. Everything leaves and comes back in a different form. So we want our producers to be able to take products and turn them into a form that adds value and creates business."

This was a great idea, but apparently easier said than done. The problem, he said, was inspiring enough of the locals to come and pay to work on these machines. Building communities centered around food is hindered by federal government policies that have for decades advantaged the national-scale industrial players over community-oriented small and medium-sized operations, laying waste to the infrastructure that once supported thriving local-food economies across the country.

With the Mission Mountain Food Enterprise Center representing one small piece of a local-food system's infrastructure back in play, Karl wondered how to get people hooked into the idea of small-scale processing as a viable route to local economic security. Each of the businesses incubated here creates jobs—good Montana jobs—and pumps money back into the local economy.

"Having food processing gives local control," he said as we admired the giant cooler and loading dock big enough to accommodate a forklift. He illustrated his point with a story about the Flathead Lake Cherry Growers, a group of conventional (that is, nonorganic) cherry growers clustered on Flathead Lake north of Ronan, the eastern shore of which has a mysterious microclimate conducive to the fruit. The cooperative, which pits and freezes some of its cherries at the center, sells to a processor in Washington, where the fruit is incorporated into a Northwest label and loses its Flathead identity. Overproduction all over the Northwest in 2009 glutted the market and sent prices plummeting, which slammed the Montana growers, whose cherries are last in the region to ripen.

"They rotted on the trees," said Karl. He paused, letting the image sink in. "Now, you go back less than a decade and they had their own packing houses and that meant jobs. Weren't necessarily great-paying jobs, but they were jobs. And they would have had more control over their products."

Most of the producers who use the center would like to build their own facilities eventually but need help getting started. Karl proudly displayed some of the products created there: Thunderhead raspberry chipotle sauce, which sells for almost ten dollars a bottle; Silent Creations bison jerky, made by Matthew Silent Thunder, a member of the Mescalero Apache tribe; Tipu's Chai, which has been so successful that the owner is taking it national.

But while the center has spawned some thirty or forty businesses, a dozen or so of which remain viable, new generations of entrepreneurs aren't exactly beating down the door. Launching a new product takes a lot of work, and most local farmers don't have time in their schedules to start making value-added products. Nonfarmers might not have the start-up capital or the expertise, or even know that the center exists to help them. And Ronan's distance from Missoula— about fifty-six miles—is enough to discourage some would-be food entrepreneurs who live in the city or elsewhere in the metro area.

So if this facility were a business, I asked Karl, would it be operating at a loss?

"Oh yeah," he said, laughing. "Oh yeah. That's a big hiccup with a nonprofit model. There's the idea that it should stand on its own. Well, we're a food development resource. So we're working with agricultural producers who don't make a lot of money. We're working with food business ventures that don't make any money generally, at least for the first five to seven years. How do you make money off of people who aren't making any money and still pursue your mission of developing local food?" Grants are fine for funding educational programming, he said, but they don't tend to pay for someone to supervise the processing floor or to fix a leaking roof.

There is hope, though, in the form of what Karl called "a cascading effect," by which he meant that each piece of a local-food system can enable and then reinforce the others until you have a robust, cost-effective network. About a year after my visit, the Lake County CDC helped develop a regional strategic plan to scale up local and regional food businesses through values-based supply chains. But even in the summer of 2010, a cascading effect was already under way in the region, where cooperatives are improving availability and distribution of local products, and farm-to-school programs are engaging local farmers. The Lake County CDC has had a hand in many of these developments. Karl mentioned his work processing local fruits and veggies too big, too small, or too blemished for farmers to sell at the market into products that local schools can use at an affordable price.

As Karl and I were winding down our visit, another of the ventures the CDC helped set up came knocking on the door in the form of a slight, friendly guy with a dirty-blond ponytail and a University of Memphis baseball cap. This was Dave Prather, manager of the Western Montana Growers Cooperative, whom I had arranged to accompany on his delivery rounds that afternoon.

"Hey Dave," said Karl, who is himself a farmer of organic wheat and veggies and a member of the co-op. Founded in 2003, the co-op is owned by about thirty member-farmers, each of whom pays a hundred dollars a year in annual dues. The members collectively sell everything from cherries to meat, and some of them are so small they're barely more than gardeners. Except for its CSA program—which supplies its prepaying subscribers regular food deliveries throughout the season—the co-op sells wholesale to restaurants, grocery stores, health food stores, universities, and the public school system.

At the beginning of each season, the co-op manager works up predictions and then secures members' commitments to grow what will be needed. The growers use the co-op's online system to log in what they have ready twice a week throughout the season and then, once customers have agreed to buy, they bring their goods to the truck for a delivery run the following day. Using this system, everything customers receive has been picked within twenty-four hours.

Karl's favorite thing about the co-op, he told me, is that it frees him up to farm so he doesn't have to focus on marketing and distribution. Then there's the advantage that comes from pooling resources to enable selling in quantity. "I took two dozen heads of lettuce to the truck last night and thirty-six things of chard, and a restaurant wouldn't even look at me if I took that amount to them," he said. "But because all these producers bring stuff together, all of a sudden you have the volume."

And doing some level of volume sales is key, considering that one major reason most small producers have been booted off the shelves of conventional grocery stores is that they don't supply in the big, efficient quantities that large-scale producers can muster. Growing and selling small amounts often jacks up the price of produce because of the logistics of getting it to market, but when you cut out the middleman like the co-op does and combine your goods into larger loads, you just might be able to fight your way back in.

"Sometimes it costs a bit more than what they're going to pay elsewhere," Dave admitted as we trundled north on Highway 93 in the co-op's refrigerated truck, heading toward the first stop in what would be a long afternoon of deliveries. But, he went on, a lot of the time it's competitive with produce of its type. Most of the co-op's farms are either USDA organic, a classification that requires adherence to very specific methods and strictly regulates inputs, or they carry an alternative organic classification called Montana Homegrown, which takes a local perspective on organic standards. For example, if there's no organic straw available locally for mulching beds but a farmer knows and trusts the practices of a nonorganic producer nearby, the Homegrown classification allows the farmer to buy that straw instead of having organic straw shipped in from afar.

Flathead Lake stretched gorgeously before us as we rose over a hill, its edges thick with pine and the sky above piled softly with clouds. That summer, Dave said, the ability of one of the co-op's growers to produce cherries in large quantities enabled the group to strike an agreement with Safeway, a development that he admitted in his understated way was "a pretty big deal." Would Safeway put the cherries out with a sign that says "LOCAL," I wondered? Has the idea of local food become so mainstream that even Safeway was starting to value it?

"That's what we're going to be pushing them on this year," said Dave. "It's going to be a learning experience for both sides." The first bit of learning involved getting Safeway to allow the co-op to deliver directly to stores instead of having their cherries processed through a central warehouse, the closest of which is in Washington. "We had to explain to them that what we are after is not to ship our Montana products to Washington only to have them shipped back to Montana," Dave said. I asked if Safeway had pushed back on the issue. I had always imagined executives of such places as stern and protocol-obsessed, apt to be impatient and unconvinced by the tiny voices of logic from small, local farmers. "They didn't really push back," said Dave. "It was just a sort of ignorance."

In the county seat of Polson, population about four thousand, Dave navigated the truck into a small street next to our first stop, Mission Mountain Natural Foods. "Jerks have decided to park right in front of the alleyway," he said good-naturedly, eyeing a van blocking our path. He pulled around into the parking lot, consulted his order sheet, hopped down from the truck, and yanked open the back doors. He rapidly pulled out boxes of various sizes, stacked them on a dolly, and then took off at a fast clip with me trailing after.

"Beautiful day today," he greeted the staff inside, where the earthy smell of bulk grains floated over a musky undertone of incense. Dave went into the back room to drop off his shipment while I browsed among the dried nuts and fruits.

It had been rainy and clammy for a long time, he told me when we were back on the road. "It's been the wettest June on record, I think." On one day the week before, the high had been a chilly forty-five, though summers in the valley are usually hot and dry. The tricky weather in this part of Montana contributes to what Dave identified as perhaps the biggest hurdle for increasing sales of locally produced foods: the difficulty of providing a consistent product week in and week out. Even the co-op's larger growers who have their production systems down pat run into trouble now and then. Dave mentioned one farm that has been producing lettuce for thirty years. "They know what works for them," he said. "But then again, last weekend they lost most of their lettuce crop. It was out in the field and a hailstorm came along and shredded everything."

What do you tell customers when that happens, I asked? "We tell people sorry," he said. "It's all we can do, really. And most people understand." Though, he added, such scenarios can leave customers scrambling at the last minute to get their lettuce—or whatever else the hail has mowed down—from elsewhere. This is a fate that big grocery stores sourcing produce in massive quantities from distant locations rarely or never encounter. If one big supplier can't deliver, another one surely can.

We pulled up at a store of a very different character from the first. A huge banner reading "SAVING YOU MONEY IS WHAT WE'RE ALL ABOUT!" greeted us as we entered Super 1 Foods, and all along our path to the storage room neon orange signs advertising rock-bottom prices bloomed like garish carnations. In the back, pallets of Froot Loops and Kraft Easy Mac lurked ominously in the shadows.

I told Dave I was surprised that a place like this would want the organic milk and eggs he had to offer. The previous store with its wafts of patchouli and bulk bins of oat groats had been more what I'd envisioned. But even mainstream shoppers want organic products nowadays, he said, and once a store recognizes they can make money on something, they'll do it, even if it's biodynamic milk being sold in the type of place that slings gallon jugs of Tampico juice drink for two dollars a pop (in the delicious flavors of orange, pink, and green).

The dairy and meat products, which the co-op can deliver all year, aren't subject to the consistency problems that vegetable growers face, so big stores can rest assured they'll have little hassle. Small, local producers need to be able to offer a consistent supply of a certain product for a chunk of time—say two months—for the big stores to find selling it worth their while. "No produce manager wants to deal with it," said Dave, referring to the trouble of frequently changing signs and displays. "It makes their lives too difficult."

We spent the afternoon hopping from store to store all around Flathead Lake, trucking by marvelous vistas rolling themselves out through openings in thick stands of evergreen. We stopped at Montana Coffee Traders, which uses some of the co-op's food in its café offerings, and Blacktail Grocery, an independent food store. We popped in at Withey's Health Foods, whose inventory seemed to be heavy on the vitamins and supplements, and Rosauers, a regional chain that sells co-op products in its Huckleberry's Natural Market.

"Another problem with the big stores is their insurance requirements," Dave said as we sped south on the far side of the lake, passing a clutch of quaint cherry farms. "We carry insurance for our growers. We have a two-million-dollar policy." That kind of liability coverage would be too expensive for most of the co-op's growers to carry individually, which would make them automatically ineligible to sell to big stores.

While the co-op enables small growers to access these larger stores, it also connects its members to individual buyers through its CSA program, started in 2008. Local customers pay up front for a full summer share or a half summer share and also have the option of buying a fall share, which provides storage crops into December. They can log on to the co-op's website to purchase additional items like meat and dairy to be included in their boxes, which the co-op delivers to drop points in Polson, Ronan, Missoula, and the Bitterroot Valley.

From what I had seen on my drive with Dave, this co-op, though admittedly tiny in the scheme of things, was offering local residents a positive alternative to the industrial produce shipped in from California. Not only that, but the co-op was slowly figuring out the formula for offering that alternative on the very same store shelves as the corporate-controlled veggies, providing direct competition in a marketplace usually sadly lacking such variety. This seemed a remarkable feat, something worth finding out more about.

So off I went to find Julie Pavlock, chair of the co-op's board of directors, organic farmer, and CSA organizer extraordinaire, at Foothill Farm in the tiny town of St. Ignatius, population about eight hundred, nineteen miles south of Ronan. Most of the Flathead Valley lies within the Flathead Indian Reservation and nowhere is this more obvious than in St. Ignatius, where a tribal health clinic squats next to the old Mission Church, which Catholic missionaries built to evangelize to local native tribes in the early 1890s and from which the adjacent mountain range draws its name. A warren of tribal housing is tucked into the southeast corner of town, down a dirt road from Julie's farm, which backs right up to the feet of the Mission Mountains.

The low ranch house and tidy barn seemed empty when I arrived, and there was no one save a family of scarecrows among the neat vegetable rows out back. The only sign of life was a couple placid cows munching grass in a far field. But as I turned to leave, someone in a plaid, wooly jacket came racing up the street on a motor scooter, honey-colored ponytail flying out from under her helmet.

"The World Cup," Julie said as she pulled into the driveway. "It's England versus Germany." She had been watching the match with her parents, who had moved down the road after they retired. This was not the person I had imagined as grand pooh-bah of the local food co-op. In my mind's eye, I had seen someone older, less pretty, more careworn. Someone not taken to watching international soccer tournaments and riding motorcycles. Someone, in short, more *farmerish.*

Inside the house, I perched on a kitchen stool while Julie fixed coffee and told me about the crossroads at which the co-op finds itself after three summers of gradual growth. "We're at this funny position where we can sell just about anything we grow," she said in between blasts of her electric coffee grinder. "But in order to sell more, we have to make a big leap in production, and no one's really willing to do it until they can be assured that we're able to sell it, but we can't sell it until it's there." It's a catch-22, but, as Dave had stressed, the big grocery stores are the ones writing the rules of the game, and they're looking to buy in quantity, so quantity is what Julie must contemplate if the co-op is to play that particular game.

"It presents all sorts of new logistical issues," said Julie. "We're thinking, Well now we need a big truck. And are we ready to make these big steps? Can we figure out how our producers can grow more than they are now?" What they'd really need, she said, is their own central storage facility to replace their current patchwork of offices, storage areas, and packing sheds scattered miles apart around the region.

Karl had told Julie he thinks the Mission Mountain Center would be perfect for the co-op, and Julie almost agrees. "It has everything we need and want, excepting that it's in Ronan, and then we'd have growers that are eighty miles away from it," she said. "If we had a facility just like that in Missoula, it would be perfect for us." No wonder Karl was having such a hard time filling up the place.

Julie put water on the stove to boil and leaned back against the counter, looking at me thoughtfully. Ironically, considering that the co-op established itself on the principle of helping small growers pool their resources to get into larger markets, the appeal of working with an ever-increasing army of small growers scattered far and wide was wearing thin. "The majority of organic vegetable growers of any size in the area belong to the co-op. It's clear that it would be easier for us to help those growers to grow more than to bring on new, smaller growers. It's definitely something that we talk about a lot. Where do we go from here?"

She turned her attention to some complex and fine-smelling

alchemy on the counter, then placed a mug of coffee in front of me. Hauling a massive jar of milk out of the refrigerator, she said, "This is raw milk. I don't know how you feel about it." She is, she admitted, one of those people who sees raw milk—that is, milk that hasn't been pasteurized using the high temperatures meant to kill pathogens—as an elixir of health. Selling raw milk is illegal in Montana, as it is in many states, and debates about its dangers, benefits, and legal status constantly pop up in the news. This milk was from Julie's own cow, and she feels so confident of its hygiene that she feeds it to her four-year-old.

I'd never had raw milk, and having written about the politics of the stuff in the past, I was curious to try, so she poured me a glass and watched with interest as I drank it down. The cool, sweet creaminess was so tasty it would surely be best appreciated with a chocolate chip cookie, but even without one I could report that it was delicious. She looked pleased. "I'm so passionate about raw milk," she said.

Dairy—albeit not the raw kind—and meat would be good ways to expand the co-op, she said, but the limitations of local meat-processing facilities, which are few and small, make that a daunting prospect. Meat production for the industrial system is "what's happening around western Montana," Julie said as she led me out into the yard for a tour of the farm. "It would mean taking on a whole different infrastructure." None of the co-op member's herds are very big—Julie has only twenty-five animals—so they can't offer the consistent supply of high-end cuts restaurants want. Co-op members sometimes sell whole or half cows or pigs, but that's not for everybody, which leaves poultry as the co-op's main meat offering.

Julie's farm's vegetable fields—five acres of garlic, tomatoes, onions, cauliflower, broccoli, cabbage, and greens—were baking under the midday sun behind the house, the white peaks of the mountains beyond shining like icicles. The short, intense growing season in Montana has always been a problem for the co-op members, leaving them stretched thin in the early spring and fall. The CSA provides income early in the year to get things moving. Julie exuded enthusiasm for the CSA and pride in its success, though she admitted that customers' ignorance about the logistics of food production could be a challenge. "Even people who know enough and who care enough to join a CSA, right now when we only have greens and radishes, they're like, 'I joined this for the tomatoes. Where are they?'"

"Mommy! Wait for me!" Julie's daughter, Evelyn, in a pageboy haircut and flowered skirt, came barreling toward us over the grass. I asked her which animal we could hear bleating so insistently in the barn.

"My goat," she said seriously. "Ramona."

In the coolness of the barn, infused with that lovely smell of fresh hay and old wood, Julie hooked the kid up to a rope and gave it to Evelyn, who began tugging the reluctant animal toward the door. The barn was nearly empty; the cows were out grazing, and Julie had recently sold her two draft horses, working animals that had made her farm completely self-sustaining. This soccer-watching, moped-riding farmer was more dyed-in-the-wool, old-school agriculturalist than I ever imagined. Was the trouble of using horses really worth the ability to swear off oil, I asked? There really is a good reason the overwhelming majority of American farmers of every stripe have embraced tractors: using draft animals seems a perniciously difficult and inefficient way to farm. "Well," she said, smiling, "I know how to work with them better than I know how to fix a tractor."

But even though she loved farming by that superintensive

method, managing the team's needs became too much. "It's hard to drive horses when you have a baby on your back," she reflected mildly, watching as Evelyn stopped and turned to her, incidentally holding up the type of backpack used to carry a baby, which she had been wearing earlier in the day with a teddy bear strapped inside.

"Mom, can we put this on the baby goat?" she asked.

"No," Julie responded with an amused smile.

"Why?" asked Evelyn. "It would look so funny."

As I headed back toward the highway, I reflected that co-ops seemed to have an important role to play in reinvigorating locally oriented food systems. But I could see that the logistics were tricky. How were other co-ops in the area faring? Were these same logistical and infrastructure problems the biggest obstacle for every group of local-food producers?

I sped up Route 93 with this question in mind and found Heidi Johnson, her husband, Gary, and their three children at the Orchard at Flathead Lake, one of the many cherry orchards overlooking the lake's eastern shore that Dave and I had trucked by the day before. Heidi and Gary, who are leading the process of forming the nascent Flathead Lake Organic Cherry Cooperative, make ends meet by putting out a range of value-added products—cherry jam, cherry chutney, cherry BBQ sauce, and Gramma Johnson's Apple Butter—which Heidi, a former chemical engineer, processes at the Mission Mountain Center.

As Heidi and I settled ourselves at a picnic table below the orchard's lone apple tree, Gary rode by on a little tractor with a bandana tied around his close-cropped hair and their four-year-old daughter Alexandra wiggled herself onto her mother's lap. With the lake spreading out below us and the sky domed above, the whole world seemed from our perch like a blue marble run through with green and white. Behind us, the farm's five hundred cherry trees rolled up the side of a gently sloping hill backing up onto a mountainside thick with evergreens.

The orchard, which Gary's parents had managed conventionally during his youth, was the third orchard in the area to turn organic and the first to secure USDA organic certification. "Cherries are one of the most heavily sprayed fruits," Heidi said. But, as she sees it, "if you can't do it without a ton of herbicides and pesticides maybe it wasn't meant to grow there." To keep pests away, she and Gary use a fermented bacteria, an organic pesticide from Dow Chemical, the draconian sound of which made me wonder how many people have entirely the wrong idea about organic food. (What? Organic doesn't mean you just sprinkle happy wishes over your fields and watch protective rainbows of joy appear over each of your tender seedlings?)

Some of the conventional cherry growers in the neighborhood— many of whom belong to what Heidi referred to as "the Cherry Mafia," otherwise known as the Flathead Lake Cherry Growers— are certainly guilty of holding misconceptions about organics. They tend to blame Heidi and Gary for any fruit fly problems, Heidi said, because they think being organic means you do nothing at all to keep pests off your fruit, rainbows of joy notwithstanding. When a neighbor found a fruit with fly larvae in his tree, another neighbor called to ask Heidi if she could do anything with the infested cherries. "I was like, 'Uh, *no,*'" said Heidi, indignant at the memory. "Why does me being organic make you think I can do something with fruit with worms in it? The crunchiest granola person you can imagine doesn't want wormy fruit."

But despite such fault lines in the area, Heidi found a tremendous amount of interest in organics when she and Gary moved back to Montana to take over the orchard after years away. "We decided to form this co-op because we have people asking us all the time to help them," she said. When we met, she was deep in the thicket of paperwork needed to properly establish the co-op—bylaws, marketing plans, feasibility studies—and her main concern was, just as I had suspected, something fairly mundane.

"Our problem is that we don't have anywhere to sort and pack and keep them cold," she said. The co-op would likely be dealing with hundreds of thousands of pounds of fruit at harvest time. "We can't just sort that in our garage." I asked whether the Mission Mountain Center could work for them, but its location—requiring more than an hour's round-trip commute during an intensely busy time at the farm—is a problem for everyday use. "It's a great facility and we couldn't be doing what we're doing without them," she said. "But it's a trek. It gets frustrating." This sounded familiar.

Despite the frustrations of making things work, however, the co-op is steadily getting off the ground, helping build up the diverse network of enterprises the local-food economy needs to thrive. The co-op was awarded a fifteen-thousand-dollar grant from the USDA under the Value-Added Producer Grant program, and Heidi has made solid connections with the dining program at the University of Montana, which buys the co-op's fresh and frozen cherries.

As I tipped my car down the steep slope of the orchard's drive and out on to the lakeside road, I wondered about how a big university like University of Montana handled buying fruit from a little producer like Heidi. Institutions are a big piece of the local-food puzzle since places like universities, prisons, hospitals, and government agencies are usually major food buyers and, thus, key players in any community's food economy. The majority of the time, massive food service operations satisfy these institutions' needs by obtaining food as cheaply as possible from industrial sources. But many institutions are starting to seek food from nearby small farms. As Heidi had suggested, hopeful news on that front turned out to be in good supply. A great example was indeed just down the road.

CHAPTER 3

Institutionalized

The biggest buyers flex their localizing muscle

FROM HEIDI'S FARM, I SPED south again, breezing past St. Ignatius and on to Missoula, the booming metropolis of the area, where the University of Montana is settled amid a cluster of leafy streets on the east side of town. There, on a quiet afternoon in the campus's University Center, I met Kyra Williams, then coordinator of the university's local-food program as an AmeriCorps VISTA volunteer and a young Vermonter with short, brown hair and a quiet confidence. AmeriCorps is a U.S. federal government program that funds deserving organizations working on a variety of causes to hire and train volunteers who earn stipends.

"Dining services' priority is to buy local," Kyra told me as we passed through some unmarked doors and a maze of drab hallways leading to the university's catering kitchen. The Farm to College program here has been building since 2003, when four environmental studies graduate students approached the dining services director, Mark LoParco, with the idea and found him extremely enthusiastic.

"In our database system when you go to order something, the items that come up first will be the Farm to College items," said Kyra. She estimated that in the summer some 30 to 50 percent of the produce the university buys is from local farms, much of it supplied by the Western Montana Growers Cooperative, along with smaller groups and individuals like Heidi. With the university's food budget over $3 million, that's a lot of money returning to the community. Here was one more piece of the cascading Western Montana local-eating network clicking into place.

We emerged into the catering kitchen, an expansive conglomeration of countertops, refrigerators, walk-in freezers, stoves, and a hodgepodge of other useful implements. Somewhere behind a bank of cooling racks, a radio crooned quietly as a couple of staff members wound down the day's work. The university, Kyra noted, is the biggest catering company in Montana, a distinction that hints at the considerable influence its buying habits could have on the local economy.

Local-food advocates like to imagine a world where universities get all their food from nearby farms, and in that vein, University of Montana is certainly a good-news story. But as pleasant as that image is, there are some real limitations to what such a large food service system can manage, especially on the residential side, which operates on a fixed budget and a set menu rotation that is planned months in advance. Incorporating new items into the agenda on the fly is near impossible, so co-ops learn at the beginning of the season what the university intends to buy. But even when local farmers know what the university wants, there are instances when small producers can't possibly satisfy the university's needs.

"We haven't had a local chicken source in a few years now because you're feeding fifteen hundred people and you need chicken wings and only chicken wings," said Kyra. Small farmers can't supply only one part of an animal in such bulk.

Another problem is processing, Kyra told me as we meandered across the quiet quadrangle on the way to the residential dining hall, comically called the Food Zoo. This was becoming a theme. The inconvenience and cost of processing raw ingredients seemed to be a universal thorn in the side of all those I had talked to about local food in Montana.

"One of the things that I learned this year is that the number one cost is labor," said Kyra. "So it makes it a lot harder to buy from local vendors because they're not able to process things in the way we need them, and we're not able to staff more people to chop all this stuff up."

By "all this stuff," she meant, for one thing, the slices of veggies along the salad bar, which the staff was laying out in the Food Zoo for that night's dinner for summer students. The students began filing in as Kyra and I talked amid the Formica tables and metal-framed chairs, their slumping shoulders suggesting a gloomy apathy. Maybe they were just tired, but somehow these didn't seem like people who would care whether their carrot sticks came from up the valley or the other end of the Earth. A study of Farm to College published in 2007, however, found that 84 percent of students found the program very or somewhat important. This is likely in part due to education being a large piece of the university's program. Dining services puts up signage for all their local foods, hosts events about nutrition, screens movies about food issues, and distributes brochures and reading lists. I was reminded that not only do institutions like the university provide a potential market for local produce, but their communications to their own members and their prominence within the larger community mean that their priorities can transmit powerful messages about the value of buying food from one's neighbors.

We pushed our way into the dining hall's kitchen, where the staff was busy filling warming trays for the night's meal. It really struck me as we stood amidst what seemed like miles of food-prep equipment: the scale on which you have to operate in such an institution is just enormous. And this wasn't even a massive university. As someone who has a hard time getting organized enough to put together the week's menu for herself, I thought how difficult it must be to incorporate local foods into a production facility that operates, with good reason, much like an industrial machine.

"There are a lot of ideals out there that can't always be met, just with the scale we're working on and the budget we're working with," said Kyra. "When I go to meetings of all these people in small nonprofits who are very idealized about the food system, I come into the group and say, 'But these are the hard facts about feeding a group of people and how the system works.' Having it so mechanized with menus on rotation is the only way to do it if you're going to be efficient and be able to save money and figure out how much waste you're producing and all of that. It's all in our system. By doing it that way, each year we get more efficient in cutting down on our waste and not buying too much."

Even though the ideal might not always be possible to meet, a program like the University of Montana's offers an optimistic example of how large institutions can transform their buying habits to support local producers while at the same time improving efficiency to reduce waste. Just the same, Kyra noted that she would like to see the university push the envelope even further. Ideally, she said Montana would have a student farm dedicated to supplying the dining facility, as is the case at the University of California at Santa Cruz, the gold standard of farm-to-college programs. Incidentally, about a year later, after Kyra had moved away from Montana to work on a farm, the university established the Dining Services Garden to supply organic produce grown from heirloom seeds to the dining facilities.

As I said goodbye to Kyra in the parking lot and revved up my little rental car, I was left with one nagging thought: While it's great to source locally when "local" means small farmers like Julie and Heidi, or the student-run farm out the back door, what about institutions in states where "local" could mean that you get your beef for the night's tacos from the industrial feedlot down the road? If you're in Iowa, that's local by the technical definition, isn't it? Were there institutions out there—land-grant schools, perhaps, focused on agriculture—with farm-to-college programs that held strong to their intended ideals in the face of what must be considerable pressure from board members and the school administration not to step on the toes of nearby industrial suppliers?

I found such a program in—surprise!—Iowa, where I arrived on the campus of Iowa State University (ISU) in Ames on a glorious July day and was taken aback by its loveliness. I had imagined Iowa as an endless flatness and the university—a land-grant school of twenty-eight thousand, twice University of Montana's size—as a huddle of institutional concrete buildings stranded amid monumental cornfields. In fact Iowa is hilly—charmingly so—and ISU looks not unlike my own New England college, only bigger, and home to students focusing on subjects like agronomy. Take, for example, Chantal Roberts, a tall, soft-spoken agronomy major and the dining services' sustainability coordinator, who met me in the student union early on a Monday. A few moments later, Nancy Levandowski, the director of the university's dining services, burst through the door in a black skirt suit with white trim and a gold name tag.

"My flight got in at eleven-thirty last night, so I'm a little slow this morning," she said breathlessly, settling between us at the little table. She had the air of someone satisfied by the hectic life of a packed schedule, someone who might be described as a "mover and shaker."

She, however, described herself as a "California girl" who brought ideas about local and sustainable food with her when she arrived at ISU in 2006. When she asked the university administration if dining services sourced anything locally, she was pleased with the answer: fifty-four thousand dollars' worth. But it wasn't quite what she had imagined. "They gave me a list," she said. "Coca-Cola Des Moines. Yeah, it's probably our soybeans that made the high-fructose corn syrup, but that's a little bit of a stretch for me." What she wanted was a program where you could trace all local produce purchased back to the farmers who grew it.

The first obstacle was funding. The dining services purchasing department defined its creditability by how much money it was saving the university, so earmarking a pot of money for the new venture was essential. Nancy asked the students on the meal plan to grant her an extra 1 percent of their dining cost to create a budget for local and organic food, a change that they agreed to despite it raising the cost of their meal plans. Her efforts have been so popular that in 2009 the students added an extra percent to the bucket, boosting the local-specific earmark to 2 percent of the dining program's $6 million food cost. In 2011, students reduced the allotment to 1.5 percent, but with the 0.5 percent difference made up in grant funding, the local-and-organic food budget still totals more than $100,000.

Soon, donors and board members began hearing of her efforts, and unlike many of the students, some of them were none too pleased. A donor who is also a pork producer told a dean at a cocktail party that he had heard ISU dining was banning confinement pork. The rumor was not true, but Nancy said she still "ended up in a working group with five deans talking about what was appropriate and what was not appropriate. When I first started all of this, we used to say, 'local, sustainable, organic.' Now we have to say, 'local, organic.' Sustainability hasn't been defined by the USDA. It hasn't been defined by anybody." Her definition of sustainable food—following the standards upheld by the Food Alliance, an Oregon nonprofit that certifies food producers on their farming practices, environmental stewardship, and labor conditions—was "considered rather radical by a lot of the administration of this university," she said. This is an unsurprising fact considering that ISU trains students in many of the industrial farming business practices that organizations like the Food Alliance condemn.

Ultimately, though, Nancy and the deans worked out a balance. "It's been an interesting path, but it's a good path," she said. "It's part of the politics of the campus. Every campus has politics. What I had to learn was anything judgmental was not appropriate. That's a safer zone to be in. On our webpage now, we define everything by referring to the USDA."

The details of the program, however, are still hers to decide, and the finer points about what constitutes "local" as she envisions it can be hard to parse out. I pulled out my question about whether a feedlot down the road would be considered local. Is there any size limit on the producers she was willing to work with? In the popular imagination, after all, "local farm" and "small farm" have come to be just about synonymous. "We don't talk about how big," she told me. "It's about local." The central question is whether they can trace the food back to the original farmer.

"Here's an interesting one," she said, leaning forward in her chair. "Hormel came to me." Hormel is a Fortune 500 meat producer best known for making Spam canned meat product. "Now, they're buying predominantly pigs from Iowa and processing them in their plant," she continued. "They asked me, 'Would we be able to count as part of your local purchases?' So I'm thinking, 'The pig farmers are local, it's processed local, so it's giving jobs to people here.'" She paused, looking at Chantal and me. "It's a moral dilemma."

She told Hormel she would have to feel confident that she could know precisely which farmer produced which piece of meat. "I've been to a Hormel plant up in Minnesota and they're processing twenty thousand hogs a day," she said. "If they're going to sell me bacon, and we know it's this bacon and this lot number and it's all local, that's one thing. But if you start getting into pepperoni and that other stuff, there's no way, because it's a blend. It's just not going to happen."

If they could guarantee that connection with the farmer, she told them, she would be willing to talk with them. They tried to compromise, asking if traceability on 60 percent of the meat would be enough. "I said, 'You're stretching it. I need to know who my farmers are.'"

The mover and shaker had to leave for another meeting, but before she did we headed upstairs for a quick tour of the dining hall, a welcoming room with tall windows and round tables. Permanent serving stations offered various types of food—deli, salad, cereal—and a few staff members were laying out the hot breakfast items in warming trays.

"Any Farm to ISU products out today?" Nancy called to a worker as we breezed in.

"No," the woman responded, glancing up from her task of arranging apples in a bowl.

"Oh well," Nancy said, turning to me. "We can't do it all the time."

In fact, she's found it important to mention to the skeptics out there that it's not like she's strong-arming the university's entire food system into some local-only paradigm. "I'm not trying to say we have to switch everything over," she said as we surveyed the breakfast station. "That would be like me saying, 'We're only going to do healthy food.' Yeah right. I'd be out of a job in a week. If I don't have chicken strips and hot dogs and some of that stuff, I'm not taking care of my customer base. But what I can do is provide them an opportunity to try new things."

Before she headed off to her next engagement, Nancy told me she's been excited lately to see that some of the freshmen are arriving at the university having already developed a sense of concern about their food and eating a little bit healthier than the students were when she started the program, a change that reflects a growing interest in the subject in the broader society. "They're starting to ask questions about where their food comes from," she said. "When I got here in 2006, [the school] really thought I was a crazy California girl. And now they're like, 'Oh, okay . . .'"

While the ISU program is remarkable and "oh, okay" is certainly a step in the right direction, I wondered after my meeting with Chantal and Nancy how much more ISU could be doing if Nancy were given full leeway to follow her ideas. What happens when an eat-local program is embraced so fully by an institutional administration that it impacts not only the institution, but also the surrounding community? Perhaps such a situation would more likely occur in an institution where the quality of the food is directly related to the business at hand.

Navigated by this question, I found myself a month later driving through New Milford, Connecticut, one of those charming New England towns with the scent of old money and a liberal peppering of venerable white churches. A sign at the town's edge announced that it was incorporated in 1712, and at nine a.m. on an August Monday, the bells of the First Congregational Church and St. John's Episcopal began to compete over the airspace in the town common.

I found the administration office of the New Milford Hospital in a peeling old house and sat reading a brochure about the institution— "your home for health"—as I awaited Marydale DeBor, then vice president for external affairs. I had come to hear her tell me how the hospital had not only transformed its entire food service to healthy, local fare, but had also taken an active role in reaching out to the wider community on issues of eating, health, and sustainability.

The door sprung open and a slim, put-together, gray-haired woman burst in with two little dogs. "Are you waiting for me?" she exclaimed, looking pleased when I nodded my assent. She left her dogs—known as "the girls"—in the outer office and ushered me into a conference room where she launched into the story of the hospital's Plow To Plate program. In 2006, she and a couple of friends (a chef and a pediatrician) had been shocked at the increasing appearance of obesity and type 2 diabetes among the hospital's patients, so they formed a community coalition of like-minded people set on addressing the problem.

Soon enough, the coalition had settled on the idea of overhauling the hospital's dining services. "I said, 'Look, I've been appalled since the day I arrived here at what we are feeding people in our hospital,'" Marydale told me. "'It's just outrageous. How can we do this to people who are sick?'" I could tell this was a woman to be reckoned with, as was her vision—to transform people's relationship to food. The idea was big enough to match the prominent role the community hospital plays in New Milford. As Marydale put it, "We have a bully pulpit."

Negotiations with the hospital's administration led to some changes in management and a call for proposals to find a new food service vendor. With the winning bidder, Unidine, at the helm since July 2008, the hospital has moved from slinging fried and processed victuals to serving freshly made meals, as much of it as possible from local farms. This change required remodeling the kitchen, teaching the staff cooking and knife skills, and restructuring the patients' food ordering process. Marydale explained that in most hospitals, patients choose what they'd like to eat for several days at once so the food can be stored on a patient's floor until it's time to serve. In New Milford, patients now order each meal separately from menus brought by specially trained staff who introduce the program and explain the importance of healthy eating for recovery. The requested food is prepared fresh and sent up to the patient's room to be eaten right away. "Our patient satisfaction scores—we use a national index—were in the low thirtieth percentile, and we're now in the ninety-ninth percentile," said Marydale. "One of the few in the country."

I was given proof of patient opinion almost immediately upon entering the low-key eighty-five-bed hospital, a squat brick building on a hill across the street from the administration building. We bumped into Chef Kerry Gold ("He's just a genius and I love him," Marydale said. "He's my partner in crime here."), who proposed a tour of the cafeteria. We were about to turn out of the hall when a smiling orderly in scrubs paused on his way by. "I just had a patient tell me that this cafeteria is the best place to eat in New Milford," he announced to us with a grin. "Granted, I'd just given her a whole bunch of drugs, but still, she was awake enough to know that she was getting out of here in time for lunch, and she wanted to be down here to have lunch." He chuckled as he moved off in his turquoise clothes, and we turned into the tiny but neat cafeteria to see what it was that particular patient so badly wanted.

Indeed, lunch at New Milford Hospital was unlike any hospital fare I'd ever heard of. On that day's menu, Chef Gold said, sweeping his arm toward the signs that stated as much, were pomegranate-glazed chicken with a fennel and walnut salsa, herb-crusted salmon with a dill sauce, grilled asparagus, and steamed brown rice. Add to that a couple different kinds of soup (including a vegetarian option), salad, and some kind of dessert involving chocolate ganache, and you begin to see how people who don't even know anyone in the hospital might end up coming here to eat.

"People come from the town," said Marydale. "We fax out our menu to the post office, the mayor, the senior centers, the nursing homes. People come here and eat like it's a restaurant." The growth in the retail trade has allowed the institution to improve patient food without running up the budget.

Marydale and Chef Gold led me into the kitchen, where a small staff of smiling—and, let's be frank, good-looking—young men were chopping vegetables and tending stew pots in chef's whites. The facility was clean and orderly, and everyone appeared to be having a surprisingly good time. Marydale pointed out where they had reconfigured the kitchen to fit a large cooler unit since they now use so much more fresh produce.

Out through the back door of the kitchen, we emerged into the hospital's culinary garden, situated on top of the loading dock. A big green sign proclaimed it the Planetree Healing Culinary Garden, and Marydale noted that anyone in the community was welcome to come enjoy it. It was all just too perfect: the sunshine of the summer day, just starting to heat up around the edges, a handful of butterflies flittering amid the greens, the fact that volunteers built the garden and a local Brownie troop maintains it.

Chef Gold was quickly running through a tour: "We have tomatoes, these are acorn squash, we're stripping down the basil left and right to make our own pesto. Over there we have Russian basil and parsley. We have thyme and garlic, chives, rosemary. We have lots of sage. Lavender. We make lavender scones. We have strawberries."

Hold the phone. Lavender scones? I considered asking if I could move into one of the hospital's empty beds. But I didn't have time to sink too deeply into this reverie—Chef Gold was off, busy with the day's schedule, and Marydale and I were headed back to the administration building where she could share with me the whole *other* side of the program. The other side? Wasn't it enough that the hospital was actually using the fruits of local farms to help its patients get well? Could there possibly be even more hopeful news in this story?

"This whole thing is about disease prevention," Marydale was saying as we crossed back over the parking lot. "I mean it may look like it's just fun, hip, groovy food. But this is public health practice. We just make it fun. Because who wants to be lectured to? And we make it participatory."

By "participatory" she meant that the hospital had gone way beyond just feeding good food to patients. They had engaged the entire community in programs meant to change attitudes about eating and food. Youth Chef Advocates, a shining jewel in Plow To Plate's crown, engages kids from the youth agency in an intensive, nine-month cooking and food education program. They learn about seasonal produce—harvesting scallops at the Stonington docks, for example, and peas at a local farm—and are taught culinary skills.

"They get proper chef's attire—an embroidered chef jacket and everything," said Marydale. "They're expected to show up with that clean every week. They're responsible. They have a professional knife kit. At first people thought we were crazy having seventh graders with these knives. But they have respect. They know that these are the knives used at the Culinary Institute of America." After learning how to cook the foods they've harvested, the students prepare a meal for friends and family and serve it to them, describing the ingredients and their preparation. "We're reconstituting the community table," said Marydale. "When we first started, half the parents showed up, and by the last dinner we had like seventy-five people. This became the hot ticket in town."

The kids in the program each do an advocacy project, which

helps spread interest in healthy, high-quality foods to other children. "Some kids helped younger kids plant lettuce," said Marydale. "Some kids wrote a book about food and read it to elementary kids. We had kids write op-eds and get them published in the local paper."

To engage the wider community, the hospital has also focused on building up the local farmers' market by doing publicity and inviting storytellers and musicians to make the event into an appealing family affair. The hospital has set up a CSA for its own employees and is working with local pediatricians to distribute five-dollar tokens that can only be spent at the farmers' market to families whose children are at risk for diet-related diseases. Marydale's team got beloved local children's author Billy Steers to write a picture book about a farmers' market as part of his popular Tractor Mac series, which they distribute to Head Start programs and child care centers.

To reach the other end of the age spectrum, the hospital started the Senior Suppers program, which partners with all the senior centers in the area to offer healthy meals for five dollars, served with a side helping of food education and an after-dinner social hour featuring interesting talks, therapies like Reiki and hand massage, and musical entertainment.

"It's full-surround," said Marydale. "This is classic public health practice. You change the environment, you work with people, you get everybody involved. You figure out every which way you can go at the problem of changing how people eat."

And while it may be relatively easy to have an impact when you're working with an eighty-five-bed hospital in a small community—an accusation that has kept New Milford from getting the greater recognition enjoyed by some other programs—Marydale is gearing up to take her show on the road, perhaps to larger institutions.

"We now have hospitals coming to us," she said, as she showed me to my car. "We're teaching them. This is all turnkey, all this material. We can do it for any hospital." She paused in the midday sunlight, considering the fast-moving health care universe. "I haven't found anybody else who's built public health programming around it the way I have," she said.

CHAPTER 4

Cultivating the Internet

The Web connects growers and eaters

So FAR, I WAS HAPPY: I had managed to rake some hope, learning that despite logistical challenges, people all over the nation are hard at work figuring out how to buy food from and sell food to their neighbors. If every community in the nation had a growers' co-op as enthusiastic and determined as the one in western Montana, a university as dedicated to connecting consumers with farmers as Iowa State, and a hospital as tapped in to the eating life of its community as the one in New Milford, things would really start changing in a big way all across this country.

But despite all the good news I had found, it was clear that the complexity of connecting small-scale growers to interested eaters is a major difficulty for the growth of local food. Big grocery chains work in ways that make it difficult for small and medium-sized local and regional enterprises to compete with large, national-scale food producers. Individual buyers are often left choosing between the farmers' market and a CSA, both good options, but not always convenient, affordable, or sufficient to keep all the small-scale growers afloat. Institutions that seek to buy local face the challenge of how to

best communicate with and order from a large number of little retailers instead of interfacing with one big industrial vendor.

Clearly things were hard out there for your smaller food producers, but it seemed to me that they had one magical ace up their
sleeve, a tool that could provide a far greater advantage to locally
oriented growers than to the big dogs: the Internet. I had already
seen its benefits; there is no way that the Western Montana Growers
Cooperative could operate as efficiently as it does without its online
system in which growers consistently record their available produce
so the manager knows what's on hand to sell. The Web, so superb at
connecting those who have something to sell with those who want
to buy it, seemed rife with potential for shifting the focus of food
retail away from industrial suppliers and toward those in the position to offer on-demand delivery of the freshest food around.

Hot on the trail of a thriving online local-food marketplace, I
made my way to Portland, Oregon, where an organization called
Ecotrust keeps its headquarters in a reclaimed historic building atop
a Patagonia store and a locally sourced pizza place. The group is
typically Portland, from its welcoming, open-plan office space to its
farm-to-school programming and its holistic view of regional environmental health. But don't think for a minute everybody is sitting around the office singing "Kumbaya": these people are all
business and their FoodHub online network, launched in February
2010, is one of the most effective innovations for growing a local-
food economy.

I sat down in the office's oddly shaped kitchen with Deborah
Kane, Ecotrust's Vice President of Food & Farms, a small, energetic woman with short brown hair wearing a slim, sporty dress.
She seemed like a straight-shooting type of person, and indeed, she
didn't waste any time getting to the point.

"For a decade, Ecotrust has been trying to connect regional food buyers and sellers. Why? We want to create a robust regional-food economy. Why? We want to create jobs, strengthen rural communities, and make sure that people throughout the region, no matter who they are or what their income is, have daily access to the region's bounty," she said. I noticed that she didn't use the words "food miles" or "carbon footprint" once, an outlook that jived with my conclusion that local food is more about job creation and community vitality than it is about environmental health.

Deborah pulled up the FoodHub homepage on her laptop, where a colorful jumble of images—a strawberry, a cow, a tractor, an ear of corn—graced the top of the page. She quickly ran down the program's specifications for me: regionally focused in the Northwest (at least at that time; it has since expanded to a national scope, organized by region), scale neutral, and production-practice neutral.

But wait, that meant that Ecotrust was welcoming the big players just as much as the little guys. What happened to the local-food movement as a means of evening the playing field against industrial producers? I had to make sure I had heard correctly. "So that means that you're prioritizing proximity over method of food production or size of farm?" I asked.

"Completely and entirely correct," she said. "You can be somebody on point oh-two acres—the size of my backyard—with a honeybee population and you can be all the way up to a rancher in eastern Oregon grazing on forty-five hundred acres. It's not just for organic farmers. It's not just for sustainable farmers. If you're a conventional farmer, we want to see you in FoodHub because we think it's a great opportunity for you to connect with the regional-food marketplace."

She signed into the system and pulled up the account's dashboard page, where a user would be able to input profile information; conduct a search of products, buyers, or sellers; see all the messages in the site's "marketplace" classified space; or launch a browsing session to see who else is out there in, as Deborah liked to call it, "the FoodHub universe." Each seller's account might contain information about business practices, contacts, minimum order amounts, delivery schedule and range, connections with mainline distributors, liability insurance, seasonal product availability, certifications, acreage, and professional associations.

Buyers, meanwhile, list their purchasing managers' information, food needs, and delivery and transaction preferences. The only restriction on buyers is that they be an institution, not an individual, a focus that makes FoodHub unique in the field. "There are few people—actually, none to my knowledge—who are doing it the way Ecotrust is doing it: trying to create that business-to-business connection in a way that would build community and allow people to share stories and keep the story intact as products move throughout the supply chain," Deborah told me. But as with the growers, these institutional buyers can be any shape and size. "It's buyers who are buying case quantities or semitruck loads," she said. "We don't just want to be worrying about white-tablecloth restaurants. We want to be worrying about food buyers of all kinds."

I was starting to get the picture. It wasn't that FoodHub planned to support small producers by prioritizing them, but simply by leveling the playing field so that they could compete as effectively as the bigger guys. And likewise, this level-playing-field setup would enable your average office complex stocking its cafeteria to access the same fresh produce on which high-end restaurants had long cornered the market. The idea was to make everything available to everybody and let the market go to work. The fact that this concept seemed novel only shows how skewed toward one type of producer and one type of institutional distributor our food markets have become.

As we talked, Deborah demonstrated how the system allows you to organize the data by many variables, including by institutions like hospitals. "You can sort by buyer or by seller, you can sort by distance, you can go into map view, you can sort by business type," she said, clicking around through various lists and finally landing on the profile for Oregon Health & Science University Hospital, which had put out a call for carrots, peaches, and Romaine lettuce.

The only thing FoodHub doesn't do is complete transactions online. Ecotrust decided to leave off the shopping cart feature after focus group testing revealed that it made users feel burdened by the requirements of constantly updating prices and quantities. Basically, FoodHub serves as a comprehensive business-to-business food-oriented bulletin board (one that also happens to help users create professional purchase orders and invoices).

Just as its creators were hoping, several months after Food-Hub's unveiling users were starting to post notices about a lot more than what fresh produce they had in stock. "It's not just about 'I've got blueberries' or 'I need okra,' but here's someone saying, 'Hey, I've got eight hundred square feet of cold storage,'" said Deborah, clicking on a notice in the site's classified section. "That's a totally wonderful thing to know about if you're trying to grow a regional-food community." After my visit to Montana, I knew this all too well. I wondered if the people I had visited there knew about Food-Hub, considering that, despite the site being at that time focused on Oregon and Washington, its regional purview also took in Montana, Idaho, California, and Alaska.

"It is a perfect tool for connecting food buyers and sellers," Deborah said as she clicked the Web browser closed. "It is a perfect tool for strengthening connections in the region." FoodHub was precisely the kind of innovation I had been looking for, and I left the Ecotrust office with a hopeful spring in my step. But I also wondered about other ways the Internet could serve local- and regional-food economies.

What about Web ventures that *did* prioritize the little guy or the organic farmer? What about using the Web to inject life back into a foundering rural economy that had been wrung dry by the consolidation of our agricultural industry?

This time my search took me to the opposite side of the country, to the little town of Rutherfordton, North Carolina, in the jewel green foothills of the Appalachians, where I located the office of the Foothills Connect Business and Technology Center in a white-columned former municipal community hall on North Main Street. The man I had come to see—Timothy Will, larger than life in a Hawaiian shirt and a massive grin—was single-handedly rebuilding the local agricultural community using a system of horticulture training and Web-based producer-consumer connections.

He was also, apparently, a hugger. A bear hug was not the kind of hello any of my previous interview subjects had given me, but then, Tim Will is a different kind of fellow. I was not fooled by the bristly gray scrim of beard and close-cropped white hair; this was clearly a man of huge heart and uncommon energy, not to mention great vision. He is, as he himself said, "a change agent," a guy who knows that when you do what you love with fervor and even ferocity, the universe responds. He had funneled his vision and energy into transforming the area's local-food system and, thereby, its economy.

"We're not foodies," he had told me in an earlier phone interview. "It has very little to do with food and everything to do with jobs. I'm in an area where the economy has collapsed." Now, face-to-face, he reiterated the idea with enthusiasm: "We are rebuilding the economic system here. Now, that's cool. That's one of the coolest things to do." He beamed at me. "I'm going to get a coffee. You up for a coffee? Okay, we're going to get a coffee."

Rutherfordton (pronounced, amusingly, "Rolfton" by locals) is a small place, one of those former manufacturing centers that are fading to gray in the bright, globalized sunlight of the new century. The town has been rocked back on its heels—even the barber said business is down because all the heads of hair have left to find work in bigger cities. But there's still one solid coffee shop, and over a couple lattés Tim told me how it had all started after he became head of Foothills Connect, a nonprofit founded in 2005 to use technology to support development of small business and entrepreneurship. His first task was to think up a new flagship project for the struggling organization. A cousin of his, a chef at a Charlotte restaurant some seventy miles away, lamented that he longed for fresh produce—the supply chain that served his restaurant sent him two-week-old produce from California, a quarter of which was so wilted it had to be thrown out. A lightbulb went off: Tim's cousin needed fresh produce and the people of Rutherfordton needed income. Many of the jobless he was meant to help were sitting on untilled family land, and all around Rutherford County there were established farmers who had few local markets for their goods. Tim had hit upon Foothills Connect's next project and was off and running.

His team created a proprietary online system—Farmers Fresh Market—that allows farmers to input their inventory and for restaurants and consumers in Charlotte to order online. Meanwhile, they worked to spread broadband Internet widely through Rutherford County, in part so that farmers could access the system. Every order that comes in gets a barcode detailing the farm providing the food, the order amount and type, an order number, and when possible, GPS coordinates of exactly where the food was grown. The system sends an invoice to the buyers and a statement to the grower, which lists the total price of the food, the amount taken out for Foothills's processing fee (20 percent), and the final profit. Producers then bring their orders to the office at the appointed drop-off times, where they're scanned with the barcode gun and put into the right box for the distributor to deliver.

The next day at delivery time, Tim took me to the loading dock behind the office so I could get a look at the action, with mostly involved farmers pulling up with their freshly harvested produce to be included in the morning's truckload bound for Charlotte. I lingered in the sunshine with Kirk Wilson, director of the program, who looked every bit the farmer in sturdy blue jeans and a stiff-brimmed mesh cap, and I watched Lindy Abrams organize the incoming vegetables into boxes. Though at age twenty-five she had left a job in arts administration to cultivate her family's land as Holla Holler Farm, Lindy seemed more like a hip city kid than a farmer in bug-eyed sunglasses and a handmade belt buckle emblazoned with the word HOLLA. She was working the drop-off to earn a little extra cash, since making ends meet on the income from a tiny farm is tough, even with the advantage of being young and unattached.

"From what I've seen, you've got to get an early start because by the time you get it all figured out, you really need some steady income," she said as she leaned against a post for a minute, enjoying the sunshine. "Right now I can adjust and live cheaply." She flicked a mark on her clipboard as the delivery driver slapped a barcode sticker on the last box of greens to be loaded into the back of the truck.

Lindy was by no means the only new farmer in the area. A centerpiece of the Foothills Connect program is training would-be local farmers in small-scale organic growing using hand tools, a method detailed by organic gardening guru Eliot Coleman. As the truck pulled away with the day's delivery, Kirk walked me down the hill to a tiny vacant lot on a side street, where a banner reading "FOOTHILLS CONNECT HORTICULTURE SCHOOL" slouched between two posts and a small hoop house lurked behind a few weed-choked beds. "This is the spring class's," Kirk said, examining some overgrown rows. "They learned how to make a raised bed and how to plant it. They had these little push-planters and seeders."

If the ambitious Tim Will has anything to do with it, the trainee farmers won't be stuck in the little square of grass much longer. Later that day, he and I drove in his old pickup to an unused high school building and stood before the playing field, braced against the chill, post-rainstorm air under a sky as flat and unshining as a cookie sheet. He swept his arm across an ample grassy acre, a rectangle of blacktop, and a playground and described his vision for the space: a working farm, a community garden, and a farmers' market. "This is where we'll grow it," he said. I wasn't sure if he meant food or the organization, but he could well have been referring to both. He told me he was also working to get permission from the city of Rutherfordton to commandeer enough of the school building to relocate the Foothills Connect offices.

He pointed to a strip of grass beside the playground. "Right in here, this acre or so, I want to be able to do a community garden so the parents would work in the garden," he said. "And this would be the end where we grow for market and training—bringing them in from Spartanburg, Greenville, Charlotte, and as far away as Tennessee—and train them how to do raised-bed, French intensive organic gardening like the Peace Corps taught me to go and teach Third World people thirty years ago."

Tim had been, I had discovered in a series of wandering conversations, a supervisor in the Peace Corps in Honduras and Fiji, a technician in a nuclear war room during Vietnam, an urban planner in New Orleans, an executive in the early days of the digital telecommunications industry, and the mayor of a town in Florida. He pursues whatever strikes his interest, often making life-change decisions on a hunch, as when he moved to Rutherfordton after seeing the area portrayed in the film *The Last of the Mohicans* and declaring it "the most beautiful place I've ever seen." (Chimney Rock, where the movie's final climactic scene is set, is about twenty miles from Tim's house.) In his professional life, he has doggedly pursued whatever stirs his passion and whatever might make life better for others, an approach that left him impatient with the usual ego- and money-driven logic of the world's workplaces.

At early stages in job interviews as an in-demand telecom manager, he had told me as we sipped coffee in the café during the torrential rainstorm earlier that day, "They'd want to talk about money. And I'd go, 'It's too early to talk about money.' They'd go, 'Huh?'" He made a face of profound confusion, mocking his long-ago interlocutors, then he laughed delightedly. "I'd say, 'It's how a lot of people keep score, but it's not the most important thing to me. If I were going to make a list, it'd probably be in the first page, probably in the first column, but it certainly wouldn't be in the first three.' And I'd leave it there. And they'd say, 'Well, what are the first three?' And I'd say, 'It has to be exciting, it has to be adventurous, and it has to be fun. Or I can't do it.'"

I loved his enthusiasm, but this list of remarkable demands for job searching struck me as a tad pie in the sky. Who has the luxury to hold tight to such ideals in the face of potential bosses and HR apparatchiks and the promise of benefits packages? I took a sip of my coffee and watched the downpour pummel the sidewalk outside.

But the story wasn't over yet. The upshot, Tim said, was that his interviewers would be so thrilled by the prospect of an employee who wanted to work for the joy and excitement of it rather than the money that they would immediately offer him a bigger salary than the job advertisement had mentioned. Plus stock options.

"So they would give you more money," I said in disbelief, "because they were so enthusiastic to have someone who—"

"—who worked for adventure, excitement, and fun." His tone of voice seemed to say, "Doesn't that make complete sense?" And I had to admit, his search for fun and adventure by helping cultivate a crop of new farmers and finding a way to supply Charlotte restaurants with the freshest local produce sure seemed to be working out swimmingly. This approach to life did hold a certain, beautiful logic.

For Tim it seemed there was no other way of being—if you said nothing else about him, it would be that he gets up in the mix and doesn't ponder regrets or make excuses. And like any man of action, he does not suffer fools gladly. He remembered his frustration with the Peace Corps volunteers he was supervising in Honduras, who had amazing skill sets but would come to him and say they didn't know what to do. "It seemed to me," said Tim, reddening with annoyance at the memory, "that *anything* they could do would be right. Do something! I had no patience for that."

His take-action method of working has helped the Farmers Fresh Market program have a greater impact than even he may have originally imagined. As soon as the trainee farmers started working with iron hand tools procured from a mail-order garden-supply shop, for example, Tim decided they could be better designed and immediately took the idea to local metalworker Thomas Elfers, who creates custom gates and metal sculpture at his workshop, Ornamentals and Finer Welding, Inc. When I was visiting, the stronger, less expensive broadforks he designed and built had just become available for sale at a new organic seed and fertilizer shop, Earthperks, which Farmers Fresh Market farmers Richard and Deborah Davis had opened on their farm. The rustic little shop filled with racks of seeds, pallets of fertilizer, and all manner of other useful items not only keeps farm dollars in the community, but also provides a focus of community life and a venue for other local entrepreneurs to sell their products. With its establishment, the Davises have reestablished a key piece of the local agricultural economy.

"We're getting second-generation jobs that are supporting the farmers," Tim told me proudly.

But according to his staff at Foothills Connect, Tim is bringing something much more valuable to the community's needy members. Out on the loading dock, Jim Brown, Tim's executive assistant and former chairman of the board, had told me about the letter he wrote to nominate Tim for the Purpose Prize, an award for people who make a difference to society in their "encore careers" after retirement, which Tim ended up winning in 2009. "Tim Will grows hope," the first sentence of the letter had read.

And on our tour of the horticulture school, Kirk had expressed a similar sentiment. Learning how to be food producers and entrepreneurs helps local people get more income, which can be vital in a region whose economy has been badly damaged by globalization and recession, he told me. But the benefits go deeper than a few extra dollars in people's pockets. The program takes such a comprehensive approach to enabling the area's people to help themselves that it has started a literacy program to teach illiterate farmers to read so they can use the Web-based ordering system.

"It's more than about the money," Kirk had said. "Teaching people how to read. What price can you put on that? Giving people hope. What price can you put on that?"

PART 2

GREEN THUMBS

CHAPTER 5

Advocating for Agriculture

Determined organizers help new farmers succeed

MY BLEAK FEELINGS ABOUT OUR food system had been considerably improved by my journey among the locally oriented pioneers doing their best to rebuild damaged food economies around the country. I was even beginning to feel a tingle of optimism somewhere under the ribs on my left side, just about in the same place I used to get a cramp at swim practice. I was ready to declare victory and take off in search of a stiff drink. (Here's to conquering the mountain passes of northern Idaho in a rental car the size of a matchbox.)

However, right when I could almost hear the ice cubes clinking in a tall, sweating glass, a troubling thought occurred to me: who exactly is supposed to be doing all the work of growing these local-food systems? The thing about having a large number of smaller producers distributed abundantly throughout the countryside servicing all of their local and regional communities is that you actually have to have *a large number of producers*. This, I could see right away, presented a problem.

We have a relatively small number of farmers in the United States, and every year their average age gets higher. According to the U.S. Environmental Protection Agency (EPA) about 40 percent of U.S. farmers were fifty-five or older as of 2002. Think about that for a moment—almost half of all the people growing our country's food are speeding rapidly toward the age at which activities like shuffleboard and pinochle gain an unfathomable appeal. In 2007, the USDA reported the average age of a U.S. farmer to be fifty-seven, a situation so dire that the EPA declared "the graying of the farm population" to be causing "concerns about the long-term health of family farms as an American institution."

Technically, the tradition of families running farms is still alive and well—in 2004, 98 percent of farms met the USDA's definition of family-owned farms—but it's the small and especially middle-sized family farms, those with sales below $250,000, that are in considerable danger. These one-time bastions of the American agricultural landscape composed 90 percent of U.S. farms in 2004 but accounted for only 24 percent of U.S. farm production value.

The commonly referenced divide between family-run farms and corporate farms is not, then, so much of a concern as the distinction between small farms and large ones. While the 2007 USDA Census of Agriculture actually saw an uptick in the number of small farms for the first time since the 1940s, the farmers who run them work more *off* the farm than the average farmer, many of them approaching farming as a part-time add-on, a retirement hobby, or an element of a rural lifestyle. Meanwhile, midsized farms across the country, as judged by both acreage and revenue—those that are the best positioned to efficiently serve regional-scale food economies—are flat-out drowning. Big farms, by contrast, whether owned by families, corporations, or family-owned corporations, are gaining strength, continuing the trend toward concentration in agricultural production. Their number has increased steadily since the early 1980s, especially among those with sales of a million dollars or more. Studies by the USDA Economic

Research Service show that little by little our agricultural landscape is being taken over by the industrial farm operation—massive, mechanized, commodity focused, and run by what is, for cultivating such large tracts of land, a very small number of people.

One impact of having fewer farmers is that agriculture is taking a diminishing place in most of our lives. No longer do most of us have grandparents, uncles, cousins, or even friends who farm for a living. Many of us don't even know anyone who grows tomatoes in the backyard. More of us than we'd like to admit don't have the foggiest notion how to cook a tomato anyway. (I'm sure I'm not the only one surprised to learn that you can actually make your own ketchup.)

Indeed, the U.S. population has become disconnected from the details of our food and the way it is supplied to us. While it might sound reassuring that almost a third of U.S. households said they were planning to grow some of their own food in 2009, as reported by the National Gardening Association, it's not at all hard to find a child who can't identify an onion or an adult, even one who frequents farmers' markets, with little understanding of seasonality. And if we aren't familiar with the ins and outs of producing food and the impacts of consolidating our farmland in the hands of very few, we are unlikely to fully comprehend the danger presented by our dwindling population of farmers.

As I guided yet another miniature rent-a-car toward yet another shoebox-shaped motel on the way from someplace to somewhere, I pondered the difficulty we seem to be in. Unless we can get a lot more people, especially young people, interested in the business of farming and food, all the best intentions of changing our food system for the better will never amount to a hill of beans. I could tell that I yet again had my hoperaking work cut out for me. Next on the agenda: find out what inspiring efforts were under way to encourage, train, and support new farmers; maintain small family farms; educate our children about farming and food; and demonstrate the value of cultivating a green thumb.

My first stop was the suburban Connecticut town of Ridgefield, where the amazingly named Severine von Tscharner Fleming, founder of the new-farmer-support organization called The Greenhorns, was working for the summer on a friend's farm. "Yoo-hoo!" she called, waving, as I stumbled out of the brambles in which I had managed to park my car. She stood in the doorway of the idyllic white farmhouse dressed in a blue striped blouse, green gardener's clogs, and a base-ball cap propped atop a frizzled mop of blondish curls.

"This is the farm and it's the last farm in the town of Ridgefield," she told me as we started out on a tour. "And this is the field and that is the ridge." She pointed down below the farmhouse, where green fields interspersed with quaint stone walls swept down toward dis-tant woods. I chuckled at her comment, but she didn't crack a smile.

"So this used to all be farms up and down here?" I asked, ges-turing in the direction of the road, a leafy lane that meandered among the landscaped mansions of the upscale neighborhood.

"You know, New England, America—all farms," she responded. "Our early presidents—all farmers." Now, she told me as we ducked into a shed housing chicks and bunnies, we don't have enough farm-ers to fill the shoes of the retiring generation. According to the 2007 USDA Census of Agriculture, farm operators aged seventy-five or older are over five times as numerous as those under the age of twenty-five. After I fumbled and dropped the tiny chick she gave me to hold—come on, I grew up eating powdered mashed potatoes, what do you expect?—we moved quickly on to the yard where a band of rowdy goats were frolicking and eating everything. One im-mediately jumped up to munch on the drawstring of my pants, bleat-ing crazily.

"Are there a lot of young people interested in taking the old-timers' places if they could only figure out how?" I asked as I tried to yank my pants out of the gobbling maw of my new best friend.

"Yes, there are." She leaned over to scratch a goat behind the ears. "Hi, goaty goat."

Young agriculturalists—who The Greenhorns's website poetically calls "rough and ready protagonists of place"—don't have nearly enough support, she told me. Severine's single-minded purpose in starting the organization was to provide young farmers the help they need to succeed. "Our whole lives are oriented around services to young farmers. Our mission is worrying for young farmers, and we're doing it in every way we can."

She led me into a greenhouse where she watered some heat-scorched plants with a hose, and then we wandered through vegetable patches and orchards under a dazzling blue sky surprisingly hot for May.

A major way The Greenhorns helps young farmers, Severine explained, is by providing a thriving network on which they can rely for advice, companionship, and resources. Any farm run by a lone farmer "is relying on that one person, their health, their mental sanity, their happiness," she said. "We thought, 'We need to start supporting the whole person.' A lot of that is having the opportunity to socialize with people when you're not trying to hustle vegetables. Because frankly hustling vegetables is exhausting."

What young farmers need instead is simply to hang out with people, to hear the gossip, the friendly advice, the warnings. Like, she said, "a bad landlord story, or knowing we can all pool up and buy seed grain together in a pallet-load, or that he's got a plucker and I need a plucker because I'm trying out my turkeys this year."

As our local-farming economies have disappeared, so has the local community life that has always played an essential role in supporting agriculturalists in their long, hard work. The Greenhorns tries to resurrect this valuable asset by creating deliberate social networks in local areas. "It's transactional, it's relational," Severine said about the way the farmers in these networks interact. "It's what every community needs. It's what every community has always had. It starts with everybody being fluent with each other, knowing where everyone's at, who has waste to share, who needs support."

The Greenhorns cultivates these communities using various methods of communication—publishing a blog with more than a thousand regular readers, maintaining an online map to track young farmers' locations, hosting a radio show on which Severine conducts farming-related interviews, and, as the flagship project that originally jumpstarted the idea for the organization, making a documentary film about this newest generation in American agriculture. To add the all-important face-to-face element, the organization puts on a series of events and mixers around the country.

"I'm an activist, an organizer. I spend five hours a day on the computer doing all this stuff," Severine said as she led me into a shady field where a crew of spirited pigs rooted around in the grass. "But the reason why I do it is that I'm in service to agriculture, and if I'm not farming I'm kind of bummed. Hi piggies! Let's make sure you guys have water."

She had recently faced one of the more difficult challenges that characterize life for young farmers—loss of her rented land. With rampant farm consolidation and real estate development taking over farmland, young farmers can rarely afford to buy their own parcels, a situation that leaves them at the mercy of landlords. When I asked about the obstacles young farmers face, access to land was first on her list. "Access to land, access to capital, access to training, access to cultural support," she ticked off. "There's also inadequate sustainable agriculture curriculum in the land-grant universities. There's inadequate expertise at the extension level about issues faced by young farmers." She rubbed the neck of a pig that poked its nose into her hand. "Oh, he loves a scratch. What do you say, pig?"

These are big problems, I pondered as I got back in my car and cruised out among the mansions on my way back to the highway. They are problems not easily fixed by wishful thinking or community confabs. The Greenhorns was doing an admirable job of building a community of support for, raising awareness about, and advocating on behalf of new farmers, but I wondered what other programs might exist to help people gain access to some of the resources they would need to succeed in farming.

After a little digging, I discovered a series of programs around the country that assist retiring family farmers whose children aren't interested in farming to transition their operations to a new generation. These state-level programs, often called Land Link and connected as part of the International Farm Transition Network, give young people unrelated to a farm's owners the chance to gradually learn about, take over the management of, and then buy the farm (literally, not figuratively, one hopes).

On the outskirts of Urbandale, Iowa, under an angry sky threatening a downpour, I pulled up to a low, nondescript building on a street lined with strip malls in search of one of the most prominent and active of these programs; this was the unlikely location of Iowa State Extension's Outreach Center, home to the Beginning Farmer Center. I was installed in a small conference room and soon joined by David Baker, farm transition specialist, who works with farmers of all types to make sure family farms, especially the small ones, remain family farms. The center's Ag Link program helps farmers create succession plans to transition operations to sons, daughters, or other related parties, while the Farm On program matches up nonrelated parties so farmers without interested children can arrange for their farm businesses to proceed into the future as family-scale enterprises.

"There's still that age-old thought that you have to pass your farm down to your oldest son," David told me as we settled into our chairs. "In the back of a lot of our culture, that idea is still there. They'll say, 'Oh, my family can't farm it, I guess I don't have anybody.' Hello! We've got thousands of young people who would love that opportunity."

The would-be farmers who seek out the Beginning Farmer Center have a deep thirst for the agricultural life. "They just want to farm," he said. "They're not worried about how many dollars an hour they earn. They're not worried about promotions. Something has said to them, farming is good. Raising my own crops, being my own boss—that's good. I value that. I just want to farm. Tell me how I can do it."

Now a handsome older man with arms defined by hard labor and the easy smile of someone who feels satisfied with his path in life, David was once such a young person. He grew up "a town boy" but felt so drawn to the farming life that he arranged to take over a five-hundred-acre farm in northwest Iowa from a retiring farmer at a time long before programs like the one he now manages existed. After more than thirty years raising corn, soy, and cattle while doing off-farm jobs and, at one point, going back to school for an MBA, he now owns the place outright after purchasing the final portion from the previous owner in 2008.

His own experience taking over an older farmer's operation made him an ideal candidate to counsel others on succession issues. "My main focus is trying to match up nonrelated parties and counsel both of them to get along and grow into the future as a family farm that's unique," he said. "I don't dwell on the relationship issue, really, because it's people." Whether they're related or not, the success of any arrangement relies on good communication. The first and most sensitive communication task in this business is "getting the older generation to accept the fact that they're going to die," he said. According to a survey done by Iowa State Extension, only 27 percent of older farmers have identified a successor for the business. "It sounds macabre, but we're all going to have to make some decisions toward the end of our lives about what we want our lives to stand for," David told me. "When I talk to the older groups, I talk to them about legacy. What do you want your legacy to be? That you cashed out all your chips and had a lot of chips that went into the bank in town, or that you helped some young people get established? That your family farm went on to the next generation?"

David seemed like the right kind of guy to be asking such questions to hard-boiled veteran farmers—he was a farmer himself, after all, a man's-man kind of guy, but one with a diplomatic way of putting things and a passion for helping people negotiate their relationships. His next career, he had already decided, would be family counseling and therapy. His enthusiasm for this work was clearly just as much about preserving the small farms of the nation as it was about a dedication to the idea of family. When older farmers passed their farms on to nonrelated younger people, he emphasized, it was a way for the older farmers to support young families dedicated to farming. He described the satisfaction of raising his own children in the rural lifestyle he loves: "You hope that your children learn how to work hard, how to manage money, how to take care of living things, how to appreciate the land for what it can provide."

David believes that attracting young families back to small towns by helping them procure farms is a key to saving rural America and its wholesome values from withering on the vine. "I think it's important for the local communities to have young families doing business in those towns," he said. "You look at Iowa; how many small farmers, young families could we have going into these small towns, going into the churches and schools and into the businesses if we had fewer five-thousand-acre farmers and more one-thousand-acre farmers? Not that I'm opposed to large farms, because I'm sure they're well run and they're efficient, but it's not in the best interest of our communities and our society."

The problem of passing down the land into the right hands, however, has already advanced beyond intransigent old farmers who don't care to think about end-of-life issues. Many of these old farmers are already gone, having left their farms in the hands of a non-farming next generation, absentee landlords who pass the land down again to new generations even further removed from the value of the life it once supported. "Second-, third-generation ownership is growing because the first generation is dying off with no plans of what will happen to the farm," said David. "So what will happen? [Their kids or grandkids] sell it to the highest bidder. Who are the highest bidders? The big farmers."

Indeed, it seemed clear from our conversation that if we don't keep consciously working to keep small and medium-sized farms up and running, then massive farms—whether run by families or corporations—will keep gobbling up all our farmland. What David is doing at the Beginning Farmer Center is proactively preventing the land consolidation that is damaging our agricultural system. "We have seventy-some-thousand farms in Iowa," he said. "That's seventy thousand opportunities for a farm business to go to someone else. I think there's so much potential there, I really do. And what's driving me is the thought of having seven ten-thousand-acre farms. All these small rural towns are going to dry up and be gone."

But with the right opportunities and support, those who have an interest in farming can gradually reestablish the roots of these wilting rural communities. And if we can provide these opportunities to the diverse subsection of the American population that wants or needs to farm, our small towns can become all the stronger and more vibrant by reflecting the larger population more accurately. The Beginning Farmer Center is already active in engaging immigrants and refugees in the Des Moines area.

"A lot of immigrants have been coming into the state for the packing plants and other manufacturing businesses, so they have forty-hour-a-week jobs," said David. "How can they help sustain their families with a small parcel of land? I've worked with several immigrants to buy land in and around Des Moines. They raise vegetables, sell them at farmers' markets, add a little bit of income to their family. Many times they're large families, so if they can raise enough produce for their own families plus sell some, boy, it's a win-win situation."

Win-win indeed. I left our meeting brimming with hope and full of curiosity about the potential of renewing American small farming, not only by transitioning from the older generation to the younger—an essential task—but also by changing the face of it, by cultivating a more diverse crop of farmers.

The 2007 USDA Census of Agriculture reveals that the vast majority of farms in the United States—1.83 million out of 2.2 million—are principally operated by white males. But as the diversity of the country increases—with current minority groups set to make up over 50 percent of the U.S. population in about thirty years, according to the Census Bureau—the uptick in nonwhite primary farm operators is outpacing overall growth. While many of the farmworkers on the nation's large farms are Latino, the number of Latinos who own and operate their own farms in the United States is relatively low but growing particularly rapidly, having increased by 10 percent between 2002 and 2007. Another important development is an increasing diversity in gender across the U.S. agricultural landscape. The number of women farmers jumped by an eye-popping 30 percent during that same period, and the number of women who gain responsibility for land they inherit from their husbands is startlingly high.

So while there's apparently a good reason I always picture a farmer as a white guy in a Monsanto hat, that white-male agricultural picture is slowly altering. There's change afoot: an increase in diversity that could really reinvigorate our food universe. A little digging around was clearly called for. Surely we have farmers of all stripes—white, black, Asian, you name it—jostling to find their places in the sun. And what specifically of the Latino farmers and women farmers who are showing such growing interest in tilling our soil? Surely, they must be hidden in plain sight, just waiting for me to find them.

CHAPTER 6

New Farmers in the Dell

Training and outreach programs draw diversity to the fields

To GET TO ALBA—a nonprofit organization otherwise known as the Agriculture and Land-Based Training Association—I shot down a long highway from San Francisco to Salinas and then wended my way through the massive fields of industrial farming operations whose workers were out spraying crops with chemicals, bandanas tightened across their faces. The organization I had come there to find was geared toward helping exactly such workers become farmers in their own right, a great example of how to support and diversify the American small-farm landscape.

At the end of an unassuming dirt road squeezed between two enormous fields, I arrived in a cloud of dust at a low, modern building fronting a wide, dirt yard. I was greeted by Deborah Yashar, ALBA's food systems program manager, a reserved young woman in a white sweater and practical shoes.

"We're an incubator," Deborah told me in what seemed to be a characteristically quiet voice as we settled ourselves in metal folding chairs in the simple, high-ceilinged classroom where ALBA runs a training course in the basics of organic farming and business. "Once they start farming here we're an incubator for them to advance and become a self-sufficient farmer. But it takes many years."

The training program is geared toward Salinas's low-income Latino population, many of whom are farmworkers; the course was taught solely in Spanish from ALBA's founding in 2001 until 2009, when it was also offered for the first time in English. Most of the program's students would never be able to launch their own farms without the kind of assistance and support ALBA offers. The training course, taught twice a week in the evenings and weekends over six months, is followed by a structured opportunity for graduates to set up their own half-acre organic farms on the 110 acres at this site or the seventy at another location. The new farmers pay 20 percent of the local commercial rate for their half-acre parcels during the first year, with the only requirement being that they farm organically and maintain the USDA organic certification by filing the proper paperwork and meeting with the inspector when necessary. With some of the richest soils in the world, Salinas boasts very fertile and thus very expensive land, so this deep discount is crucial to these beginning farmers' ability to get a start. The discount decreases each year thereafter, with the price of students' land jumping to 30 percent of the going rate during the second year and so on, until the graduates are considered commercial farmers and pay full commercial rates by their seventh year on ALBA land.

The new farmers' small parcels contrast strongly with the massive tracts that characterize the surrounding megafarms. The classroom was decorated with a few colorful posters, one of which was an aerial photo of the surrounding area showing a vast carpet of monochromatic green squares unbroken by trees or other barriers. The section in the middle of this chessboard, ALBA's little 110-acre section of the world, was cheerfully striped willy-nilly with different shades of green and interrupted by stands of pine trees that serve as windbreaks and promote biodiversity.

Deborah and I went out into that patchwork landscape, where we strolled beside a procession of neatly tended fields bursting with lettuces, strawberries, tomatoes, and many other crops. It was a windy, cold day in Salinas, a bleak Wednesday with gathering clouds and a bedeviling wind that kept my hair flipping into knots as we wandered up and down the multicolored fields. We stopped to admire an idle tractor, and Deborah noted that along with access to affordable land, ALBA offers graduates access to water, equipment, and technical and marketing assistance. The organization also runs ALBA Organics, a company housed on the property that was set up specifically to provide a market for these beginning farmers and that distributes their produce all over the area to groceries, schools, hospitals, and other institutions.

Dealing with ALBA Organics is part of the new farmers' training. "If they were selling to another company and the farmer brought them a box of squash that wasn't perfect or that had issues, chances are that after the second or third time the company won't talk to them anymore," Deborah explained. "Whereas here every time something like that happens, there's a learning process that they go through. That way they can be more successful when they go out and sell to other buyers."

Once they earn their spurs, the farmers can branch out, including selling at farmers' markets. A few of the beginning farmers run CSAs. A recent college graduate who had been an ALBA intern banded together with his parents, former farmworkers, to start J&P Organics, which has a successful CSA serving about three hundred customers. As in that example, it's not unusual for these small farms to be family affairs. Deborah mentioned another family enterprise, two brothers not much older than eighteen who lost their younger brother in a gang shooting. "The two brothers who farm here are basically holding up the whole family through their revenue," Deborah said. "It's pretty amazing."

Such violence is not uncommon in the area. When I asked Deborah whether she lives in Salinas like most of the program's students, she said no, "I'm not that hard-core," making reference to the fact that the area is, as a friend of mine put it, "a perfectly beautiful town that's been overrun by gangs and drugs." Many of ALBA's students and farmers are impacted by the crime endemic to the place, and those who work on the conventional farms in the area also face other threats to their health and safety, mostly from the liberal use of toxic pesticides in the fields where they spend their days. The program's graduates, even those initially skeptical about the organic style of farming ALBA teaches, often embrace the organic method because they want to feel confident about having their children playing nearby and family members involved in the work.

Daniel Zamora, for example, a stocky guy with a blondish brown mustache, had started his ALBA strawberry farm with his father, who used to pick strawberries on a conventional farm. We hailed him down as he drove a truck in the dirt lane beside his field, and in accented English he told me how he grew up in Salinas and came to ALBA three years ago after a stint in a construction job. Now he grows four acres of strawberries under the name Heritage Farms and employs four people at harvest time.

I asked what he loves about farming. "I love to watch them grow," he said, gazing affectionately at his fields. He'd like to branch out and get land of his own—really graduate from ALBA—but his biggest problem is finding land. Large-scale landowners want to rent thirty acres at once, he said, not just a few acres to a little guy, an intractable problem that many of ALBA's farmers face.

"It's a scary world to leave ALBA," Deborah noted. "Not only are the staff and equipment not available to you, but finding land is very hard, very expensive."

But while finding small parcels of land is difficult, it is not impossible, and plenty of the program's graduates set off on careers as independent small farmers. However, Deborah noted, "A thing we're realizing more and more is that becoming a farmer is not the only positive outcome and it's not the only goal. [ALBA's program is] improving their lives in so many ways. So many of them come out of the program with new confidence. So many of them haven't had education past elementary school, so the whole experience is so empowering. We meet people who don't want to talk, who are so extremely shy, and six months later they're like different people. It's really transformative."

For farmers who speak no English, as well, the Spanish-language training and support is invaluable. Rigoberto Bucio, a twenty-one-year-old Mexican immigrant, admitted that he wouldn't be farming right now if it weren't for ALBA. Standing in the middle of his three-acre field of mixed vegetables and fruits wearing a brown sweatshirt over a collared shirt and jeans, he was intense and soft-spoken. I flailed about for a moment with a set of half-remembered Spanish words, then surrendered to Deborah's translations, by means of which Rigoberto told me that he came to the United States in 2003 in search of better opportunities and at the time of my visit lived in Salinas with his wife and three-month-old baby.

After working as a field hand for another ALBA farmer for four years, he decided to try it himself in 2007 and now grows, among other things, broccoli, squash, tomatoes, and strawberries. He likes farming because he can be in the fresh air in the countryside, he said, looking out across his field and absently playing with the leaf of a tomato plant that crawled up a stake to the level of his waist. His markets so far are ALBA Organics and a mini-farmstand that he runs once a week at St. Mary's by-the-Sea Episcopal Church in Pacific Grove. Deborah establishes such relationships, which have proved very successful for a handful of ALBA's farmers. The churches "kind of adopt them," said Deborah, which allows individual farmers to capture a small market instead of competing against many others at a traditional farmers' market. Opportunities like this can make an enormous difference to a newly minted small farmer. "It's good to sell my own products at a good price," Rigoberto said in Spanish, his dark eyes smiling. "Every Sunday more people come."

As Deborah and I wandered back through the fields, the wind snapping at us, I thought about how much more diverse and secure our country's cadre of small farmers would be if there were more programs like ALBA helping dedicated young people like Rigoberto gain skills and get their start. If, as David Baker had argued, the consolidation of small farms into larger ones is not in the best interest of our country, then more nonprofit and even government funding should support ALBA-style small-farm incubators to reinvigorate agricultural landscapes and bring greater diversity, more jobs, and new energy to farming communities thereby ensuring that rural towns don't become ghost towns.

Indeed, engaging the interest of populations who have traditionally been left out of the American farming landscape will help us grow the new farmers that we need as the older cohort retires. Not only does ALBA advance the interests of Latino growers, but, as I was surprised to learn, 30 to 40 percent of ALBA's students are women. These women, according to Deborah, "are actually the main driver of the farm, not just helping out the husband, but really running the show."

I thought back to something Severine von Tscharner Fleming had said—that she believed young women were entering farming at an unprecedented rate. "There's a joke—well, more like a fact—that the fastest-growing demographic in Vermont agriculture is women under twenty-five," she had told me. "That's why I sent my brother there." She laughed, but her story pointed to a very real shift that is taking place.

However when I went to find out more from Leigh Adcock—executive director of the Women, Food and Agriculture Network (WFAN)—I was surprised to learn that young would-be female farmers are hardly the front line in the battle to get women more involved in our agricultural system. The women who are best positioned to make a difference in our farming landscape, it turns out, are actually much older and much less aware of their own potential.

WFAN is headquartered in Ames, Iowa, the same town where I had met Nancy Levandowski at Iowa State. Since it was a weekend and Leigh was stuck at home without a car, she requested I come to her house in Gilbert, ten miles north. On my way there, I again marveled over how wrong I had been about Iowa. I found myself rolling through a landscape that unfurled in gentle waves like an inviting green sea. However, I did find the corn I had expected: vast fields of it hugged the straight road toward Leigh's house. A pungent tang of manure lay heavily in the air.

In the kitchen of her ranch house amid the cornfields, Leigh, a thin woman with short brown hair in a pink sleeveless shirt, poured me a glass of lemonade as she lamented that ten of her fourteen chicks had drowned in the thunderstorm that had rolled through overnight. Sighing, she sat down with me at the table with a tall glass of iced tea and regarded me with pensive brown eyes.

Was this a farm, I asked? I imagined it must be; cornstalks were the only neighbors. But no, it was just a rural house, though they did have a kitchen garden in the back (featuring hops her husband grows for home brewing) and a motley assortment of animals in the side yard, including the four remaining chicks. And she does co-own with her mother the 360-acre corn and soybean farm in north-west Iowa where she grew up and where her septuagenarian mother now lives alone.

Single, landowning women like her mother are, in fact, the ones women's agriculture organizations like WFAN are most eagerly seeking to engage nowadays. Throughout Iowa and most likely beyond, older women are increasingly becoming the sole owners of farmland through inheritance when husbands and fathers pass away. Most people don't realize, Leigh told me, that 47 percent of the land in this country is owned by women. If a woman and a man own a plot of land together, they're both considered owners, so that statistic isn't as surprising as it seems at first. But, with the rising trend of single women owning land—which they largely engage tenant farmers to cultivate—women are now the sole owners of some 20 percent of Iowa land, according to Iowa State Extension. Not only that, but about one in every ten acres of farmland in Iowa is owned by a single woman over seventy-five years old.

This all sounds positive for women, I was thinking, but Leigh told me that a problem arises because in many cases these women are unaccustomed to making decisions about the land's management. Tenants can often get away with practicing the most destructive forms of farming and disregarding environmental concerns—which tends to increase their profits—because the women landowners either don't know what to demand or are not bold enough to lay down the law.

WFAN's Women Caring for the Land program brings such women together to have peer-to-peer conversations about their goals for managing their land and how to attain them. "They have very strong conservation ethics and values," said Leigh. "But they're not used to making the decisions about the land for one thing, and they don't know the information they need to get to the goals they want to reach." The idea is to help the women find ways to manage their land more sustainably, whether in the type of agriculture being practiced by tenants or through conservation measures like fencing to keep livestock out of waterways, planting buffer strips of vegetation to manage pollutants, or dedicating portions of the land as wildlife habitat. And there's always the lingering question, as David Baker at the Beginning Farmer Center would surely point out, of what these women will prioritize in passing the land down to the next generation of prospective farmers.

"When our aging population's gone in the next twenty years, that's going to be a big turnover," Leigh told me, as if reading my mind. "Already the number of out-of-state landowners is growing because the heirs are leaving Iowa, they don't want to farm. A lot of them want to hold on to the land because they have sentimental reasons or maybe they want the income. They're renting the land to tenant farmers, they rarely come back to look at the land, so the environmental stewardship could be anywhere. You might have a good tenant that wants to take care of that land and you might have a horrible tenant, and you'd never know if you never come and look. That's a scary trend, which is another reason why we are reaching out to women as an important chunk of that inheritor population."

The group discussions WFAN organizes are engineered to help this particular inheritor population open up and feel empowered. "Our approach is to treat the women as experts on their own land, and they can tell each other a lot," said Leigh. "We really want it to be a conversation, not just a talking head up front." Such a conversation is only likely to happen, however, if the sessions are for women only. "They are more comfortable in a women-only atmosphere, in an informal atmosphere, with a woman facilitator, and that's what we're trying to offer them. We're trying very hard to make these women-only events. We occasionally get a little push back from staff people about that because men don't like to be left out, but I've seen the dynamic between the ones with men there and the ones with women only there, and it's different: they don't talk if there are men there."

WFAN pays particular attention to issues of women's land ownership in part because it was founded in an international context—it was started in 1995 as an outgrowth of a working group at the Fourth World Conference on Women in Beijing—and it was responding to the fact that women perform up to 80 percent of the agricultural labor worldwide, but own less than 2 percent of the land and have little say in farming practices and food policy.

"I think the organization really was created to help redress that inequality, that imbalance," said Leigh. "And it's also evolved over the years as a social support network for women who are involved in all aspects of sustainable agriculture, from the farmers themselves to people who are advocates to consumers who are concerned with helping support that form of agriculture. Over the last two years, our mailing list has grown from three hundred to over eleven hundred people, which shows me that the interest is growing and people are really passionate about this."

One of the groups increasingly interested and passionate is, as Severine had pointed out, young women. WFAN runs an apprenticeship program called Harvesting Our Potential, which places young women on women-owned Iowa farms for six to ten weeks of hands-on training and provides them each with a one-thousand-dollar stipend. Though the program is small—it had seven apprentices in the summer of 2010—there is more than enough interest from young would-be farmers. "It seems to be a program that's needed and wanted," said Leigh. "We had more applicants than we were able to fund."

One of the season's apprentices had been assigned to Rolling Acres, the farm of WFAN's founder, Denise O'Brien, near the tiny town of Atlantic, Iowa, a couple hours' drive west of Ames. Denise is a person of no small stature in the sustainable agriculture community, having built herself a storied career in food policy and advocacy, even coming close to being elected Iowa Secretary of Agriculture in 2006. To find her, I fishtailed my rental car up and down a hilly dirt road in the rain at nine a.m. on a Sunday, mud spraying behind, and finally turned into a drive beside a picturesque blue farmhouse surrounded by a carnival of colorful flowers.

As Denise poured me a cup of coffee at the kitchen table, her husband Larry appeared, his white hair in a ponytail and his eyes smiling. Liza, one of the farm's two interns, came in to scrounge for breakfast in the refrigerator before heading out for a much-needed day off. She's from Iowa, she told me, leaning against the counter as she nibbled on some toast. She had moved home to try farming after having found herself unhappy working for a nonprofit focused on homeless preschoolers in Washington, DC. She was now helping Denise and Larry all summer with their thirty-share CSA, working alongside the other intern, Gwen, who had come through the WFAN apprenticeship program.

Denise sat down across from me cupping a steaming mug of coffee, and I asked about how she got her start in farming. "I came out of feminism, and when I started farming with Larry, it took me a couple years to learn everything I needed to learn, and I learned the language of farming," she said. "And when I got through this period of time, I felt that I was a farmer. I'd done my apprenticeship, and I was a farmer. So I'd call myself a farmer. I'd go to public meetings, especially in the turmoil of the eighties, and I'd say, 'I'm a farmer.' And women would come up to me afterwards and say, 'You call yourself a farmer?' and I'd say, 'Well, yeah, I farm alongside my husband.' And I'd say, 'What about you?' They'd say, 'I'm a farmer's wife.' I'd say, 'What kind of work do you do?' They'd say, 'I feed the cows, or I milk the cows, or I feed the pigs, or I raise chickens, or I run the tractor.' And I'd say, 'Sounds like a farmer to me.' And they'd say, 'No, I'm a farmer's wife.' It's a generation thing. I came out of a different generation. Now, those women, twenty years later, own the land. And they don't understand that they can make decisions about the land and they could influence policy. They could influence change, and it could really help beginning farmers start farming. There's a rich, rich source of knowledge and resources and maybe some capital that we need to plug into, to get young people on the land."

Women, it was clear, need to help women when it comes to gaining more say in how our land is farmed and our food produced. "We've got to continue nurturing a class of farmers," Denise insisted. "Those people who have that burning desire and passion to farm, we need to nurture that, whether it's a man or a woman or whoever." But because women hold the lion's share of responsibility for feeding their families healthfully and are so often the ones doing the farming in developing countries, women's inclusion and empowerment will be vital to ensuring a sustainable global food supply.

"Women are the key to food security in the world," Denise said. She finds the issue so important that although she ceded control of WFAN to Leigh in 2007, she still volunteers her time to advise on the project of getting women to take control of their land. "It is really critical work," she said.

is like the antithesis of the Xbox," Tony said as we
oss some neat vegetable gardens and into a small
e trees housing a rustic wooden table set around with
sat down and contemplated the tree canopy silently for
I want them fully immersed in this," he said. "Listen, I
birds. There's butterflies around, you know? Let's slow
wn so they get to be children again."

cher in the school system can bring his or her class here
rip, and the subject matter that can apply runs the gamut—
ath, art, history, physical education, you name it. The kids
volved in all sorts of activities, including planting, harvest-
g for the farm's resident goats and chickens, growing mush-
rotten logs, cooking meals. Tony is in the process of restoring
e kitchen in one of the buildings, and he mentioned an art
t had recently built a clay oven for making pizza.

is little patch right here is our grow-your-own-pizza patch
e kids love pizza," he said, pointing out an area under a hoop
blooming with tomatoes and basil. "I want kids to be fully
ed in the pizza process. I want our kids to be able to come to
lace and plant it, grow it, harvest it, cook it, eat it. And then it
er changes the way they look at food. It's not consumption;
omething more powerful than that. If they are part of that pro-
, they think differently, they act differently."

ndeed, he finds that students are much more likely to want to eat
d they've had a hand in growing, as many school garden propo-
ts attest. The farm serves in part as a testing ground for food Tony
thinking of incorporating into the school system's lunch menu.
his is a place where I can figure out the things that my kids like to
t and then go into the ag community and say, 'These are the things
want you to grow because these are the things that I'm going to
uy,'" he said.

CHAPTER 7

Seeds of Learning

Inspired educational efforts bring kids closer to their food

I WAS SATISFIED TO KNOW that there were efforts designed specifically to encourage and support aspiring agriculturalists and land
stewards of all types, young and old. With programs like the ones I
had visited crisscrossing the nation, how could we not but end up
with a larger, more diverse, and more robust set of farmers?

Well, of course, programs such as these always need new aspirants to fill their ranks, and since most of us nowadays are divorced
from the sources of our food, it isn't a given that an ever-increasing
stream of young people will see the appeal of a food-and-farming
kind of life. We won't ever end up with enough farmers—not to
mention healthy eaters or advocates of good, affordable food—
unless we make sure our children are exposed to the possibility of
such a career path.

I am not advocating that we turn all our kids into back-to-the-
landers, but considering our aging farmer population, it would be
myopic for us not to at least familiarize our young people with where
food comes from. The less we collectively know about our food
sources, the more control of our lives we cede to those who manage
that aspect of our society. And as our cadre of farmers is whittled

down, those in control of our food—and therefore of us—make up an ever-more select, wealthy, and powerful group. Food is as much about civics and democracy as it is about biology; teaching our kids about food is tantamount to fighting for the future of our country.

With that stirring patriotic notion in my head, I headed to my next stop by way of a depressing stretch of road outside Baltimore. I sped past sad strip malls, fast-food chains, and used-car dealerships before turning into a street that seemed to dead-end at a parking lot full of school buses. But a hand-scrawled wooden sign attached to the chain-link fence pointed me to the right, up a small wooded lane and finally into a wide clearing populated with a few old stone buildings and a greenhouse fronting an array of small vegetable fields. This was Great Kids Farm at the Bragg Nature Center, brainchild of Tony Geraci, the food service director of Baltimore City Public Schools since late 2008 and one of the leaders of the national farm-to-school movement. He accepted the job only because he was promised free reign of this property, which is located outside the city limits but owned by the Baltimore City school system.

I found him in a big turquoise room in the largest stone building, sporting a green cap, a white goatee, and a yellow tie dangling across his rotund belly. On one side of the room under soaring banks of windows, a few students sorted vegetables into bags for the farm's fifty CSA members, who provide a large segment of the facility's funding. Although Tony runs the thirty-three-acre farm as a resource for the city's schoolchildren, the school system doesn't supply a penny, so he funds his efforts through the CSA, direct sales to local restaurants, and whatever grants he can get his hands on.

Tony launched into our tour with gusto, describing how the farm had originally been founded as an orphanage called, remarkably, the Maryland Home for Friendless Colored Children. "What a name," he hooted. "They could have used a good marketing guy." The facility

was in an advanced state
"This was a throwaway p
this property to a group of
gally so they couldn't." He g
lot of friends."

Tony didn't seem like th
people liked him or not. He was
awesome stuff—and good ridd
Somehow I wasn't surprised to lea

He led me outside and into a sn
building, where rows of microgreens
under the care of an earnest volunteer.
on, all right?" he said, fingering the tin
He pointed out a tray of miniature plant
couple leaves and popped them on my to

"It's a little spicy," I said. "Mustard g

"Radish. Every time a group of kids
with the makings of a school garden that so
planted," Tony said. "So we want to encoura
notion that 'you're part of a greater communi
has some really significant issues around territ
the East Side growing stuff for kids from the
realize, 'We're just kids.'"

How had we leaped right from tiny radish lea
I could see that operating a learning farm in the
system was a much different project than many of
what more precious school gardening programs I had
This was not a question of teaching kids the differ
mustard greens and radish greens, but a matter of recl
small piece of their childhoods by acquainting them w
world many of them would never have experienced othe

But while this food-service angle certainly has its utility, it is definitely the sense of deep engagement Tony is trying to cultivate that comes across most strongly in the way he talks about the farm. "This is a place to inspire. This is a place to enlighten," he said as we strolled past the beehives, which students had painted brightly with pictures of insects and butterflies. "As they're walking through the farm, we want them to touch it, to smell it, to taste it. We encourage grazing. They play with the worms in this vermiculture thing, play with goats, play with the chickens, see the bees at work. That's what this place is about. This is a place that they can take these ideas and go back to their own communities, their own schools, their own neighborhoods and re-create."

It's a philosophy that is really making a difference in some kids' lives. He told me about a couple of troubled students—"kind of hard-core thugs"—who had been ordered to come to the farm by their probation officers. It wasn't a surprise when they arrived there, as Tony put it, "completely under duress," sulking angrily at their plight. "But something happened here that spoke to them," he continued. "First time maybe that they've ever been at a place like this. As you well know, this is in the heart of Babylon. This is surrounded by strip malls and fast-food places and housing projects, and there's this little chunk of green that lives in the midst of that. Maybe this is the first time that those kids just got to sit and be with this. But they went back to their community and they started creating gardens in their 'hood. They started connecting with older people in their 'hood. We got them hooked up with an internship to come out here and work for the summer. And they started leading tours around the farm. One kid now has a scholarship to the University of Maryland and he wants to be a farmer."

Setting up programs that have that kind of legacy might take a lot of work, Tony noted, but building strong resources that will serve future generations is thoroughly worthwhile. "There's this old Sicilian proverb, and, loosely translated, it goes, 'The farmer who plants the orchard is often not the farmer who gets to rest under the canopy of the trees,'" he said while showing me a few fig trees beside the greenhouse, grown from cuttings of trees his family had brought with them from Sicily when they immigrated to the United States. "In the work that we do, we are orchard builders," he continued. "And these orchards aren't for us. These orchards are for our children and our children's children. And it's important that we don't stop the building, you know? These are really simple things that we can do for this country. As a first-generation American, I'm pretty excited about that."

We headed past the chicken coop ("These are our girls," Tony said proudly. "LADIES! BUCKAW!") and down a leafy drive toward a larger field beyond a patch of woods. The back field is where the farm staff and students grow most of the crops and where Tony has plans to restore a broken-down greenhouse to serve as a farm market and retail job skills training program for the students. On the way there, we paused at a particularly woodsy portion of the property, where a little creek ran beside a clearing. "This little trail right here, it's kind of overgrown," he said, pointing into the tangle of green. "I've got a group of Eagle Scouts who are going to build a campsite right over there. My vision is to have these urban kids come here and—"

"Camp out?" I interrupted, thrilled to imagine Baltimore City kids spending their first night ever in the woods.

"Under the stars." He ran his eyes over the patches of brambles that would soon give way to his vision of kids learning to be kids again. "They get up in the morning," he said. "They go collect their eggs. They cook 'em." He looked at me expectantly. "You know?"

Yes, indeed. I had been infected with Tony's enthusiasm, and I left the farm that day—armed with eggs, scallions, and strawberries from its fields—brimming with excitement to explore what other similar programs might be getting kids' hands into the soil and their minds off their video games.

That quest took me to a rural spot in Hillsborough, North Carolina, outside Chapel Hill, where I found myself lingering beside a duck pond with Bob Nutter, an energetic eighty-one-year-old sporting a red cap decorated with pictures of black-and-white Holsteins and matching red suspenders.

"Have you ever seen geese that small?" Bob asked, pointing out some goslings in the water, his wrinkled face lighting up with delight behind thick glasses. He chuckled as he gingerly made his way up the path from the pond. His two great-granddaughters sprinted past and into the animals' area to the left, where goats, cows, horses, sheep, and a llama were loitering in pristine enclosures labeled with neat wooden signs.

"This place is a wonderland for kids," their mother, Bob's granddaughter, told me as she rushed by after her children, who had barreled into the horses' pen to say hello. The menagerie composes a section of the Maple View Agricultural Educational Center, an agritourism enterprise tucked into a twenty-acre corner of four-hundred-acre Maple View Farm. Bob, a fifth-generation farmer once named a "town treasure" by the Chapel Hill Historical Society, operated the dairy farm for decades after relocating from Maine in 1963. His son Roger now co-owns and runs it. The center, founded in 2009, exposes kids to the farm and the animals and teaches them about food, seeds, bugs, alternative energy, and other related topics. The facility was the brainchild of one of Bob's long-time employees, Allison Nichols, who became a teacher after working summers in one of Maple View's ice cream stores.

"The kids she taught didn't know where their milk came from,"

Bob told me as we toured the center's two-acre working garden. "They didn't know anything. We thought it would be good if they learned something about where their food comes from."

The center's only building, a six-thousand-square-foot ware-houselike structure fronted by a spacious gravel parking lot, contains a series of brightly decorated classrooms filled with hands-on activities designed to teach kids the intricate details of agriculture and the science behind food. In one room, an incubator warmed duck and chicken eggs on their way to hatching, while in another a seed-planting station was ready for the next class to try out their green thumbs. In the soil science room, materials were poised for kids to test the rate of water flow through various types of soil, and next door, cages full of butterflies, ants, roaches, and other creatures were set to offer students a firsthand look at the role insects play in farming.

Allison, a young, sweet-faced woman with a businesslike air, explained that the center was—at that time—run as a for-profit, charging fees for access to the facilities and classes and hosting birthday parties for a price (the noise from which has unfortunately caused trouble with the neighbors). Agritourism, a sector of the tourism industry focused on facilitating rural and agricultural experiences, is rapidly expanding, having almost tripled in value between 2002 and 2007, according to the 2007 USDA Census of Agriculture. Bob and Allison had never expected to do more than break even, and in fact switched the center to nonprofit status about a year later so as to more easily expand its programming to adults and to be able to offer financial aid to help both students and adults visit.

As I toured the rest of the farm with Bob ("Look, am I ever too busy to take a pretty girl around?" he responded cheekily to my request that he show me the place. "I don't get that busy."), I wondered whether turning food and farming education into a commodity might give people an idealized vision of what it means to be in the business of growing food. The tidy garden and idle animals on display at the center seemed more like museum pieces than elements of the messy life of a real working farm, and it was possible that visitors would come away from their time there ever-more enthralled with a quaint vision of rural life and just as clueless as before about the reality of small agriculture as a demanding, financially unstable, and increasingly threatened sector of our farming landscape.

On the other hand, the whole point was to give kids access to information about food and farming, which the center was equipped admirably to accomplish. And here I was, bumping down a dirt drive past a paddock where cows and their calves meandered over lush fields glowing in the radiant sunlight of the clear April day. The center, after all, was part of a working dairy farm, a small family farm that has adapted to the times to remain financially viable and is nothing if not quaint. Visitors to the center don't get full access to this portion of the farm, but they can buy its milk in glass bottles in stores around town, proof positive that in some corners of the country, a rural idyll is still a realistic vision.

Maple View had very nearly gone under amid the changes wrought by a quickly consolidating milk market. When the price of milk sank so low that Bob feared he'd have to shut down, Roger returned from a career in construction to reconfigure the business into one that could tap a higher-end niche market: Maple View started bottling its own milk, a rarity in the state. Roger, a taciturn, mustachioed fellow, showed me the milk-processing center, which can pasteurize and bottle seven thousand gallons a week, a quantity that a big dairy operation could dispatch in a mere two hours. The smaller-scale operation, of course, results in higher-priced milk, but consumers who shell out the extra find it worthwhile to keep a small family farm running and to know about the treatment of the cows that produced their milk.

Plus, of course, there's the taste. Roger led me into the cooler room, which was stacked high with crates filled with glass bottles of regular and chocolate milk. He plucked a half-pint of chocolate milk from a box and handed it to me with a proud smile. As I took a sip of the cool, sweet stuff, I silently agreed he had something to be proud of. If an educational center can teach kids about farming while simultaneously bolstering the stability of a farm that created milk this good, I decided, well, that's what one might call a win-win situation.

Both Great Kids Farm and Maple View Agricultural Educational Center were great projects, places designed to get kids intimately in touch with the details of what they eat every day. But as I said good-bye to Bob and rolled off through the verdant hills of North Carolina, I wondered whether there were any projects designed to give students more regular and frequent access to such learning. In all the many school-garden projects out there in the vast educational universe, could I find one that treated the agricultural space like an actual classroom—even a multidisciplinary classroom—instead of a separate realm designed for a different kind of learning divorced from the regular curriculum?

Naturally, I headed for Manhattan. What better place to look for such a thing than a big city with little space for school gardens? That might sound like sarcasm, but really, if a school administration on this cheek-by-jowl island is going to set aside precious school space for a plant-growing environment of any size, you can bet they'll be making good use of it. It turns out that I had come to the right place, though a tad early to see my theory about city school gardens tested. In August 2010, when I dropped in on the Manhattan School for Children, a middle school on West 93rd Street otherwise known as P.S. 333, the new greenhouse on the third floor was still under construction.

The air was roasting when I arrived with Benjamin Linsley, a

CHAPTER 7

Seeds of Learning

Inspired educational efforts bring kids closer to their food

I WAS SATISFIED TO KNOW that there were efforts designed specifically to encourage and support aspiring agriculturalists and land stewards of all types, young and old. With programs like the ones I had visited crisscrossing the nation, how could we not but end up with a larger, more diverse, and more robust set of farmers?

Well, of course, programs such as these always need new aspirants to fill their ranks, and since most of us nowadays are divorced from the sources of our food, it isn't a given that an ever-increasing stream of young people will see the appeal of a food-and-farming kind of life. We won't ever end up with enough farmers—not to mention healthy eaters or advocates of good, affordable food—unless we make sure our children are exposed to the possibility of such a career path.

I am not advocating that we turn all our kids into back-to-the-landers, but considering our aging farmer population, it would be myopic for us not to at least familiarize our young people with where food comes from. The less we collectively know about our food sources, the more control of our lives we cede to those who manage that aspect of our society. And as our cadre of farmers is whittled down, those in control of our food—and therefore of us—make up an ever-more select, wealthy, and powerful group. Food is as much about civics and democracy as it is about biology; teaching our kids about food is tantamount to fighting for the future of our country.

With that stirring patriotic notion in my head, I headed to my next stop by way of a depressing stretch of road outside Baltimore. I sped past sad strip malls, fast-food chains, and used-car dealerships before turning into a street that seemed to dead-end at a parking lot full of school buses. But a hand-scrawled wooden sign attached to the chain-link fence pointed me to the right, up a small wooded lane and finally into a wide clearing populated with a few old stone buildings and a greenhouse fronting an array of small vegetable fields. This was Great Kids Farm at the Bragg Nature Center, brainchild of Tony Geraci, the food service director of Baltimore City Public Schools since late 2008 and one of the leaders of the national farm-to-school movement. He accepted the job only because he was promised free reign of this property, which is located outside the city limits but owned by the Baltimore City school system.

I found him in a big turquoise room in the largest stone building, sporting a green cap, a white goatee, and a yellow tie dangling across his rotund belly. On one side of the room under soaring banks of windows, a few students sorted vegetables into bags for the farm's fifty CSA members, who provide a large segment of the facility's funding. Although Tony runs the thirty-three-acre farm as a resource for the city's schoolchildren, the school system doesn't supply a penny, so he funds his efforts through the CSA, direct sales to local restaurants, and whatever grants he can get his hands on.

Tony launched into our tour with gusto, describing how the farm had originally been founded as an orphanage called, remarkably, the Maryland Home for Friendless Colored Children. "What a name," he hooted. "They could have used a good marketing guy." The facility was in an advanced state of disrepair when he arrived to take over. "This was a throwaway place," he said. "They were going to sell this property to a group of used-car guys, but I got it tangled up legally so they couldn't." He grinned mischievously. "I didn't make a lot of friends."

Tony didn't seem like the kind of guy who cared whether people liked him or not. He was the guy who would get stuff done—awesome stuff—and good riddance if you didn't get on board. Somehow I wasn't surprised to learn that he lives on a sailboat.

He led me outside and into a small greenhouse next to the main building, where rows of microgreens were sprouting in plastic trays under the care of an earnest volunteer. "These are meant to be grazed on, all right?" he said, fingering the tiny plants. "You gotta try this." He pointed out a tray of miniature plants, and I obediently plucked a couple leaves and popped them on my tongue.

"It's a little spicy," I said. "Mustard greens?"

"Radish. Every time a group of kids comes here, they leave with the makings of a school garden that some other group of kids planted," Tony said. "So we want to encourage this pay-it-forward notion that 'you're part of a greater community' because Baltimore has some really significant issues around territory. I want kids from the East Side growing stuff for kids from the West Side. So they realize, 'We're just kids.'"

How had we leaped right from tiny radish leaves to turf battles? I could see that operating a learning farm in the Baltimore school system was a much different project than many of the other somewhat more precious school gardening programs I had learned about. This was not a question of teaching kids the difference between mustard greens and radish greens, but a matter of reclaiming some small piece of their childhoods by acquainting them with a natural world many of them would never have experienced otherwise.

"This farm is like the antithesis of the Xbox," Tony said as we wandered across some neat vegetable gardens and into a small clearing in the trees housing a rustic wooden table set around with benches. We sat down and contemplated the tree canopy silently for a moment. "I want them fully immersed in this," he said. "Listen, I mean there's birds. There's butterflies around, you know? Let's slow our kids down so they get to be children again."

Any teacher in the school system can bring his or her class here for a field trip, and the subject matter that can apply runs the gamut—science, math, art, history, physical education, you name it. The kids can get involved in all sorts of activities, including planting, harvesting, caring for the farm's resident goats and chickens, growing mushrooms in rotten logs, cooking meals. Tony is in the process of restoring a massive kitchen in one of the buildings, and he mentioned an art class that had recently built a clay oven for making pizza.

"This little patch right here is our grow-your-own-pizza patch because kids love pizza," he said, pointing out an area under a hoop house blooming with tomatoes and basil. "I want kids to be fully engaged in the pizza process. I want our kids to be able to come to this place and plant it, grow it, harvest it, cook it, eat it. And then it forever changes the way they look at food. It's not consumption; it's something more powerful than that. If they are part of that process, they think differently, they act differently."

Indeed, he finds that students are much more likely to want to eat food they've had a hand in growing, as many school garden proponents attest. The farm serves in part as a testing ground for food Tony is thinking of incorporating into the school system's lunch menu. "This is a place where I can figure out the things that my kids like to eat and then go into the ag community and say, 'These are the things I want you to grow because these are the things that I'm going to buy,'" he said.

But while this food-service angle certainly has its utility, it is definitely the sense of deep engagement Tony is trying to cultivate that comes across most strongly in the way he talks about the farm. "This is a place to inspire. This is a place to enlighten," he said as we strolled past the beehives, which students had painted brightly with pictures of insects and butterflies. "As they're walking through the farm, we want them to touch it, to smell it, to taste it. We encourage grazing. They play with the worms in this vermiculture thing, play with goats, play with the chickens, see the bees at work. That's what this place is about. This is a place that they can take these ideas and go back to their own communities, their own schools, their own neighborhoods and re-create."

It's a philosophy that is really making a difference in some kids' lives. He told me about a couple of troubled students—"kind of hard-core thugs"—who had been ordered to come to the farm by their probation officers. It wasn't a surprise when they arrived there, as Tony put it, "completely under duress," sulking angrily at their plight. "But something happened here that spoke to them," he continued. "First time maybe that they've ever been at a place like this. As you well know, this is in the heart of Babylon. This is surrounded by strip malls and fast-food places and housing projects, and there's this little chunk of green that lives in the midst of that. Maybe this is the first time that those kids just got to sit and be with this. But they went back to their community and they started creating gardens in their 'hood. They started connecting with older people in their 'hood. We got them hooked up with an internship to come out here and work for the summer. And they started leading tours around the farm. One kid now has a scholarship to the University of Maryland and he wants to be a farmer."

Setting up programs that have that kind of legacy might take a lot of work, Tony noted, but building strong resources that will serve future generations is thoroughly worthwhile. "There's this old Sicilian proverb, and, loosely translated, it goes, 'The farmer who plants the orchard is often not the farmer who gets to rest under the canopy of the trees,'" he said while showing me a few fig trees beside the greenhouse, grown from cuttings of trees his family had brought with them from Sicily when they immigrated to the United States. "In the work that we do, we are orchard builders," he continued. "And these orchards aren't for us. These orchards are for our children and our children's children. And it's important that we don't stop the building, you know? These are really simple things that we can do for this country. As a first-generation American, I'm pretty excited about that."

We headed past the chicken coop ("These are our girls," Tony said proudly. "LADIES! BUCKAW!") and down a leafy drive toward a larger field beyond a patch of woods. The back field is where the farm staff and students grow most of the crops and where Tony has plans to restore a broken-down greenhouse to serve as a farm market and retail job skills training program for the students. On the way there, we paused at a particularly woodsy portion of the property, where a little creek ran beside a clearing. "This little trail right here, it's kind of overgrown," he said, pointing into the tangle of green. "I've got a group of Eagle Scouts who are going to build a campsite right over there. My vision is to have these urban kids come here and—"

"Camp out?" I interrupted, thrilled to imagine Baltimore City kids spending their first night ever in the woods.

"Under the stars." He ran his eyes over the patches of brambles that would soon give way to his vision of kids learning to be kids again. "They get up in the morning," he said. "They go collect their eggs. They cook 'em." He looked at me expectantly. "You know?"

Yes, indeed. I had been infected with Tony's enthusiasm, and I left the farm that day—armed with eggs, scallions, and strawberries from its fields—brimming with excitement to explore what other similar programs might be getting kids' hands into the soil and their minds off their video games.

That quest took me to a rural spot in Hillsborough, North Carolina, outside Chapel Hill, where I found myself lingering beside a duck pond with Bob Nutter, an energetic eighty-one-year-old sporting a red cap decorated with pictures of black-and-white Holsteins and matching red suspenders.

"Have you ever seen geese that small?" Bob asked, pointing out some goslings in the water, his wrinkled face lighting up with delight behind thick glasses. He chuckled as he gingerly made his way up the path from the pond. His two great-granddaughters sprinted past and into the animals' area to the left, where goats, cows, horses, sheep, and a llama were loitering in pristine enclosures labeled with neat wooden signs.

"This place is a wonderland for kids," their mother, Bob's granddaughter, told me as she rushed by after her children, who had barreled into the horses' pen to say hello. The menagerie composes a section of the Maple View Agricultural Educational Center, an agritourism enterprise tucked into a twenty-acre corner of four-hundred-acre Maple View Farm. Bob, a fifth-generation farmer once named a "town treasure" by the Chapel Hill Historical Society, operated the dairy farm for decades after relocating from Maine in 1963. His son Roger now co-owns and runs it. The center, founded in 2009, exposes kids to the farm and the animals and teaches them about food, seeds, bugs, alternative energy, and other related topics. The facility was the brainchild of one of Bob's long-time employees, Allison Nichols, who became a teacher after working summers in one of Maple View's ice cream stores.

"The kids she taught didn't know where their milk came from,"

Bob told me as we toured the center's two-acre working garden. "They didn't know anything. We thought it would be good if they learned something about where their food comes from."

The center's only building, a six-thousand-square-foot warehouselike structure fronted by a spacious gravel parking lot, contains a series of brightly decorated classrooms filled with hands-on activities designed to teach kids the intricate details of agriculture and the science behind food. In one room, an incubator warmed duck and chicken eggs on their way to hatching, while in another a seed-planting station was ready for the next class to try out their green thumbs. In the soil science room, materials were poised for kids to test the rate of water flow through various types of soil, and next door, cages full of butterflies, ants, roaches, and other creatures were set to offer students a firsthand look at the role insects play in farming.

Allison, a young, sweet-faced woman with a businesslike air, explained that the center was—at that time—run as a for-profit, charging fees for access to the facilities and classes and hosting birthday parties for a price (the noise from which has unfortunately caused trouble with the neighbors). Agritourism, a sector of the tourism industry focused on facilitating rural and agricultural experiences, is rapidly expanding, having almost tripled in value between 2002 and 2007, according to the 2007 USDA Census of Agriculture. Bob and Allison had never expected to do more than break even, and in fact switched the center to nonprofit status about a year later so as to more easily expand its programming to adults and to be able to offer financial aid to help both students and adults visit.

As I toured the rest of the farm with Bob ("Look, am I ever too busy to take a pretty girl around?" he responded cheekily to my request that he show me the place. "I don't get that busy."), I wondered whether turning food and farming education into a commodity might give people an idealized vision of what it means to be in the business of growing food. The tidy garden and idle animals on display at the center seemed more like museum pieces than elements of the messy life of a real working farm, and it was possible that visitors would come away from their time there ever-more enthralled with a quaint vision of rural life and just as clueless as before about the reality of small agriculture as a demanding, financially unstable, and increasingly threatened sector of our farming landscape.

On the other hand, the whole point was to give kids access to information about food and farming, which the center was equipped admirably to accomplish. And here I was, bumping down a dirt drive past a paddock where cows and their calves meandered over lush fields glowing in the radiant sunlight of the clear April day. The center, after all, was part of a working dairy farm, a small family farm that has adapted to the times to remain financially viable and is nothing if not quaint. Visitors to the center don't get full access to this portion of the farm, but they can buy its milk in glass bottles in stores around town, proof positive that in some corners of the country, a rural idyll is still a realistic vision.

Maple View had very nearly gone under amid the changes wrought by a quickly consolidating milk market. When the price of milk sank so low that Bob feared he'd have to shut down, Roger returned from a career in construction to reconfigure the business into one that could tap a higher-end niche market: Maple View started bottling its own milk, a rarity in the state. Roger, a taciturn, mustachioed fellow, showed me the milk-processing center, which can pasteurize and bottle seven thousand gallons a week, a quantity that a big dairy operation could dispatch in a mere two hours. The smaller-scale operation, of course, results in higher-priced milk, but consumers who shell out the extra find it worthwhile to keep a small family farm running and to know about the treatment of the cows that produced their milk.

Plus, of course, there's the taste. Roger led me into the cooler room, which was stacked high with crates filled with glass bottles of regular and chocolate milk. He plucked a half-pint of chocolate milk from a box and handed it to me with a proud smile. As I took a sip of the cool, sweet stuff, I silently agreed he had something to be proud of. If an educational center can teach kids about farming while simultaneously bolstering the stability of a farm that created milk this good, I decided, well, that's what one might call a win-win situation.

Both Great Kids Farm and Maple View Agricultural Educational Center were great projects, places designed to get kids intimately in touch with the details of what they eat every day. But as I said good-bye to Bob and rolled off through the verdant hills of North Carolina, I wondered whether there were any projects designed to give students more regular and frequent access to such learning. In all the many school-garden projects out there in the vast educational universe, could I find one that treated the agricultural space like an actual classroom—even a multidisciplinary classroom—instead of a separate realm designed for a different kind of learning divorced from the regular curriculum?

Naturally, I headed for Manhattan. What better place to look for such a thing than a big city with little space for school gardens? That might sound like sarcasm, but really, if a school administration on this cheek-by-jowl island is going to set aside precious school space for a plant-growing environment of any size, you can bet they'll be making good use of it. It turns out that I had come to the right place, though a tad early to see my theory about city school gardens tested. In August 2010, when I dropped in on the Manhattan School for Children, a middle school on West 93rd Street otherwise known as P.S. 333, the new greenhouse on the third floor was still under construction.

The air was roasting when I arrived with Benjamin Linsley, a thin, hip-looking Brit from BrightFarms, the company that had designed the greenhouse and was helping manage the project. On the third floor, Benjamin shoved open a metal door onto the rooftop, where the bones of the structure were already intact above a broad expanse of tar paper flooring—a skeleton of metal beams forming low walls then pitching steeply upward to a classic triangular greenhouse shape. As the glass panels were not yet installed, temporary white plastic siding luffed in the hot breeze while two sweating workmen pieced together a ceiling beam to the sound of pop hits on the radio.

I had thought the day outside was steamy, but the temperature in the heat-trapping space was incendiary. Two ventilation fans stood maddeningly still, and I felt sweat trickle down my stomach. "I bet you wish your girlfriend was hot like me," the radio crooned.

"In terms of school greenhouses, it will be far and away bigger, more expensive, more sophisticated than any other," said Benjamin, mopping his brow. "This is designed to be the mother of all school greenhouses."

The idea, he explained, was to integrate the facility into as many aspects of the life of the school as possible. "This is not just a place to grow food, this is not just about biology," he said. "There's a potential to design this system as a hands-on place for kids to learn across most of the curriculum. If we set it up in the right way and if we help with curriculum development, really most of the school— teachers, areas of the curriculum, and school life—should in some way be able to interact with this space. Our principle is to try and make these facilities right central in school life and school curriculum."

This was exactly what I had been looking for. The 1,440-square-foot hydroponic greenhouse will serve as one of the school's science classrooms—containing "a whole suite of different growing systems and aquaponic systems and some environmental science equipment" according to Benjamin—and will supply food to the school cafeteria, as well as housing a variety of teaching tools to make it a flexible learning environment for a range of subject areas. The school administration planned to assign a staff member to care for it, thereby ensuring that its maintenance wouldn't fall between the cracks.

"We've seen a lot of schools with smaller greenhouses that fall by the wayside because it's not integrated into school life but also because it wasn't any one person's responsibility," said Benjamin. He gave credit for the different approach at P.S. 333 to the parents Sidsel Robards and Manuela Zamora, who spearheaded the project and fought tirelessly to make sure no financial, zoning, or administrative hurdles got in the way of its construction. "Part of the achievement of the parents was getting the school to own this project," Benjamin said. No doubt that element will be part of the model the two women plan to replicate in other New York City schools through their initiative, the Greenhouse Project, which they started under the auspices of BrightFarms' nonprofit partner, New York Sun Works.

The parents had gotten the idea for the school greenhouse upon visiting New York Sun Works's original greenhouse project, the Science Barge, which is, as the name suggests, a greenhouse on a barge. In Yonkers, where it is now permanently moored after an initial two-year residence at Pier 84 in midtown Manhattan, Benjamin gave me a thorough tour of the floating farm, describing how it was opened in 2007 as a research and demonstration project but soon revealed its unique suitability as an educational facility.

"We discovered almost by accident that putting a set of technologies together in this way in a city like New York provides a fantastic place to teach kids about food, about agriculture, about ecology, about environmental sustainability," he told me as we stood on the barge's deck looking up at an array of solar panels that provide 80 percent of the energy needed to heat and cool the greenhouse. Small wind turbines and a biodiesel generator produce the other 20 percent. Along with supplying its own energy, the Science Barge is also water self-sufficient and almost devoid of agricultural waste, collecting the water for its hydroponic systems from the rain and the river (with purification) and then cleanly dispensing with any nutrified wastewater, of which there is little, via an onboard constructed wetland. "The barge, the delineated area, acts as a nice way of talking about resources and closed-loop resource systems," said Benjamin.

Swaying a little as the water underneath us rocked, we went to see the greenhouse, which covers more than half of the barge's deck and is laid out to accommodate school groups and other visitors. A handful of students were gathered in the back section of the greenhouse watching Gwen Hill, the Science Barge's director of education, explain how to maintain the tomatoes that were growing up wires out of receptacles called Dutch buckets. Classes from schools in Yonkers, Westchester, Manhattan, and New Jersey account for most of the barge's visitors, but kids also come from Queens, Brooklyn, and the Bronx. Schools pay a fee to send classes there on field trips, a charge that's necessary to help Groundwork Hudson Valley, the nonprofit that now runs the facility, pay for the barge's lease. Grant programs, however, cover the costs for low-income schools, including transportation to the facility, and Gwen is focused on encouraging equal access. "I never turn schools away from the barge," she said.

Teachers without access to "the mother of all school greenhouses" or any other such facility find it worthwhile to take their students all the way to Yonkers to experience this unique urban farm. "It's hands-on learning—being able to see and touch things," said Benjamin. "Teachers bring their school groups and say, 'You don't understand how powerful it is to be able to talk about food and nutrition and agriculture when there are actually tomatoes here. Our kids have never seen a tomato plant before.'"

CHAPTER 8

Farming Their Futures

Field-based learning prepares students for agricultural careers

EXPOSING OUR YOUNGEST KIDS TO the details of food and farming is essential. But while getting our children acquainted with the character of a tomato plant or the purpose of vermiculture will surely enrich their lives and make them more likely to be informed about and interested in their food system, facilities such as the Great Kids Farm and the P.S. 333 greenhouse won't necessarily help restore the vibrancy of our agricultural community on their own. We also need hands-on training programs that build on such educational efforts, ways to channel the natural enthusiasm of any student who is developing a more serious interest in growing food.

Surely such programs must be proliferating, just as school gardens for elementary-age youngsters are popping up all over in the midst of increasing concern about the sustainability of our food supply and the eating habits of the next generation. And not only would such programs aimed at older kids and teenagers be a welcome discovery, but what about initiatives targeted at college kids and even at working-age young adults who are looking for a new direction?

My first stop was San Francisco, situated next door to the city of Berkeley, where the current enthusiasm for school gardening was first ignited by Chef Alice Waters's now-famous Edible Schoolyard program. There is no dearth of related efforts in the Bay Area, one of the most notable of which is called Urban Sprouts, a multifaceted initiative focused on providing "garden-based education" in underserved communities. The program reaches more than 750 middle and high school students at seven schools, 60 percent of whom are low-income students and over 95 percent students of color, to encourage "eco-literacy, equity, wellness, and community." The program incorporates students' parents into some of its activities. What I was most interested in, however, was the organization's Summer Sprouts program, a two-week intensive gardening-oriented job-training program that takes place every summer at the Garden for the Environment, a demonstration garden run by a nonprofit in San Francisco's Inner Sunset neighborhood.

Summer Sprouts was in full swing during my visit on a warm July day, a diverse group of young people buzzing with activity amid the raised beds and flower borders of the meandering garden. As I entered under a wooden trellis, I passed a clutch of students huddled in one corner learning how to make cheese. Along the fence by the road, other kids were picking and arranging flowers for an Urban Sprouts fund-raising dinner that night, and at the other end of the garden path, another group was helping a visiting chef prepare a lunch of tacos featuring fresh veggies from the garden and handmade tortillas.

Program Manager Audrey Roderick, sunglasses propped on her head, welcomed me with a smile and a handshake. As the one in charge of things while the executive director was out on maternity leave, Audrey was in the middle of a hectic couple of weeks, but she still looked like she was having fun as she greeted students and showed me briefly around the garden.

Students must interview for their positions in the program, she told me, and once enrolled, they get paid for their time. Juniors and seniors in high school serve as mentors to younger students in the gardening work. In the summer of 2010, seven high school group leaders, each paid ten dollars an hour, were supervising seven junior leaders—younger high schoolers—and twelve middle schoolers, who all received stipends.

The interview process, hierarchical structure, and compensation are designed to introduce students gently to some of the requirements, responsibilities, and benefits of a workplace, which means the program doubles as garden education and job training. They are able to learn basic workplace skills like interviewing, leadership, and group communication in a safe and structured environment.

Incorporating the food preparation component into the program focuses attention on healthy eating, which Urban Sprouts strives to make a core issue in all of its programming. "Healthy food is a right," said Audrey as we strolled toward the taco station where the students were gathering for lunch. Students with an interest in culinary arts can develop their skills by focusing on these elements of the program.

As hungry kids lined up by the folding tables equipped with portable stoves to get their freshly made tacos, I got a word with one such culinarily inclined individual, Kevin Rodriguez, a student at Ida B. Wells High School. As the current kitchen manager, he was directing the students in making lunch, a role he said he enjoys because he has a brother in middle school and feels comfortable mentoring kids that age. While auto mechanics is his thing at school, he was thinking he might be interested in going into food or cooking. He excused himself to jump back behind the lunch table, joking with friends as he checked over the status of the taco service.

Like Kevin, Michael Mejia, a senior at the June Jordan School for Equity and a group manager in charge of one junior staff person and three middle schoolers, appreciated the program's focus on mentoring younger students. "It's really a program not only about gardening, but it's about peer leadership," he told me. "As seniors, we're about to go out into the world, so we need skills. We get to understand how to lead." His favorite thing about the program was "working with the kids and building community," he said. Though spending time in nature and learning about healthy eating weren't bad either. "We're in the city all the time. There's all these cars, all this cement—it's great to come here and be with plants," he said. "And I've been trying to influence my family" to eat healthier.

"Do they listen to you?" I asked.

He smiled. "No, not at all."

Michael's junior leader, Walter Pan, an earnest kid with a mop of black hair and a white T-shirt, had found that exploring healthy eating was only one way the program was expanding his consciousness. As he prepared for his junior year at Lowell High, he was participating in Summer Sprouts for the fourth time (he had been one of the original students to enroll when it first began) and credited the program with helping him question received wisdom in a way he never had before. He had always thought that things were a certain way for a reason, he told me—that adults treat the environment how they do, for instance, because that is how it is supposed to be treated. But the program had encouraged him to think critically about the choices people make—in food, in the environment, in everything. "After joining this program, I realized that a lot of things people do are wrong. And one of the reasons is that no one is speaking up about it," he said. "I learned all this knowledge I never knew about."

But before he got to that point, the program had given him confidence and leadership skills, helping him turn from a shy seventh grader into an eighth grader self-assured enough to be elected student body president. "This program really opened me up," he said.

"It gave me a lot of leadership skills." Now, his dreams are as big as his newfound confidence: he plans to learn to fly and to become an engineer—perhaps an aerospace engineer—so he can create more environmentally friendly planes. In the meantime he was working on turning his friends and family into environmentalists and enjoying the idea of another year in the program next summer. "It gives me something to look forward to," he said.

Before I left the garden, I learned that Audrey had attended the University of Montana, where I had learned about the Farm to College program from Kyra Williams. While there, Audrey had participated in the Program in Ecological Agriculture and Society (PEAS) focused on sustainable farming, which I had also happened to check out while I was roaming about Missoula. Incidentally, the program provides a great example of an avenue for students at the college level to explore their interest and develop their skills in agriculture and food issues.

I had met Josh Slotnick, cofounder and director of PEAS, at the picnic tables outside Bernice's Bakery in Missoula on a late Saturday afternoon in June. The tree-lined street was sleepy; the sunlight was turning gold and students drifted silently by on bicycles. Josh appeared abruptly and slid into the picnic bench opposite me as I munched on a cookie, his baseball cap and dirty T-shirt lending truth to what he had told me on the phone: he was taking a break from a long afternoon's work on his own farm, Clark Fork Organics, to speak with me. He works there whenever he's not at his full-time job directing the ten-acre PEAS Farm, where students complete the intensive farming internship that serves as the core of PEAS.

Josh spearheaded the establishment of the program in 1997, drawing inspiration from the ecological horticulture apprenticeship program he and his wife, Kim, had completed at the mother of all sustainable farming programs, UC Santa Cruz's Center for

Agroecology and Sustainable Food Systems. PEAS is a partnership between the University of Montana, which employs Josh as a lecturer in the environmental studies department, and a nonprofit organization called Garden City Harvest, which Josh also cofounded and for which, incidentally, Audrey of Urban Sprouts used to work after completing PEAS.

Garden City Harvest covers all the farm's operating expenses, including leasing the land long-term from the Missoula County Public Schools and providing a farm building, tractor, and all other necessary equipment. The university, in turn, supplies Josh and the students, who are involved in the program from February through October, with the summer session being the most intense time. During the summer, students work on the farm Monday through Thursday from eight a.m. to noon and cook lunch for each other using produce they have grown. On Fridays, they attend an agroecology class in which, said Josh, they "talk about bugs and weeds and tractors and irrigation and things like that." They also go on field trips to local small farms to learn about the realities of the business. The PEAS Farm isn't, after all, a business proposition: although it runs a CSA, it supplies a majority of its food to the Missoula Food Bank.

As nurturer of young would-be agriculturalists, Josh has developed an intimate perspective on the profound ways the training program can influence college kids at a formative stage in their lives. What they get from the experience goes far deeper than information on how to grow broccoli. More important than agricultural training, he told me, is "a sense of what work is like, how you feel fully committed and attached to the people around you and the ground right under your feet." The dynamic arises organically in the atmosphere of shared labor and learning that the program fosters. "It has to happen on its own, and when it does happen it really is magical," Josh said. "People have a sense of ownership over where they are and what they're doing and their allegiances to those around them." The students get to be "involved in an activity where they understand their own personal necessity," sometimes for the first time ever. "If they weren't there, things wouldn't go the way they're supposed to go. The carrots wouldn't grow, the beets wouldn't grow. And they feel like they belong to a group. That sense of belonging and that sense of personal power or personal effectiveness are really transformative."

To use that transformative experience to help kids who need it most, Josh and colleagues started a program called Youth Harvest, which engages small numbers of Missoula teenagers who are in trouble with the law for drug- and alcohol-related offenses to work on the farm alongside the college interns. These young farmers, aged sixteen to eighteen, are paid a minimum-wage stipend and stand to have their records wiped clean if they participate successfully. Working with the university students provides these troubled teenagers a window into a different world.

"The university students are only a few years older, but they're worlds apart," Josh told me, his gentle eyes taking on an intensity under the brim of his cap. "The university kids are on a whole other path. The university kids are all optimistic. They're excited. The Youth Harvest kids are pretty cynical. Their lives are really deeply screwed up. They, for the most part, have just been in the way. And to watch them discover that sense of being necessary and belonging to a group, tangible results coming from what they do, helping make beauty and importance. It isn't 'jail to Yale'—the issues are way too big—but what I found with these kids is that that summer experience proved to be a reference point that they held close to them for many years to come."

The fact that people working together to grow food forge a sense of deep connection and meaning among the rows of vegetables is nothing less, Josh told me, than "the central truth of my adult life." It's a bold statement, but one that he defends emphatically. "What we found over the years is that agriculture is a catalyst for the creation of community," he said. The vibrant communities that have sprung up around Garden City Harvest's seven community gardens and two other neighborhood farms in the city bear this out. "These places are hubs for human activity, people working together in close contact creating new things, actively caring about each other and the ground under their feet. The experience for the people involved is so much greater than the food for the food bank. That doesn't mean they don't need it—we bring them fifteen thousand pounds of food. But for the people at the food bank it might as well come from Wal-Mart. For the people who created the food, it was a transformative experience."

After Josh rushed off to finish his work before sundown, I went to get my own look at this mystical place that has impacted so many lives. In a quiet, suburbanish neighborhood called the Rattlesnake, I pulled up next to a Garden City Harvest truck in a parking lot beside the PEAS Farm's neatly arrayed, well-tended fields. Beyond the far rows, a man was running a ride-on lawn mower over a soccer field, the distant growl of his engine mingling with the soft grunting of pigs from a nearby enclosure. I wandered around to the porch of the rustic wooden farm building, where I found a few college-age kids relaxing in a porch swing, cutting vegetables, and poking at the coals in a grill. They invited me to have a burger— a local, grass-fed one, of course, on a bun made by producers in a local wheat cooperative—and were amazed when I told them it would be my first burger in sixteen years. (I was a vegetarian for eleven years, but that's a discussion for another chapter.)

As I settled myself in the porch swing and rocked with a comforting creak, the only girl in the group, Alex Kuennen, a native Montanan and University of Montana student in a worn T-shirt ripped under the arms and a straw cowboy hat, told me she was the caretaker of the place. She was living in a room upstairs and doing all the daily maintenance chores to keep the farm running, a job she ended up with because she liked the program so much that she "just never left." She laughed, but her friend Benjamin Courteau chimed in to say that really was the way it happened. Alex was coming around to help on the farm so often, he said, that it just made sense to have her there all the time. If she weren't graduating after the next semester and then moving to a heifer farm in Arkansas to learn about animal husbandry and environmental education, she said, "I could probably stay here for a good, long time."

Benjamin was similarly love struck with the farm, describing the program as "life changing." He had come back as an alumnus of the university to do the program after he got a master's degree in international relations and had trouble finding a job. "There's something about doing humble manual labor with other people that just brings you very close together and levels the playing field in a way that builds incredible community," he said, as if channeling Josh. The experience inspired him to switch directions: He eventually moved to Seattle to start a company offering mentoring on how to farm urban patches and produce value-added products in the city.

In an era when farming has by and large become so mechanized that farmers managing industrial operations rarely spend much time with their hands plunged into the soil, it was heartening to see young people so inspired by and articulate about the value of labor-intensive farming as a way of life. And of course I was happy to find what I had come looking for—a project that was giving young people interested in farming the skills they need to make a go of it. Alex was certainly equipped with all the knowledge required to work in agriculture in whichever way she chooses. I followed along behind as she went to feed the scraps of dinner to the pigs and admired her ease with their strange ways as they jostled into the trough. "It's amazing," she said, watching them affectionately. "They eat all day and then they're still hungry."

I appreciated the existence of a program like PEAS, especially considering the infectious enthusiasm it seemed to inspire in its director and participants, but I wondered what might be out there for people who don't have the college-internship path available to them. What about young adults who have arrived at a profound transition point in their lives and think they might like to try out farming? Or even those who might not think of farming as an option until they get the chance to try it?

At a food-related event one night with this question lingering in the back of my mind, I met Michael O'Gorman, an approachable farmer built like a fire hydrant who had founded an organization called the Farmer-Veteran Coalition in 2008. He smiled, pumping my hand with his solid fist, and told me that he started the organization after his son joined the military in the wake of 9/11. He was forced, as he put it, to "open his mind," grappling to understand what it means to be a soldier and a veteran in our country today. Considering this question from the vantage point of the large-scale organic farms he has managed for years in California's Central Valley brought him a realization that changed his life: veterans would make good farmers. And, boy, did farms need them.

He told me he would be speaking the next day on a panel about creating rural jobs at a meeting of the Coalition for Iraq and Afghanistan Veterans. Would I like to come hear more? That's how I found myself attending my first-ever military-related conference, part of the modest audience gathered in a hotel meeting room. Michael stood up front with the session's panelists and explained the logic behind his campaign to get vets and farmers to join forces.

"One of the instigating pieces of information that motivated us to start the Farmer-Veteran Coalition was a report that showed that one-sixth of the American population is classified as living in rural communities, but 45 percent of the military comes from rural communities," he told the audience. "At the same time we have a crisis in the United States of a lack of young people going into agriculture, so we thought, well, what better place to go look for new farmers than the young men and women who went into the military with a sense of service and came out with the discipline and the leadership and the work ethic and are looking for something new to do?"

He flipped through a PowerPoint, rattling off a few more statistics about the disproportionate role of America's rural areas in our fighting forces and sharing anecdotes about the enthusiasm veterans show for the idea of returning to their roots. "This is a very exciting time to go into agriculture," he said. "There's more support and there's a lot you can do."

To illustrate his point, Michael introduced Adam Burke, one of the first veterans the coalition worked with, who returned from duty in Iraq with a Purple Heart and an injury that required him to walk with a cane. Now he has little more than a limp and runs two farms and a nonprofit organization aimed at exposing other veterans to agriculture, both as vocational training and therapy.

A thin, blond guy with a piercing gaze, Adam stood up and told the assembled crowd that he had grown up on a blueberry farm in Florida, which was the only place he wanted to be when he came home from his deployment. The peaceful surroundings and satisfying manual labor of farming seemed just the right balm for a war-battered body and soul. As soon as he got back there, it occurred to him that other soldiers would surely find farm life as healing and engaging as he did.

"I decided that the best way to provide therapy for myself and others was to find something other than what [Veterans Affairs] was offering, which was just a lot of medication that was really hurting us," he said. He made up his mind to start a blueberry farm where vets could come to heal their bodies and minds and to learn a new career. His program, Veterans Farm, now has two locations in Florida, a two-and-a-half-acre plot in Webster and an eight-acre blueberry farm in Jacksonville. The latter location Adam chose because the city has the third-largest military presence in the country but no VA hospital. The fourteen-week program he offers at the farms provides veterans a monetary stipend, agricultural training, and a sense of belonging and camaraderie. One of the most important benefits, however, is something even simpler but frequently more elusive for returning soldiers: an avenue to help vets reacquaint themselves with the rhythms of civilian life.

"Our goal is to really help the guys reintegrate back into society," Adam told the panel's audience. "Go to farmers' markets and sell. Go to commercial markets. Get out in the community. Really work with the community. And then go out and start their own farms. Or, if they decide not to do that, we have a pile of farmers who are looking for workers. They need the help."

With vets and farmers teaming up to help each other, this program offers a vision of agriculture-as-civic-enterprise, which is exactly the approach we must adopt to help our food system—and our society—thrive.

PART 3

GROWING EMPOWERMENT

CHAPTER 9

Cultivating the Urban Jungle

Advocates fight to bring food and fairness to inner cities

THE MOVEMENT TO TRANSFORM OUR food system is at its heart an effort to restore a dynamic of democratic fair play in a part of our society that has become far too dominated by moneyed corporate interests. Large-scale food companies have consolidated at an alarming rate over the last several decades, asserting their identities as profit-driven corporations first and their role as purveyors of nourishment second. The corporatization of our food sector has brought with it an increasing disregard for the role of food as a social good that has a value deeper than money and on which the well-being of our society depends. Taking power back from the Big Ag players, both by taking one's money elsewhere and by once again recognizing food's important social value beyond its role as a money-making commodity, is a profound act of self-empowerment.

Viewing things through this lens, I could see that all the people I had met so far along my journey were working—in their disparate ways—to advance the simple cause of fairness in one of the most fundamental aspects of our lives. Why, they were asking, shouldn't we be able to buy the food produced at farms near our homes? Why shouldn't a small-scale producer who wants to grow food for his neighbors be able to make a decent living? Why shouldn't we support people who dream of becoming farmers? Why shouldn't we teach our kids about the healthy food that keeps them alive?

Many actors in the industrial food system have been trying for decades to keep people from asking such questions. The answer they'll never admit to, for each of these queries, is that we shouldn't do those things because they will keep the big food companies from making as much money as they could if we'd just shut up and keep eating our Cheetos. The government agencies whose policies sustain this industrial food system in its all-or-nothing form have by and large served as yes-men to the corporate power players.

Nowhere is the nondemocratic unfairness of our food universe more obvious than in our inner cities and poor rural communities, where millions of people live without reliable access to healthy food. The problem is not only that they cannot afford fresh food, though that can also be the case, but that they have nowhere to buy it. Grocery stores in these areas, unable to make profits equal to what they could find in more prosperous neighborhoods and scared away by the logistical challenges of operating in higher-crime areas, have packed up and moved away, leaving residents with few places to turn. Many inner-city residents rely on corner stores and liquor stores, where they can get mainly processed foods and maybe some low-quality produce (usually things that store well like onions and potatoes). Mix in the ubiquitous fast-food joints, and you have a recipe for obesity, diabetes, and heart disease. While a common term for these areas is food deserts, I prefer food swamps. There's food in these places, after all; it's just not the good stuff.

I figured that just as there were people all over the country fighting for fairness for our small and middle-sized farmers, there must be people fighting for fairness for the eaters in our inner cities as well. To find out what kind of hopeful projects might be under way, I headed to the poorest neighborhood in the San Francisco Bay Area, West Oakland, which has poverty rates of over 40 percent in many sections, according to Alameda County Public Health Department, and contains a single full-service grocery store, Mandela Foods Co-operative, for its more than twenty-three thousand residents. The area is part of the city of Oakland, a former industrial center that ironically used to be a center of food processing and canning and is neighbor to Berkeley, the liberal enclave whose chefs and gardeners helped shift attention toward food fairness in the first place.

On a cold, bleak morning in early July, I walked up MLK Jr. Way, a desolate strip in the shadow of a freeway, as everything in West Oakland seems to be. In the side streets, a warren of small, well-kept houses brought a cozier feel, and things looked up even more when I arrived at the dead end of a quiet street and met Barbara Finnin, ex-ecutive director of City Slicker Farms, a smiling, diminutive woman who came briskly along with a grass green scarf tucked into the top of her jacket and a coffee mug in hand.

"Typical day in the Bay," she said, indicating the solid gray cur-tain of clouds above.

The garden she was planning to show me, one of seven that City Slicker Farms operates, was called the Secret Garden, and the name was fitting: Barbara couldn't figure out how to open the lock on the wooden gate because the workers had changed the combination. Fi-nally, after a few phone calls, we emerged into a long, thin plot snak-ing along the left side of a large house, whose owners had given the organization permission to use the land and access to water. Along the garden's far side, rusted chain-link fences cordoned off the weedy little backyards of the adjacent houses, where obstreperous dogs barked warnings. A cat watched us from a nearby rooftop.

Barbara gave me a tour through beds of greens, carrots, and Brus-sels sprouts. She pointed out the little dishes of beer the gardeners had put out to kill slugs, which apparently dive in and drown in an intoxicated stupor. "It's well known," she said, shrugging. "Slugs love beer."

Barbara explained that the organization refers to the plot as a "community market farm," which means it is professionally managed to produce food to be sold at a central market stand, instead of consisting of plots farmed by individual community members, the typical community garden model. Young apprentices who earn a stipend and live in a house together in the neighborhood cultivate all seven market farms, which produce around seven thousand pounds of food a year on land that totals less than an acre. The produce is offered to low-income area residents at a farm stand every Saturday in exchange for suggested donations. People who come to the market from other parts of town are politely told that the food is reserved for West Oaklanders, and if they want to help, monetary donations are badly needed.

City Slicker, Barbara explained, is a nonprofit working to improve food security for at-risk people, not a business looking to make a buck. "Foundations will be like, 'Why can't you make some money on your produce?'" she told me as we sat down on some cut logs arranged under the shade of a mammoth tree beside the vegetable beds. "It's because the money goes into the programs. We can't make any money. It's not possible for us to go beyond covering some of our costs."

The programs she was referring to are, in addition to the market stands and the apprenticeship program, a paid internship program for West Oakland youth and a busy backyard gardening program, which Barbara called "our community garden method." When a family applies for help starting a garden in its yard, City Slicker first assesses the space and the soil quality and then sends a team of workers and volunteers with the needed materials—planter boxes, soil, seedlings—to set up the garden. Families receive ongoing access to free materials as well as guidance from a volunteer mentor, who commits to help them for two years. There are around a hundred families currently maintaining such gardens, which produce a total of around fifteen thousand pounds of food. After eating what they need, the families give surplus to their neighbors or donate or sell it to City Slicker.

"The idea is building tools for self-sufficiency," said Barbara, hugging her arms tight against the chilly air. "It started out from seeing not only the need but that it's utterly wrong that people don't have a real choice for health. If you're living in West Oakland and you don't have access to food that boosts your immune system, and you're surrounded by freeways, there's a lot of industry and toxicity; your immune system isn't going to be able to deal with it very well."

Giving people more choice about the sources of their food and thereby the status of their health is, of course, a key goal of the democratizing push of the larger food movement. People are demanding choices other than hormone-laced meat and pesticide-covered vegetables trucked long distances. But it is important to realize that in some corners of the food movement, the word *choice* means something far more basic. In West Oakland, people want choice about issues much more profound than whether their tomatoes are heirloom or not. With this in mind, it can seem that there are two parallel food movements: one populated largely by affluent white people worrying over the fate of local family farms, and the other the province of low-income people of color preoccupied with whether their families survive, let alone thrive.

"A lot of the divide has to do with class and race, and that needs to be talked about," said Barbara. The majority of West Oakland residents are low-income people of color, with over 60 percent of them African-American, a part of the U.S. population that suffers disproportionately from obesity and diet-related diseases. Unfortunately, issues of class and race seem to be the third rail of the food movement. "It's a taboo subject for a lot of people and they don't want to talk about it for a variety of reasons," she said. One reason might be that the challenges involved here are those of systemic inequality and institutional racism, which quickly draw many food activists out of their comfort zone. "With toxic projects," said Barbara, offering a prime example, "where are we going to put them? Hey, let's put them in West Oakland. Let's put this freeway through West Oakland. This polluting industry, we'll put it in West Oakland. And you see that throughout the country. You never want to discount or neglect to talk about issues of racism when you have primarily people of color and primarily low income."

While the food movement must learn to navigate this terrain, the problems that West Oakland faces are far too profound to be solved by focusing solely on food. These are issues of poverty that must be addressed at the highest levels of policy. Of course food is a key element in their solution, and a movement working for fairness in our food system should be a major avenue for advocacy on this front. However, I couldn't help but think that the cause of blighted cities devoid of grocery stores was beyond the purview of the food system alone, no matter how messed up our farm policy has become.

In spite of that—or maybe because of it—it is important for the food movement not to divide itself into two disparate camps that don't see their common interest in promoting democracy, fairness, and choice. "I think we need to be very honest about what the conversation is about," said Barbara. "All these conversations have to be happening everywhere: wealthy people, poor people, everybody in between. And that conversation is starting to happen. I'm fueled because the Kellogg Foundation and others are saying that racial equity and social justice have to be in the forefront of this movement. That's awesome. Once large foundations like Kellogg start saying that, people will start saying, 'Who are running these organizations?'" She paused, pointing to her white face and light brown hair. "They can't all look like me."

My next stop, naturally, was to visit another West Oakland food justice organization that had recently made a management shift influenced by that idea. People's Grocery, a nonprofit founded in 2002 and initially focused on providing fresh food to local residents via a roving grocery truck, was now shifting toward a community-engagement activism model, teaching West Oaklanders how to demonstrate healthy food preparation techniques to their neighbors and training young people to advocate for food justice. The organization still provides fresh food to neighborhood residents via "grub boxes"—pre-ordered supplies of organic produce—but, unlike City Slicker Farms, it does not grow most of it. The majority of the produce comes at a wholesale price from Veritable Vegetable, a San Francisco–based company that aggregates and distributes the fruits of local small farms.

Brahm Ahmadi, the organization's Iranian-American founder, knew that the obvious differences between himself and those he was serving prevented the community from fully engaging with and investing their trust in People's Grocery. In an essay titled "Why Leaving Is My Greatest Accomplishment," Ahmadi wrote, "While I'm multi-racial and have experienced racism toward my Iranian heritage, I still very much benefit from my white skin privilege and my male gender. And while I did partially grow up in a low-income neighborhood in East L.A., I have never personally experienced real poverty. So even in founding People's Grocery, I always knew that, for People's Grocery to reach its greatest potential, I'd eventually have to replace myself with a leader who was more appropriately aligned with the experiences of West Oakland residents and more qualified as a leader for that community."

He found that person in Nikki Henderson, the most intimidating twenty-five-year-old I've ever met. She was so composed and put together that I felt like a troll when I came ten minutes late after getting lost, frazzled and out of breath, hair flying and frumpy in my reporter's road clothes.

"Not a problem," she said coolly in response to my apologies. Her striking hooped earrings swayed as she moved to shake my hand. "It happens."

We sat down at a small table in her office, a square room off a central open space with the battered looking furniture typical of small nonprofits. I asked her about what Ahmadi had written: What does it mean, I asked, for an organization like hers to be headed by an African-American woman?

The LA native answered by way of an anecdote. "The first time I went to the East Coast and got off the plane, I was surrounded by more people of color—black people specifically—than I've ever been in my life, and I carried myself differently. I was more relaxed. I laughed more. I just felt more comfortable. My guard wasn't up. I didn't realize how much my guard was up before I went to the East Coast and found myself surrounded by people who look like me. That visual trigger of having someone who looks like you, who you can identify with, being in a leadership position is very important. Brahm knew that. He could have as many people of color under him as he wanted to, but if he was still the face of this organization, people weren't going to identify with it as closely and take as much ownership of it, even if they wanted to."

The fact that she isn't from West Oakland is a hurdle, she admitted, but one that can be readily overcome with careful networking and community engagement. The organization's program director, Jumoke Hinton Hodge, has been an activist in West Oakland for fifteen years and knows everybody. "I'm planning on networking through her," Nikki said. "I think that's the best way to go. Because even though I'm a woman of color, an African-American, I don't have relationships with people here. So I need people here who have relationships with people here."

I wondered aloud what organizations could do to encourage more leadership from the communities they serve. It must be a tricky business if so few organizations succeed in doing it.

"My honest answer is that it's always going to be a tension, because if you're working in a low-income community or a community of color—any community that's been economically depressed—usually you have a high drop-out rate in schools," Nikki responded. "The K–12 education is probably falling apart." Indeed, according to Alameda County Public Health Department, more than one-third of West Oakland residents aged twenty-five and older did not have a high school degree as of 2000. "Which means," she continued, "that the people who are unemployed are usually not qualified for the job. Community organizations often sacrifice capacity for keeping it in the community, which keeps a lot of community-based organizations moving slowly and not accomplishing their missions and just kind of stuck. If that's a commitment of yours, you need to have checks and balances set up within the organization so that there is a rapid pathway for leadership development there. You need to be committed to [employees'] growth."

People's Grocery's evolving model, which focuses heavily on empowering community members young and old to build up useful skills, both in eating healthily and advocating for change, is a reflection of this grow-from-within attitude. Nikki compares the struggle for a better food system to the fight for civil rights, insisting that those invested in the movement have to organize themselves and teach each other the ways to move forward.

Her hope, she said, "lies in the movement. But we have to actually be a movement. And we haven't had to be a movement yet. There's been no civil disobedience around food." She looked at me frankly. "Unfortunately I think more people will have to be hurt by the food system before the movement is going to galvanize itself to move forward."

Of course I knew people had been hurt by our food system, not just in terms of diet-related chronic diseases, but also illness and death by salmonella poisoning, farmworkers suffering in conditions approaching slavery, and disease brought on by pesticide spraying and groundwater contamination, to name a few. But Nikki was talking about food in a way that was new to me. Her words conjured images of organized resistance and vociferous political struggle.

"We need more raucousness and we need more organization as a movement because we need to push things now," she said. "Now is the time to take risks. I don't have hope that anything will change without that."

Fair enough, but what exactly is this movement that isn't yet a movement, I wondered? As I had discussed with Barbara, we have deep divides that people are afraid to talk about. The fact that we are unified by a desire for choice about our lives seems too cerebral as a battle cry. And the "Down with Big Ag" declaration that drives so much passion feels too negative, too focused on what we don't want and not enough on an alternate vision of what we do (along with the obvious problem of demonizing all of "Big Ag" in a single unexamined stroke).

"It goes back to common sense," Nikki reasonably said. "We are a common sense movement. In any logical system, if there's no food somewhere, you should be able to get paid for growing it. And the larger system prevents things like that from happening."

I had rarely heard a more level-headed statement, in fact, and it struck me that this movement is really about ascribing to food the value it deserves: a social value, not only an economic one. If food is valued as a social good—something that keeps our society running and our people thriving, not just our companies getting rich—then the government would put its resources into making sure that people have good food to buy and eat and that those who want to make a living growing it can do so. And such change is in fact starting to occur: in August 2011, First Lady Michelle Obama got several major grocery chains to pledge to open stores in poor neighborhoods. This development is a good start, but much more commitment is needed, especially in the realm of government policy.

In the meantime, everyday Americans are taking matters into their own hands. Myriad urban gardening efforts all over the country are exploring the question of what it would take to make a living growing and feeding one's neighbors with the most local produce of all. It's a difficult equation, as city land is often so valuable as to render the idea of urban farming laughable. But in sections of cities where land is not so precious—where there are abandoned lots, say, or private land not worth building on—gardeners can make a go of putting down roots in the concrete jungle.

The most prominent example of this is Detroit, where there is so much cheap, available land—an estimated forty square miles of vacant property—that the entire city has become a veritable experiment in urban food production. The slew of small organizations and motivated individuals that took over empty lots for food production sparked a food-focused renaissance of hope and activity in the city. Gardens and farms—from tiny plots in churchyards to proper farms stretching across entire blocks—have sprouted up across the city, supported and championed by the Garden Resource Program Collaborative. An umbrella organization called Detroit Black Community Food Security Network promotes fresh, urban food as a path to a healthier African-American community, and documentary filmmakers are producing a film called *Urban Roots* to document the city's rampant agricultural activity. The business community has also taken notice: investor millionaire John Hantz hatched plans to create for-profit Hantz Farms, which is promised to be the world's largest urban farm and a key to reversing the city's fortunes. According to the company's literature, the farm will "attract tourism, increase the tax base, create jobs, and greatly improve the quality of life in Detroit."

In all manner of other places around the country, efforts to cultivate our cities are on the rise, and many of them approach food, as Nikki suggested, as a social as well as an economic good, a force that can empower disadvantaged people as well as fill their bellies. I found a promising example in the gritty Manchester neighborhood of Richmond, Virginia, where an organization named Tricycle Gardens was setting up a new half-acre urban farm in the summer of 2010. I pulled up at a neat, green oasis sandwiched by tightly clustered townhomes, parking lots, and a highway at the corner of 9th and Bainbridge Streets, an intersection a couple blocks from one of that area's most popular food sources: a McDonald's. Lisa Taranto, the organization's director, stood between two planting rows under the crystal blue sky instructing a group of teenagers—volunteers working as part of a Baptist day of service—in the technicalities of garden tools.

"This is called a spade fork. This is not a pitchfork," she said, addressing her audience from behind bug-eye sunglasses under the brim of a jaunty purple cap and holding a metal implement aloft.

"A pitchfork has longer, skinnier tines. A spadefork is kind of like a cross between a shovel and a pitchfork, right? This is also good for breaking up the soil. You gotta get in with your foot, press that in, and turn the soil over." She plunged the fork into one of the rows and uprooted a clump of rich, black earth.

The farm is the newest and most ambitious project for an organization that started almost a decade ago with a single community garden and a goal to foster civic engagement through working in the dirt. Lisa told me that for a long time the idea of urban farming seemed to be perceived by most in Richmond as a quaint, oddball venture. The organization carried on in spite of general skepticism, setting up more garden sites, including learning gardens; offering classes, workshops, and lectures; organizing potlucks, and by and large creating pockets of thriving horticulture-based community within Richmond's staid atmosphere.

Then, in the last few years, the upsurge of interest in local food, including urban farming, has made people take the project a lot more seriously. Where before the organization was frequently ignored, people are now beating down its door. On the day I was there, the Baptist teenagers had been joined by another group of last-minute helpers from a nearby university, bringing the total of volunteers up to a number Lisa had to scramble to manage. She raced around the farm with an exuberance only matched by her authority, joking one moment, issuing directives the next. I cornered her for a moment to ask her opinion of urban farming.

"To me, it's essential," she said. "Not necessarily just for survival. It's essential to humans moving forward and not being such assholes." She broke into full-throated laughter. "Because right now, it's not workin' out, what we're doing. Things are not getting better, they're getting worse. We seem to live in this fantasy that things are getting better. And they're not. Diabetes is on the rise. Poverty's on the rise. Environmental degradation's on the rise. It's bad, you know? People are not getting richer. They're not getting healthier. Their resources are not being shared more equally. Though a lot of people try to make you think they are."

The farm she was working so hard to make a success, she said, "is a little tiny drop in the bucket." She looked around, measuring the area with her glance. "This will feed maybe seventy-five, a hundred families, provide a couple jobs. A developer is renting this to us for a dollar a year. If we can't make this work on a dollar, then, you know, we are losers." She burst out laughing again, and started moving off. "Let's walk over here," she said. "I want to check on these guys."

Weaving my way after her amid raised beds bursting with leafy stalks and earnest youths slapping red paint onto the walls of a shed, I bumped into the chairman of the organization's board, William Snyder, a young, amiable guy in a fleece accompanied by two big dogs snuffling around in the grass.

"We want to prove that this scale of farming could work and make money," he told me. The organization's goals had changed over time as it became clear that urban agriculture could be so much more than a miniature community project. Tricycle Gardens was moving into an entirely new league. Food politics thought leaders Michael Pollan and Marion Nestle had even come around for a peek the prior year, he said.

"We had been subsistent," William said. "The idea was community. And now, with the farming, it becomes jobs and economic development."

The model is receiving a lot of interest and support, including from the local brewery, Legend, which uses the hops the farm plants to make small-batch barrels of beer. Local donors were offering the use of their large yards and empty lots for the organization to expand into.

With supporters behind them, "the challenge is to figure out if we can replicate and become an umbrella for other farmers who want to come into the city," William told me. "We can give them the training they need to get off the ground."

This upsurge in urban farming might just be the beginning of a tidal shift in our understanding of what type of food—and accordingly, what quality of life—belongs in urban centers. As Barbara Finnin of City Slicker Farms sees it, it's all about what we expect. "Normal right now is McDonald's, for rich people and for poor people and everybody in between," she had told me. "We don't have produce stands in our urban centers. We have McDonald's. We have KFC. 'Normal' used to be that you had your meat market and your veggie market. If you have urban centers that have gardens, it's re-focusing what's normal and what you want to advocate for."

Advocating for the prominence of fresh food in our urban jungles? As Nikki Henderson might say, that's just common sense.

CHAPTER 10

To Market, to Market

Incentives bring fresh food to the poor and income to local farmers

PROVIDING BETTER ACCESS TO FRESH food in inner cities—whether through garden programs, farm stands, grub boxes, or the development of grocery stores—is essential to promoting food security for low-income urban residents. Such programs, however, are focused on areas with little or no other access to fresh food. What about all those people who have grocery stores or other markets within striking distance but find the produce there more expensive than their budgets can manage?

A general rule of our society's food culture is that the less money people have, the less healthfully they tend to eat. Studies show that economically depressed neighborhoods usually have high rates of obesity and type 2 diabetes, especially among women. In fact, according to Population Reference Bureau, 35.6 percent of women in the lowest-income bracket in the United States are obese, compared to 15.5 percent of the highest-income women, and a study in the *American Journal of Epidemiology* tells us that women living in neighborhoods of the lowest socioeconomic status exhibit the highest rates of diabetes. This has to do in part with the access issue, but also with cost, perception of cost, an entrenched culture of and taste for fast food, lack of education about food and cooking, and insufficient time, facilities, and motivation to prepare fresh meals and to exercise. For people on highly restricted budgets living in underserved areas, these are very real problems difficult to overcome, ones that demand aggressive public policy, full-surround social programs, and incentives other than a scolding repetition of "you should eat well for your health."

Recent debates about how recipients of food assistance dollars spend their money have laid bare some of the fault lines in this debate. Is it fair to restrict food assistance recipients from buying soda with that money, or is that a condescending interference tantamount to saying poor people don't know how to feed themselves? And if you can restrict soda, can you cross Doritos off the list? If so, do somewhat healthier processed snack foods like pretzels also go? What about sugary breakfast cereals? If those are forbidden, then who decides what's "sugary"? Following this logic, what about white bread, which has little nutritional value, or jam, sugar, coffee? These are not health foods, either. This conversation smells like trouble.

Most likely a better way of helping food assistance recipients use their money in the best interest of their health is to provide a financial incentive to draw them to the produce aisle, or better yet, the farmers' market. Many of those on government food assistance would love to eat more fresh fruits and vegetables but find that such items quickly suck up the lion's share of their checks. If only food assistance were designed to go further in covering produce than in paying for processed foods, recipients might well opt for healthier fare.

A nonprofit called Wholesome Wave, headed by Chef Michel

Nischan and former USDA Under Secretary Gus Schumacher, has taken up this idea. The organization partners with farmers' markets across the country to set up versions of its Double Value Coupon Program, which matches dollar for dollar any food assistance money spent at the markets, where the food is, by definition, healthy. A food assistance recipient who signs up to use ten dollars of his or her assistance money at the market will receive an extra ten dollars from the market's organizers to spend there as well. The logistical details and specific rules of the arrangement vary from market to market, but everywhere the principle is the same: provide a powerful incentive for low-income people to buy fresh food, and they will. The program has expanded to more than 200 markets in twenty-seven states, in cooperation with more than fifty nonprofit partners, since its launch in 2008.

Wholesome Wave provides seed funding for its partners to get their programs started, along with technical support and capacity-building assistance. The organization follows up with development assistance aimed at helping markets and nonprofit partners gain continuing funding from private foundations and a range of municipal, state, and federal programs. Meanwhile, Nischan and Schumacher have set their sights even higher: They are building a case for various policy initiatives, including the insertion of the incentive in the Farm Bill itself. The Farm Bill, a monstrous kitchen-sink piece of legislation that is debated and renewed every five years, dictates much of the country's agricultural policy but also lays out the details of and allocates the funding for food assistance programming. Food assistance, in fact, accounts for the lion's share—$209 billion—of the current Farm Bill's $307 billion cost, so changes like Nischan and Schumacher are aiming for amount to no small change. The plan, which Nischan described to me as a "repurposing of taxpayer dollars to have more of an impact on food choices and health," has the potential to transform the eating habits of millions of people.

That might sound good, but the matching incentive program is even more brilliant than it seems at first, considering that drawing new shoppers to farmers' markets puts more money in the pockets of the small, local farmers who sell there. And the money coming to them isn't just any money: half the dollars food assistance recipients are spending at the markets is government money, Farm Bill money. While the majority of the Farm Bill goes to food assistance, millions are still allocated to subsidies for the nation's farms, some of them—amazingly—in the form of direct payouts that farmers receive whether they grow any crops or not. The structure of the subsidies in the bill is stacked against smaller growers. Sixty-two percent of subsidies granted by the current Farm Bill go to large commercial farms growing commodity crops like corn, soy, and wheat. Government payments go to 7 out of 10 commercial farms, while only 3 out of 10 "rural residence farms" (small family farms) are supported and only 4 out of 10 intermediate farms see this kind of support.

The Farm Bill uses U.S. taxpayers' money to give the already powerful Big Ag players a competitive edge in the form of government handouts. And some very powerful lobbies are determined to make sure it stays that way. But in a perfect world, the subsidy structure would be tilted the other way, supporting the types of farms that strengthen our communities, create good local jobs, provide a sustainable way of life, and offer us local, healthy foods. The current state of politics makes a massive shift in this direction a pipe dream, so the beauty of Wholesome Wave–style programs is that they offer a way for the small farmers in a local area to capture some of the federal food money they don't have access to any other way. While food assistance money would usually go straight to giant food corporations via the grocery stores where most recipients shop, this program instead allows those funds to help our small farmers make ends meet.

Clearly, I needed to see this type of remarkable program in action; anything that beats the Farm Bill at its own game is certainly a thing to behold. In Kansas City, Missouri, Gayla Brockman, president of the Menorah Legacy Foundation, has been spearheading a coalition of diverse partner organizations in a push to get no less than fifteen markets participating in an incentive matching scheme called the Kansas City Beans&Greens program, an independent project designed on the Wholesome Wave model but not officially part of the Wholesome Wave network.

I arrived in Kansas City two weeks after the program launched in June 2010 and spent two days zooming around town visiting markets with Gayla, a slim firecracker of a woman and a fourth-generation Kansas City native. She had returned to the area after years away in Boston, where she earned degrees in health care administration, furiously climbed the corporate ladder, and eventually had a revelation that she was "beyond miserable—doing the wrong job, dating the wrong men, living in the wrong place." She returned to Missouri to start over, albeit with a good bit of Boston spirit intact. "Welcome to Boston driving," she said, grinning, after backing the wrong way down a one-way street to reach a parking spot in a busy downtown area. "But I just gotta say, score one for me."

Before we commenced our tour, we stopped in her office, where she slurped a quick noodle-soup lunch at her desk while I asked about the Menorah Legacy Foundation's interest in the program. The foundation, according to its website, aims to "promote . . . health in the Jewish community," and I doubted whether many of the city's Jewish residents were on food assistance.

"That's not our only mission," she told me. A certain category of the grants the foundation makes—tagged Healthy for Life—focuses on transformative programs that change institutions and how people interact with them, promoting health and well-being for any and all of Kansas City's people. Her lunch dispatched, she launched into a flurry of organizing boxes of flyers for the program while filling me in on some details. Participating markets match up to thirty dollars per week for recipients of the food assistance program commonly known as food stamps—now called the Supplemental Nutrition Assistance Program (SNAP)—using a system linked to electronic cards on which they receive the money. Each market can receive up to ten thousand dollars in matching funds per season, which the Menorah Legacy Foundation pays for both from its own coffers and through fund-raising from foundations and state agencies like Healthcare Foundation, Blue Cross Blue Shield, and Missouri Department of Agriculture.

The Menorah Legacy Foundation has purposely kept the rules of the program streamlined to enable as many markets as possible to participate. "We have very few criteria," Gayla said. "One is you're local, two is you take food stamps, and three is that you will honor the match." At the time of the program's launch, six markets were already signed up, with another one set to join before the end of the summer. Gayla was pushing to get others on board and was also busy dreaming up a prototype for a mobile market that would take anything left over from the other markets to sell to food assistance recipients on both the Kansas and Missouri sides of the river. Prior to 2010, only two of the city's twenty-four markets had even made themselves eligible to accept food assistance. I noted that the program sure seems to be off and running. "This is a nice start," Gayla said, hoisting a box of flyers to take out to the car. "There is so much work that needs to be done. It needs to be much bigger." When I checked in with her more than a year later, in fall 2011, it was clear her determination had paid off: The program had expanded to fifteen markets plus a mobile market covering three "food desert" neighborhoods, and the amount of matching money Beans&Greens distributed in 2011 had almost doubled since 2010.

I was fortunate to see this remarkable program in its infancy. Our first stop was a small farmers' market that would almost triple its share of Beans&Greens match money between 2010 and 2011. We drove down a street called the Paseo, a wide boulevard with an expansive grassy median that Gayla told me used to be the province of the elite citizens of town. Now, it's down-at-the-heels in places and downright dangerous and blighted in others. The once-glorious mansions have fallen into disrepair, and the street passes through some areas plagued by drugs and crime. At Paseo and 52nd, we pulled up next to a large, tidily kept white house with two porches—perhaps not up to its former glory, but no inner-city hovel either. This is the location of what Beans&Greens refers to as Troostwood Market, which amounts to a couple folding tables set up in the front yard three days a week selling vegetables grown in the gardens that dominate the lawns on either side of the house. Such a setup might not seem like much, but there turned out to be a whole lot more to the story.

It wasn't a market day, so the yard was deserted except for Ericka Wright, forty-two, manager of the market and the garden, who came bumping over the grass in her electric wheelchair dressed in a pink tank top, pink-and-gray plaid shorts, and small glasses with sparkly, pink embellishments on the edges. Muscular dystrophy had left her rail thin and limited in her movements, but she brought an infectiously positive attitude and tireless energy to running the summer gardening program for youth she established here eleven years ago. The Troostwood Youth Garden, as her yard's vegetable patches are called, was thriving in the heat of the summer— rows of cabbages, collard greens, okra, and chard were growing exuberantly on the side of the house where we stood.

"When my mom got legal custody of my brother's kids, we were the only ones in the place that had a swing set," Ericka explained when I asked how it all began. "So all the kids in the neighborhood were here. How do you tell them to go home when it's time for the other ones to eat? I was like, well, we could do some planting and see how it works. I had never done it." At around that same time, her doctor had told her she badly needed to improve her eating habits. "I had no clue what that meant," she said. "But I like greens and broccoli and all that stuff you're not supposed to eat. So I figured, if I like this, I gotta figure out how I can eat it."

I asked what she meant by "all that stuff you're not supposed to eat." Weren't fresh greens and broccoli the kind of stuff everyone keeps telling us we *are* supposed to eat?

"You don't know what's on it when you buy it at the store," she said. It had never occurred to me before that fear of pesticides could be one reason some people gravitate toward less-healthy processed foods instead of reaching for the fruits and vegetables. "So I thought, if I do it myself, I know," she concluded.

She contacted a master gardener for help and learned everything she could about growing things organically. Soon enough, she was paying local kids a stipend—including a pair of brand-name sneakers—to work in the garden for certain hours each week during the summer. There is no shortage of willing helpers because the garden has become "a big thing in the neighborhood," she said. "Everybody knows about it. You can go down any block and they'll be talking about the garden."

The young gardeners, for their part, gain more than just a few bucks and a pair of basketball shoes. "They learn all of it, from weeding to composting," she told us. "This is our outdoor classroom." Additionally, kids living in straitened circumstances are allowed to take home what they need to help their families, and when Ericka has any extra cash, she takes the kids to do fun things around town. "I try to do things for them that otherwise they would not get to do," she said. "Last month we went and saw *Little House on the Prairie.* We take them to the plaza for a horse and buggy ride."

She led us around the house to the garden on the other side, where broccoli, bell peppers, cherry tomatoes, and green tomatoes were just about ready for harvest.

"Look at all the green ones you have," Gayla swooned, inspecting the tomato plants. "Oh my goodness. If I need green tomatoes I'll come here. Because I'm always frying up green tomatoes. It's my thing."

When Ericka first tried to start a market in the yard, she was stopped short by a local ordinance that forbade home gardeners and community gardeners from selling produce at the site where it was harvested. Gayla and a coalition of other activists including Katherine Kelly, executive director of Kansas City Center for Urban Agriculture (KCCUA) and a vocal urban agriculture advocate, fought the law until the city council repealed it, opening up the way for any small-scale gardener to create his or her own front-yard market. When the Menorah Legacy Foundation was deciding which markets to target with the Beans&Greens program, research showing the overlap between food assistance usage and farmers' markets pinpointed Ericka's little enterprise as an ideal one for the matching incentive program. Gayla helped Ericka get set up to accept SNAP dollars and then made Troostwood one of the first Beans&Greens matching markets.

The market is tiny by the usual standards, but it does enough business that Ericka said she hoped to begin using it not only to support the youth program, but also to bring in personal income to supplant her disability checks. The prospect of gainful employment was one other reason she had gotten serious about the garden project after her first experimental forays into cultivating the yard. In her youth, she was convicted of a Class A felony for dealing drugs and had been casting around for a suitable legal job when she saw the good prospects in fresh produce. "I realized I could sell watermelons at ten dollars apiece and make as much money as I could selling dope," she said. At the time of our visit, she had just received a grant to have portions of the yard paved so she could more easily look after the garden from her wheelchair. "I could live off of the garden if I managed it right," she said. "And that's my goal." Beans&Greens, which was increasing the number of shoppers and their spending allowances, was set to help her on her way.

The next morning, Gayla and I set off for City Market, a huge masterpiece of an urban market established in 1857 that should be the envy of any major city. Located in a permanent space in downtown Kansas City, Missouri, the eleven-acre market maintains five parking lots, 146 farm stalls, more than thirty crafts booths, and a collection of buildings that house more than thirty permanent, standalone businesses such as gift shops, ethnic food stores, and restaurants. On the steamy Saturday we visited, the place was packed—it was hard even to maneuver through the crowds—and the atmosphere had something of a carnival about it. People in Renaissance costumes were milling about for reasons unclear to me. A man on a little vehicle pulled a train of colorful cars filled with children, and performers tied balloon animals. Food vendors hawked "kettle korn" and fresh-squeezed lemonade, and long lines of shoppers waited for free samples at a farm-to-table cooking demonstration.

The market hadn't always thrived this way. At the yellow information tent, we met Deb Connors, a trim, together woman with short red hair and a gentle, no-nonsense attitude who had snapped the market into shape in the last seven years she has managed it on behalf of the company Copaken Brooks. The Saturday spots at the farmers' stands are now so coveted that growers must establish a track record by selling on Sundays to work their way up. Deb has ruled that only those vendors who have signed contracts are allowed to accept the Beans&Greens tokens, an incentive to get vendors to come more regularly.

She checked in with the two women manning the info tent, asking if they had enough of the tokens. When a SNAP recipient comes to the tent and swipes his or her food assistance card in the reader machine dedicated to that purpose, the staff gives out the wooden tokens in a matching amount up to the weekly thirty-dollar limit set by Beans&Greens. These tokens can only be spent at the stands of participating growers in the farmers' market, which are identified by signs. Only a couple weeks after its launch, the program had proved so popular that by one-thirty p.m. on Saturday, the women at the info booth had already rung up $650 in SNAP money, more than half of the previous weekend's $1,100 total. This put the market on track to far exceed its total of $8,000 in SNAP sales from the previous year. The participating farmers, who benefit most from this uptick in sales, were predictably thrilled. "They're happy campers," Deb said as she brought out a new tray of tokens.

Deb directed us into the market and led us through the crowd, fluently naming off the towns and life stories of the various farmers and craftspeople we passed. Her job entails making sure all the vendors at the market are in fact small-scale, local enterprises with suitably hygienic facilities and honest practices, so she spends enormous amounts of time visiting their farms and kitchens and becoming familiar with them, their families, and their businesses. She pointed out the stands selling value-added food products like jam and chocolates, a feature that makes City Market special. "You can't just have produce," she said. "You've got to have the variety."

We paused in the middle of a milling throng of shoppers armed with canvas bags and watched as one stand did a brisk business in corn and summer squash and another found a crowd of buyers for bouquets of fresh-cut flowers. Tomato Taxis—yellow wagons pulled by inner-city kids who, as Deb said, "need to be involved in things"—forged paths through the hubbub, transporting shoppers' purchases to their cars. We marveled at the buzzing activity among the stalls.

"This is the way commerce used to be," Gayla gushed.

"If anyone tells me they didn't do well today," Deb commented, "they're lying."

Troostwood Market, obviously a much more modest affair, was also attracting SNAP recipients that day. We found Ericka under a tree in her wheelchair next to a couple folding tables, where her niece and another teenager were selling the garden's produce.

"I'm going to make you happy. We used the machine today," Ericka said to Gayla, referring to the SNAP card swiper.

"How many times?" asked Gayla, smiling.

"Four."

Beans&Greens was up and running. The amount Ericka distributed in match money that first summer was $674. By the next summer, it would climb to $1,805.

Gayla bought two green tomatoes to fry and admired a photo of Ericka's niece's new baby.

"Are you going to have collard greens next week?" asked a woman buying a bag of chard. Ericka smiled with characteristic warmth as she handed the shopper her change.

"Yes," she said.

When Ericka suddenly passed away in November 2011, about a year and a half after my visit, she left behind a powerful legacy of cultivating hope and self-empowerment through food.

CHAPTER 11

Putting Down Roots

Gardening programs offer a connection to community and place

THE MANY PROGRAMS I HAD visited so far didn't just serve as grocery purveyors, but also as loci of community engagement, citizen empowerment, skills training, and good old-fashioned bonding among neighbors. If food is a social good, then growing and selling food is by its nature a social act. And just as making food into nothing more than a commodity prompts the fraying of our social fabric, an approach to food that views it as a vital aspect in the life of a community will reinforce that community's vitality, and, ultimately, the vitality of the nation. This is such an important factor in an alternative vision of our food system that I wanted to find projects that showcased the dynamic more explicitly. Surely there must be projects out there that approach gardening and farming as being more about the larger social purposes—community cohesion, skills building, empowerment, for example—than about the provision of food itself.

I started by heading to Oakland's neighbor, San Francisco, where I took a light-rail train down 3rd Street past a phalanx of check-cashing outlets and corner liquor stores to the predominantly black, low-income neighborhood of Bayview Hunters Point. The area has spent the last several decades building a notorious reputation as one of the city's most dangerous, and is now, as evidenced by an extension of the light rail, feeling the first effects of gentrification. I passed a nail salon with a few teenagers loitering out front and an impromptu vegetable stand—LEMONS—4–$1.00—then turned at a corner where a group of old-timers sat observing the world.

Quesada Avenue bloomed before me like an oasis in the desert. A remarkable median strip running steadily uphill overflowed with a cascade of colorful flowers, succulent cacti, and regal palm trees. Butterflies hovered and birds trilled. This was the centerpiece of the urban gardening effort I had come to see—Quesada Gardens Initiative—the unlikely spokesperson of which was one Jeffrey Betcher, a balding white guy in a snug, brick-red T-shirt and rimless glasses. "Over here," he called, smiling enormously and waving from the front steps of his townhouse. As soon as I came over, he enfolded me in a hug. "I hope you don't mind," he said. "I'm a hugger."

He ushered me into his beautiful, high-ceilinged kitchen and sat me down at the table with a glass of water and a bowl of tamari almonds. He moved here in 1998, he told me, when this block was the epicenter of the neighborhood's booming drug trade. Desperate to buy a house and unable to afford one anywhere else, he knew the area's reputation but realized too late that he had gotten more than he bargained for. "When I left for work in the morning, there were drug dealers on my front steps, substance abusers asleep under the steps, people defecating on the median strip, and lines of cars waiting to do their drug deals," he said. "It was that bad."

In retrospect, the desperate surroundings didn't seem to have bothered him as much as the fact that his friends wouldn't come visit, and those that did, especially the women, would get hassled. "I'm gay and I love my women friends," he said, munching on an almond. "I was working in the anti-violence-against-women move-ment, and [the harassment] was horrifying to me. But I'm stubborn. I felt like, 'I'm not leaving.' Out of all the options, that wasn't one."

Then, in 2002, a small act of kindness changed everything. Two of Jeffrey's neighbors, Annette Smith and Karl Paige, began plant-ing flowers on a small section of the trash-filled median strip. And then Jeffrey came home from work one day to find that Annette had been busy cultivating a little corner of his yard. "Even though there was a throng of people—drug dealers, who were carrying guns, pretty scary folks—she had planted flowers on this little strip of dirt by my driveway," he told me. "I was so moved by that; here's this woman who knows me a little bit—we have a nice friendly relationship—on a block where people don't meet one another, where people stay isolated and are very fearful, and here she spent part of her day to till and plant some beautiful flowers . . . for me." He smiled at the memory. "I thought, that's what life is about. That's what community development is about. That's what's going to change this block faster than any public investment or outside strat-egy. And in fact it did."

Jeffrey's background as an organizer for women's issues allowed him to see the opportunity that had presented itself. A group of neigh-bors got together for a barbeque, and Jeffrey led what he calls an "asset mapping and consensus building exercise"—basically a con-versation about the positive aspects of living in the neighborhood. That was the first step in a long-term, consensus-based, community-building process that has led to the creation of a series of gardens on vacant land in the immediate neighborhood, including the gorgeous median strip and several food-producing plots. One positive devel-opment snowballed into more and more positive energy, leading to cooperation, action, and ownership. "The [first] garden provided a safe space for us to meet and it provided us something to talk about that wasn't negative stuff," Jeffrey said as he led me outside to get a look at it all. "So it's an asset-based, strength-based approach to community change that was organic. It was happening already."

We wandered uphill along the median, admiring the sprays of purple and red flowers and bunches of leafy vegetation growing between the venerable Canary Island date palms, which are home to a resident parrot. At the top of the hill, a wall around a paved cul-de-sac that used to serve as an open-air drug market sported a joyful mural bursting with color. Anyone who feels moved can organize such an art project or take responsibility for an uncared-for portion of one of the gardens. Decisions on matters that concern everyone or need more organization are taken up consensus-style at regular community meetings.

Up some steps and a block to the left, Jeffrey showed me a beautifully designed garden meant for teaching schoolchildren about growing food. Behind a chain-link fence, a stand of corn waved its emerald leaves in the breeze next to a proud cluster of tall sunflowers and a tidy patch of leafy greens. Though corn is not the most practical food crop for such a tiny space, the garden's designer wanted the kids to see it in its original state, not just in the form of their Cheetos.

The other gardens aren't as carefully planned—each one is a continually evolving collaborative project. At another one a few blocks away, Jeffrey cheerfully greeted a neighbor working on a car and then pointed out to me the section maintained by a Chinese family nobody knows how to speak to. Beside the vegetable beds, a sandbox and rope swing indicated that the garden was for more than growing food. Kids had, in fact, played an important role from the beginning. It used to be a thoroughgoing dumping ground ("Old mattresses," commented Jeffrey, "huge dead fish"), but when the community started cleaning it out children painted signs that said "don't dump on my garden," and the dumping stopped immediately. The space was soon transformed completely and now serves as a hub of community life.

"The change that we've created is not about the garden, it's about the gardeners," said Jeffrey. "It's about people meeting one another through that process." This approach, he said, is fundamentally different from the one taken by most of the actors in the urban agriculture movement, and even the larger food movement, where the garden and the food it produces are king.

"Food folks have organized an urban agriculture coalition and are frustrated that people of color won't come play their game," Jeffrey told me as we strolled back along 3rd Street. "They don't understand why. But it's *their* game." A better strategy for organizers, he noted, is to come find the people you are interested in organizing and learn about their priorities and needs. "Go invest in what *they're* doing and really form bonds," he said. "That's what changes the world."

Indeed, the effectiveness of this community-building paradigm for transforming a neighborhood is obvious on Jeffrey's street. Surrounding blocks are still almost unchanged from the bad old days, whereas Quesada Avenue is now the safe route through town. "The bullets have for the most part stopped flying" on his street, "but they're still flying elsewhere," Jeffrey said. Not only that, but the block's residents now maintain a thriving community life. As if to illustrate that point, Jeffrey stopped to greet a neighbor as we rounded the corner onto Quesada, introducing himself to her one moment and planning a barbeque with her the next. As we turned away, he regarded me with a smile. "We realize we have done something right here."

The success of Quesada Avenue's residents, of course, came from using gardening as a means to an end more profound than a harvest of tomatoes and peppers. While the fruits of the soil are of course fundamental to any gardening enterprise, growing food can also—and, one might argue, *should* also—serve other important social purposes. That purpose can be as simple as cultivating a culture of civic engagement, as necessary as promoting economic development in poor neighborhoods, or—in the case of the New Roots for Refugees program in Kansas City, Kansas—as complicated as helping new Americans integrate into the life of our country.

As I drove through the Juniper Gardens housing project, a poor community squeezed against some train tracks in a desolate section of Kansas City, Kansas—the smaller, dumpier twin of the more well-known Kansas City, Missouri, just across the river—residents sat here and there outside their screen doors in a warren of low-slung apartments, and a band of raggedy children roamed, using half of a summer squash as a soccer ball.

The squash had come from the expansive garden that flowed out from one side of the apartment community like a green ocean from a dilapidated pier. This was Juniper Gardens Training Farm (or, as I amused myself by calling it, the Juniper Gardens Gardens), home to the New Roots for Refugees program. A partnership between KCCUA and Catholic Charities of Northeast Kansas, the program has been operating at the six-acre organic farm at Juniper Gardens since 2008, helping newly resettled refugees from all corners of the world get started in urban farming to provide supplemental food and income for their families.

I located the farm's office in one of the apartments in the block closest to the garden fence, and the doorbell summoned Cathy Bylinowski, the program's farm business development coordinator, a short-haired, bespectacled woman in a mint green T-shirt. The interior of the office was about as bare-bones as possible: a table and two folding chairs on a linoleum floor and a bulletin board displaying some of the program's materials on the wall. "They let us take over a vacant apartment this year," Cathy said as we sat down together.

She explained that the program started because the newly re-settled refugees, most of whom were farmers in their home countries, were frustrated because the jobs available to them were ones with which they had absolutely no experience. They had asked the staff at Catholic Charities, which was providing them social services, whether there was a way they could at least use their farming skills to supplement their income. "I really like the idea that they're in this process of adjusting to their new lives here, and that agriculture is a way they can continue some of their cultural identity from their past," Cathy said.

The refugees participate in KCCUA's Farm Business Development Program, which gradually introduces participants to the ins and outs of running a small farm business. From November through April, trainees attend a weekly workshop covering everything from horticulture to marketing strategies and do biweekly field walks with Cathy, during which she checks up on their progress, helps them with problems, and offers advice. Participants must attend at least ten farmers' markets during the growing season, the logistics of which Catholic Charities arranges. (Farmers in the program are in fact some of those accepting SNAP incentive tokens as part of the Beans&Greens Program Gayla Brockman manages across the river.) The program staff organizes major farm inputs such as irrigation, organic pesticide application, and soil preparation, and it also helps the farmers get signed up for sales tax as small businesses.

The program then provides a series of diminishing subsidies over the course of one to three years. In the first year, the refugees receive market supplies like a tent, scales, and totes, as well as seeds worth up to six hundred dollars and other necessaries like t-posts to make tomato trellises.

"The idea is that as they become more independent and successful farmers and small business people, those subsidies fade away," said Cathy. "The second year we're still subsidizing a certain amount, and some famers will be ready to be cut loose the third year. It'll vary from farmer to farmer. Some of the refugees might still be learning English, still adjusting, so it can go on a little longer." After that, the organizations ideally help the refugees relocate their farm businesses to vacant land, which is abundant in the county.

Cathy popped on a straw hat and we went out into the heat of the day. The sky blazed blue overhead, horsetails of white cloud painting the expanse, against which the green of the garden was arresting. The gray skyline of downtown Kansas City, Missouri, huddled in the distance beyond a stand of bushy trees and a beige strip of river. The farm was laid out in orderly quarter-acre plots, each allotted to one of the seventeen participants of the 2010 training program, fourteen of whom were the resettled refugees participating in the New Roots programs. The plots were bursting with life: corn, chard, lettuce, cabbage, squash, cucumbers, tomatoes, and many other plants.

Some of the crops the refugees grow are staples in their home countries, like Asian long beans and Burmese pumpkin, which Cathy described as "like a skinny, flattened pumpkin." Not all of the typical American crops are familiar to the new farmers, so they require some basic education and training. "We have to tell them, you know, these green beans are ready now," said Cathy. "Or, yeah, maybe in your country you like your corn on the cob to be more starchy and chewy, but that's not going to sell here, so you have to adjust to things like that."

We strolled over to an open-sided shed where some of the refugees were sorting, washing, and packing their produce for the markets they'd be attending the next day. People from Burundi, Somalia, Bhutan, and Sudan worked side by side. A Burmese family squatted over cardboard boxes, neatly arranging their greens. On one side of the shed, a couple young summer employees helped the farmers weigh their vegetables, and on the other, a small box truck sat with its back open, waiting to receive the produce. Bands of grubby children circled in and out, alternating between helping their parents and playing in the grass.

As we were turning to go, a Burundian woman in a yellow traditional dress and her adolescent daughter flagged Cathy down. The daughter, who attends the local public school, translated for her mother: Why didn't they come spray her plot with the organic chemicals like they were supposed to?

"They didn't get to her farm?" Cathy asked the daughter. "Did you see Erica this morning? She was supposed to spray this morning."

"She didn't see," said the girl, looking at her aggravated mother. "She say she doesn't know."

The mother shot back something in a language nobody but her daughter could understand, and the girl tried to shrug it off.

"What? What?" asked Cathy.

"She say Erica didn't come," said the girl, obviously embarrassed to be caught in the middle. "She don't know. She just saying that."

Clearly, making such a program work is a delicate balancing act. But it's one that those involved find is worth any amount of hassle, not least because the refugee farmers' efforts provide perhaps the only source of healthy food they and their neighbors have access to. When I visited in 2010, the program was about to open a farmers' market in a nearby church parking lot so that all the produce wouldn't end up being sold in other parts of town.

"I think in a community like this it can be a real important supplement to people's diets," said Cathy. "The fact that some small percentage of food can be produced locally is a real eye-opener and something that governments and different organizations need to look at ways of supporting. There's no reason why—if you've got adequate soil and land—urban landscapes can't to some degree be a source of food. And there are other ways that it serves our culture than actual pounds of food production."

Indeed, the refugees in Kansas City are using the business of growing and selling food to carve out new lives for themselves in a strange country. Similarly, a Philadelphia urban gardening program called Teens 4 Good is using food to teach at-risk teenagers skills and values that will help them succeed in life. Young people are particularly well suited to learning from a garden, as the task of caring for plants can be a powerful lesson in personal responsibility and efficacy, the value of hard work, and the benefits of healthy eating. Teens 4 Good, run by the Federation of Neighborhood Centers, focuses on helping teens from around the city gain valuable personal and professional competencies by managing a series of urban gardens.

On a boiling day in August, I visited one of the garden sites at 8th and Poplar, where it shares a bleak intersection with two empty lots and a police building. A homeless man with a shopping cart piled high creaked by across the street as I parked my car. Behind the garden enclosed by a high fence secured with padlocks, commuter trains chugged along elevated tracks in front of an abandoned factory pocked with broken windows. A silver SUV pulled up, and out hopped the program's director, Jamie McKnight, an athletic-looking woman with serious sunglasses and short blond hair, not unlike my junior high gym teacher. She handed me a tray of broccoli and cabbage seedlings to carry, opened the padlock, and led me into a space split down the middle by a winding mosaic path and decorated around the edges with whimsical mosaic-covered sculptures. We admired the fig trees in the orchard on one side and then

wandered among the set of raised beds on the other, Jamie fingering the plants and muttering about how the students hadn't weeded
like they should have. She pulled treats from among leaves, offering me a cornucopia of delicacies: sweet raspberries, plump black-
berries, tiny orange tomatoes that exploded in my mouth like candy.
She assessed the state of the cucumbers crawling up trellises, the
squash sprouting blossoms like fluffy tails, the kale that was ready
for harvest, the perfect purple eggplants.

The high school students in the program, she told me, take un-
mitigated pride in growing these things themselves. "When I came
here last week, they were like, 'Ms. Jamie, look how big they got.
We just put these in a couple weeks ago,'" she said. "Literally, the
fruits of their labor, they're starting to see it now and starting to
make that connection."

The students spend their six-week paid summer internship
maintaining the gardens, selling the food they grow, and doing a
loose curriculum focused on healthy eating, food politics, and business skills. "They live in a cement area," said Jamie. "All they see
is trash thrown on the streets of this city constantly every day. I talk
about how important it is to keep a green space, how important it is
to eat healthy food. And we teach them leadership skills and business skills, something they don't learn in school, where everything
is taught to a test score. Out here we're teaching them life skills."

In addition, the program gives them the opportunity to be part
of their communities. "We maintain the space all around the gardens," Jamie said. "They give back by giving to food cupboards.
They're at the Mayor's Market; they can show off what they're doing. When people come to buy fresh produce at the market, they
just love to talk about it—'We grew this right here in Philly.' It's
really cool to see them do that." The students also sell to private

clients that include restaurants, supermarkets, and even a high-end chocolate company, John & Kira's, which makes "Urban Garden" chocolate bars using the students' mint and rosemary.

There are far more students interested than the program can accommodate, even though there are anywhere from fifty-five to eighty slots, depending on funding and other circumstances each year. "This year we had 135 applications for sixty slots," said Jamie. "We did a whole interview process. We interviewed everyone and one question I asked—especially to the fourteen-year-olds, fifteen-year-olds—was, 'Why do you want to work?' And they say, 'There's nothing for us to do in the city that's productive.' And they say, 'My friends sleep till twelve or one and then they do nothing but hang out on the street and I don't want to do that. I want to do something.'"

Two or three of the most engaged students at each garden site are recruited to form leadership teams, which meet with the program staff twice a month throughout the school year to work on additional skills such as researching grants, website maintenance, and public speaking at media events. Through an emerging partnership with the 11th Street Family Health Services Center, some leadership students may get the chance to participate in a nutrition education program with dietitians and nurses and then teach what they've learned to other students.

"We're really trying to teach them how to eat better, just a healthier way of living," said Jamie. "Some kids get it. After our viewing of *Food Inc.,* I was getting texts from the kids, saying, 'If it says organic, does it really mean organic?' They were trying to get a grasp of it, you know? Some kids will walk through here and they'll say, 'I don't eat tomatoes.' And I'll say, 'Well, try one.'"

The students were gathered across town for an educational program the day I visited, so I followed Jamie's Toyota 4Runner through Philly traffic, keeping my eye on her bumper stickers—

WOMEN WHO BEHAVE RARELY MAKE HISTORY and JERSEY GIRL. We traversed a hectic, treeless street under train tracks with light blue trestles, where dollar stores jostled with fried chicken places and check cashing joints. The students, ages fourteen to eighteen and all African-American save one Latina, were congregated inside a church's social hall in rows of metal folding chairs. They were reluctant to talk at first, but when I asked them their favorite thing about the program, everyone seemed to have an opinion.

"Being able to taste your products," said Jessica, and then, with a smirk: "My coworkers, 'cause they keep me young." Elizabeth raised her hand and said she liked "getting to work out on the farm. My favorite thing is being out in the sun and working for hours." Not exactly what I was expecting to hear from an inner-city teen, but I was rapidly learning to pack away my preconceived notions.

"I never knew before I came here how to grow my own food from nothing," said Tiffany. "Fifty or a hundred years ago, everybody learned this, everybody did this. I think it should be like that again." Jessica chimed in again to back her up: "The hardest part is to start your own garden, but after you get it going it's cake."

A girl named Amber focused on a different aspect: "We've gotten into the business side of it. So we learn how to keep track of revenue and expenses. I like that we're getting different skills." Also, "I learned that I have a right to know where my food comes from," she said.

"Even though it's cheaper to eat fast food, you should eat healthy," said Saleem, who was dipping his hand into a big bag of Cheetos as he spoke. He smiled self-consciously when one of the teachers pointed out the conflict and informed him that Cheetos are made from processed corn and flavored with chemicals. The teachers were eager to find teaching moments whenever they could, and a moment later Saleem offered another reflection that indicated they were doing a good job. "I learned that I have to listen before I can lead," he said.

As if that wasn't heartwarming enough, a girl named Shardae spoke up to deliver the ultimate recommendation for getting kids out in the garden: "I learned that anybody can make a difference."

CHAPTER 12

From Prison to Prep Cook

Food production offers hope and opportunity

THE TEENS 4 GOOD PROGRAM is noteworthy on its own, but its story gets even better. As part of Philadelphia's City Harvest program, which engages forty-two community gardens throughout the city to grow an average of thirteen thousand pounds of fresh produce every year for food cupboards and soup kitchens, Teens 4 Good gardeners are actively giving back to their communities. Not only that, but the seedlings the students and community gardeners use to grow the food destined for donation are cultivated by inmates in the Philadelphia Prison System in a job training and placement program called Roots to Reentry.

I was dazzled to learn this. Not only were at-risk students learning to grow and sell food, but hungry people were getting healthy rations, residents all around the city were using their gardens to volunteer for the cause, and prisoners were gaining valuable skills by producing the raw materials needed to put the entire process in motion. This type of high-impact, food-inspired initiative was exactly the type of hope I had come raking for. And what better illustration of the social utility of food production than a program that helps rehabilitate prisoners by getting their hands in the dirt?

Although I pretended to myself that the Philadelphia House of Correction was just another stop on my itinerary, I arrived there on a bright August morning in a flutter of nerves. I had never been to a prison before, and the sight of the fortress-of-solitude-style brick building that loomed above the parking lot only reinforced my visions of menacing criminals brandishing sharp garden tools.

But then plaid-shirted Sharat Somashekara, the program's coordinator, putt-putted into the parking lot in his beat-up little car, peering at me through wire-rimmed glasses and offering a toothy, cheerful smile. He motioned for me to hop in, and I relaxed as we rolled through the guard station and toward a yard set to the side of the minimum-security units. In the garden out behind a greenhouse, two orange-jumpsuited men were at work with a hose and a lawn mower. It was a slow day for the program; there were usually more workers.

More than four hundred inmates have participated in the four-to-six-week program since it began in 2005, Sharat told me as he showed me the greenhouse, which was lined with empty wooden shelves ready for the next batch of seedlings. Each year, the inmates produce as many as sixty thousand seedlings here during the fall, winter, and spring for the City Harvest gardeners. Over the summer, they also grow thousands of pounds of food in their own garden, the majority of which goes to food cupboards around Philadelphia.

The day before, I had visited the offices of the Pennsylvania Horticultural Society (PHS), organizer of the famous Philadelphia International Flower Show and the coordinating force behind City Harvest and Roots to Reentry, where slim, soft-spoken Senior Director Joan Reilly (who has since moved to another organization) had told me that the fruits and vegetables from the prisoners' seedlings and garden feed about a thousand needy families every week. The prisoners also participate in cooking and nutrition classes, do training in life skills like anger management and résumé writing, learn about aspects of landscaping and horticulture, and have the opportunity to try out for a work-release program in landscape management and maintenance at historic Bartram's Garden, a Philadelphia landmark.

"The main garden is back here," said Sharat as he headed around the side of the greenhouse and into the large, L-shaped plot of green surrounded by a chain-link fence bristling at the top with rolls of razor wire. Disconcertingly, a steady barrage of gunshots sounded in the distance. "There's a shooting range over there," Sharat said with a wry smile, gesturing toward a nearby ridge, then turned his attention back to the garden. "These are blueberries. This is a hazelnut tree. We got some nuts off of it last year, but I think it needs a friend. I don't know how self-pollinating it is. These are cherry tomatoes." He looked around, his eyes skipping from plant to plant then landing on the inmate with the hose. "Hi, Angel. Can you wet this bed down when you get a chance?"

As I watched the men working among the neat raised beds and trellised tomato plants, I felt silly to have been afraid. As Joan had told me, "These really big guys who grew up around lots of concrete and pavement are now very gently protecting and taking care of this habitat. What they've learned and the connections they've made to it, it's palpable, it's powerful, it's profound."

Sharat turned back to me and pointed to a small tree, noting how it had accidentally been weed-wacked. "I can't really establish order here," he said good-naturedly. "It's just chaos. I'm just trying to get the basics right. If this were my own place, it would be organized differently, but it's a compromise between different priorities."

The priorities he referred to were those of PHS, the Philadelphia Prison System, and the various other partners involved in the program. "Partnering with the prison was a big learning curve," Joan had said. "By nature their work is to keep people in boxes. They need to have lots of boundaries and parameters and rules." To qualify for the program according to prison rules, inmates must have already been sentenced and only of a nonviolent crime. Most of the program's participants are in trouble for substance abuse, theft, or parole violations and are serving terms of a few months to a couple years. Participants can volunteer for the program, but for most it's an assignment, a job like any other, two to four hours a day, five days a week. Since men and women inmates aren't allowed to be in the same place at the same time, men work the garden and greenhouse in the morning and women come in the afternoon.

On the other side of the equation, the people at PHS, a creative nonprofit, thrive on making up the rules as they go along. "We're always pushing envelopes and we're always extending boundaries and imagining new ways to get things done with a little bit of re-sources," Joan had told me. "That was a pretty big collision in the first year. We didn't understand them and they didn't understand us. But we persevered."

The program has indeed become a fruitful marriage between force and inspiration. Tom O'Neal, the solidly built would-be farmer who oversees the program at the House of Correction, chuckled when I asked him what strategies he uses to get the participants to engage with the work. "Well, you have to coerce them initially to put a couple plants in the ground and water them," he said. But the heavy-handedness invariably gives way to a productive working relationship with the prisoners. "Then they start seeing them grow and produce fruit and all, and they say, 'That's cool. I'm going to go take care of my plants,'" he said. "It can be a battle initially, but most of the time, most guys love coming out here. They get to be around nature. They're accomplishing something, which some of these guys have never done."

Indeed, Joan had emphasized that the program was about some-thing much more profound than either food or job training. "Our view is that a percentage of these folks might just love this work and want to go into some aspect of that industry, whether it's working for a landscaper, becoming an urban farmer, or working in a garden center at Home Depot or Lowe's," she had said. "But whether they go into any of those fields or not, we think it's a great basis for any work they'll do. Because you learn about discipline and being focused, you learn about sequencing tasks, you learn about working as a team. You learn to find effective ways to communicate. And you learn the deep satisfaction of a job well done, which is really reinforcing and motivating. We feel that this is a great springboard for next steps."

At the core of its success is a deep lesson the participants absorb: what they do matters. "They get to see and taste the fruits of their labor," said Joan. "It's very concrete and tangible. When they're doing the work well, they see good results. When they neglect the work, forget to water, things die. So it's very immediate, and the fact that they're giving back to communities that they came from, that many of their families still live in—that we've created a connection between the gardeners and the volunteers in the food cupboards and the inmates—is very affirming."

Exposed to such an environment, participants are apt to get ideas about continuing this kind of work on the outside. Marcial Lloyd, the inmate with the lawn mower, told me he had developed the idea of keeping a garden in his neighborhood. "There's a little plot around the corner on my block," he told me with a grin that revealed a missing front tooth. "This older Chinese lady had it but after her husband died she just let it grow up. So I told my daughter, me and her are gonna go in and clear everything out and we're gonna plant some vegetables and things we can use right there in the house."

He looked happy at the thought, leaning casually on the handle of his mower as if we were enjoying a chance meeting at the park instead of standing in a yard barricaded by fences. I asked whether he thought it is important for people to grow their own food. "I think it helps, you know, because when people see other people do things like that then they'll start getting involved," he said, then revved the lawn mower back up to finish his yard work. Watching him move off, the bright orange of his suit striking against the rich, enveloping green of the garden, I thought of something else Joan had said: what's going on here is difficult but powerfully important in a human way. "It's not easy work," she had told me. "It's very complicated work. And these folks who we are working with are on big journeys. And yet I think all of us who have been close to the program feel that it's been a complete blessing. I think we've all become wiser and better people because of this program."

Among those who have gained the most are the inmates whose clear enthusiasm and skill for the work land them spots in the work-release program at Bartram's Garden, which had a 100 percent job placement rate in 2009, its first year. The Horticultural Society is so enthusiastic about this success that it is positioning the program to become a national model for a comprehensive approach to job training and reentry work. Tom O'Neal offered a firsthand account of the effort's impact: "One of the guys we sent down, oh, about eight weeks back, he's foreman down at Bartram's Garden now. He's doing very well. And he was one angry young man when he came in. I didn't think he was going to make it. I went down and saw him . . . totally different man, self-esteem, standing up straight, smiling, shook my hand. Wow. What a turnaround."

This use of gardening and food to turn lives from despair and anger to productivity and engagement is one of the most compelling examples I had yet found of the idea that what we eat has just as much power to transform our society as the nutrients that compose it do for our bodies. Food has the power to heal, both physically and psychologically.

Intent on digging deeper into that idea, I searched out another equally powerful program in Washington, DC, a nonprofit where ex-convicts cook forty-five hundred meals every day to feed hungry people at shelters, schools, nonprofits, and agencies offering services like job training, addiction recovery, English as a second language, after-school care, and protection from domestic abuse. On the day I visited, DC Central Kitchen (DCCK) was in full swing. The former prisoners, most of them African-American and all graduates of DCCK's culinary job training program, supervised a diverse army of volunteers in stirring vats of soup, loading pasta into trays, and sealing them with plastic wrap.

"These are men and women who could be second- or third-generation felons, second- or third-generation addicts, never had a family, never had a job, never had anybody who cared about them," Mike Curtin, DCCK's energetic, straight-shooting CEO told me as we observed the bustle from one side of the large kitchen. "These folks have been incarcerated, many are in recovery, they've lived in shelters, been in the system somehow for a long period of their lives."

The organization employs seventy-six full-time paid staff with full benefits who feed others and help one another overcome their demons. The program veterans serve as positive examples for the newcomers, who are recently out of prison and usually have few role models to look to. Mike said that he, a self-described "white kid from the suburbs . . . who's had every break in the world," would be ill-advised to try some tired bit of "today is the first day of the rest of your life" inspirational leadership on these guys. Instead, Mike suggested, the established staff can offer their own relevant perspective: "You were in prison for five years? I was in prison for twenty. Now I have a job, now I have vacation pay, now I have a retirement plan, now I'm back with my family."

Mike likes to call such guys "empowerment billboards." The program doesn't run on some theory handed down from on high; the power lies in the new recruits' exposure to "people who have been there in that same situation for a long period of time and now are in a different place," he said. "We want to be able to show, not explain it theoretically—this is what can happen. This is what does happen. This is what *has* happened. That's very, very important."

Curtis Cunningham, a DCCK chef who has wholeheartedly embraced the organization's self-empowerment model and is working his way up the kitchen's ladder, got involved with the program in 2008 after serving fifteen years of a twenty-year sentence for armed robbery. He was a cook in the prison's kitchen, he told me in a soft voice, and he loved the look on people's faces when they bite into something he had prepared. Now that he's learned he can transfer that passion into a job he loves in the outside world, he coaches the program's new recruits every day that the DCCK program is "about *you*" more than it is about food. He wants to make sure they understand that they have a chance to craft new futures for themselves with the help of other people who have been in their shoes. "I tell them about my own experience," he said, and he lets them know that, at DCCK, "what you put in is what you get out."

Another key piece of DCCK's model is the participation of a wide range of volunteers. On the day I visited, helpers from the audit firm KPMG and the Chapelgate Presbyterian Church had helped prepare chicken stir-fry with wheatberries and a salad of fresh, sliced cantaloupe. "Not only are we interested in their help to produce the meals," said Mike, "but what we're really interested in is an opportunity for them to have, even on a limited level, a conversation with our staff. We want these folks to walk out of here saying, 'Oh my goodness, I just had a conversation for an hour and a half with a guy who spent fifteen years of his life in prison and who was a crack addict. That's not what I was banking on when I was coming down here.'" Mike half-jokingly guessed that what they typically expect is something more like a "sort of dark, dreary place, with crazy homeless people running around with hypodermic needles and knives" and beleaguered volunteers preparing "crusty bread and watery soup." Instead, what helpers find is "this joyous, bright kitchen" where fresh produce is abundant and everyone works together to get the task done. That last part is particularly significant: Mike wants to demonstrate that everyone can give, learn, teach, and be part of the solution.

In addition to providing food to shelters and social service agencies, DCCK runs a catering business, which Mike glibly calls "seven-digit philanthropy" because you can do good simply by dialing DCCK's phone number to order the food for your office party or club meeting. "You get the same wraps, or maybe ours are a little better," said Mike as we surveyed the separate, smaller catering kitchen, standing clean and quiet that afternoon. "You get the same salads, same brownies, lemon bars, iced tea, lemonade, same price, same service, but the check you write to us goes directly to support our programs and employ the men and women who work here, many of whom would be very difficult to employ outside because of their criminal résumés."

Mike led me to his closet-sized office, plopped down in front of his computer, and offered me the only other chair as he told me how the catering side of the organization's work allows DCCK to earn income and remain sustainable and even to grow. Toward that end, Mike has overseen the establishment of another lucrative business as a distributor of produce from local small farms. Mike started buying produce directly from local farmers after having what he called "a sort of epiphany moment" in which he realized the tomatoes DCCK was buying "came from Belgium, were grown in a greenhouse, picked preripe, put in a jet, gassed so they'd be ripish when they got here, put in a truck, taken to a warehouse, put in another truck, taken to another warehouse, put in another truck, and taken to us." He set about making contacts with local farmers and quickly realized that DCCK could afford to buy whatever produce was too small, too blemished, or too strangely shaped to sell at full price.

Now DCCK is one of the largest buyers at the Shenandoah Valley Produce Auction in Dayton, Virginia, where local Amish growers bring their fresh fruits and vegetables by horse-drawn carriage. DCCK has developed such close and dependable relationships with some of the farmers that Mike plans to begin contracting with them at the beginning of each season. Buying and selling this way, he said, is much more efficient for the growers than selling at farmers' markets, and just as—or perhaps more—cost-effective for DCCK as buying the industrially produced veggies on offer through wholesalers like Sysco. Additionally, buying local has allowed DCCK to vastly expand and enrich its own menu. Before, said Mike, "we were buying bagged iceberg lettuce heads, which is basically crispy water. We said, 'Aren't we good? We're doing healthy salads.' But now we're buying these beautiful Bibb lettuces and Romaines, hydroponically grown."

DCCK now profits by offering buyers fresh, local, whole produce (dealing, for instance, with "white-tablecloth restaurants that want beautiful purple Cherokee heirloom tomatoes") and processing this coveted food—chopping, slicing, dicing, and freezing whole fruits and vegetables, and making and bottling sauces—for resale to other nonprofits. Meanwhile, DCCK can offer healthier food to its beneficiaries, and the extra processing work allows for the creation of more jobs for its client population and the engagement of even more volunteers from the community.

"I think we had three or four thousand more volunteers than the year before just because we added those shifts," said Mike. "That's a whole other group of people who get to be involved in what we do, understand what we do, get this conversation bigger and growing. Then we need staff to run and manage those shifts, so we get to hire more people from our training programs. We get to promote more people from our training programs to supervise those positions."

On the other end of the equation, DCCK's business bumps up the revenue of local growers. Mike told me about one lettuce farmer who had just built a new greenhouse to keep up with the increased demand. Even with that good progress, however, "the frustrating thing is that even doing the volume that we're doing, we are barely, barely scratching the tippy-tippy top of the iceberg of the millions of pounds of food that are wasted every year, that literally rot in the ground, either for aesthetic reasons or because distribution is a big problem," he said.

DCCK's leadership in making local, healthy food available to needy District residents inevitably led the organization in a new direction—toward the touchstone of the healthy-eating issue: school food. The organization started by taking over the lunch operation at Washington Jesuit Academy, a tuition-free private school for at-risk boys. The ex-con cooks whip up healthy meals and serve them to the kids, offering not only better health but also in-person examples of street-tough black men who have chosen to do right by themselves, their communities, and their families. The students have taken to the new fare with enthusiasm. "These guys are eating tilapia, they're eating Brussels sprouts, they're eating artichoke soufflé and quiches," said Mike. "I've had parents who come to me and say, 'My kid never used to eat anything that didn't come out of a bag or a box, and now every weekend he makes us drive to the grocery store to get vegetables like they have at school.'"

On the success of that venture, in 2010 DCCK was awarded a contract to provide three meals a day to seven DC public schools in Wards 5 and 7, some of the most underserved in the city. The program was set to start in a week at the time of my visit, and Mike was confident of success. "Once we start, I'm one hundred percent confident that we'll rock it out," he said. When I checked back in with him after the first semester of school, he reported that his prediction had been correct; his staff were providing thirty-four hundred healthy, handmade meals every day, and the kids were eagerly gobbling up delicacies like corn-crusted catfish with carrots and peas and whole-grain rolls; Turkey Bolognese with whole-wheat pasta, zucchini ratatouille, and homemade applesauce; and herb-roasted chicken with garlic Swiss chard.

Mike sees feeding kids healthy food and helping them understand its value to be part of DCCK's larger vision of societal transformation, as a new generation raised with positive values will pass those values on to their own children. He told me of one of the program participants who never knew his father and whose mother was a junkie who would leave her three children for months at a time. The family often lived without water, electricity, or gas, and they were regularly evicted, prompting frequent journeys across town to crash on the floor at relatives' houses. "That's what he grew up in," said Mike. "That was what life was." Not expecting to live much past twenty anyway, he got mixed up in the world of the streets and ended up spending more than half his life in prison. Now he has turned his life around at DCCK and just had a little girl, who will grow up without the expectation of disaster and disintegration that defined his childhood. Her life will be profoundly different from her father's, all because food changed his.

"We want to offer a vision of possibilities," said Mike. "To say that, yes, you can employ felons, and yes, you can pay a living wage.

And yes, you can provide one hundred percent of health insurance and paid vacation and all these other benefits that we do. And make money. Our budget is over eight million dollars. We're an eight-million-dollar business. Our product happens to be empowerment."

PART 4

HOW DOES YOUR GARDEN GROW?

CHAPTER 13

Organic Idyll

Organic farms keep an alternative agricultural vision alive

MY HOPERAKING MISSION WAS BEARING fruit; I had discovered much
to be glad about in our changing food system. But the projects and
programs I had visited mostly focused on the social dynamics of
food and farming: who does the farming, how the food is distributed, what the act of growing food can teach the next generation, or
how it can feed the needy. But I hadn't yet turned my sights on a
fundamental question that might impact all of these other questions
and many other things besides: How should we produce the food
we eat?

It was time for an investigation into some of the ideas on which
today's unconventional farmers and businesspeople are staking
their claims. What are the worthiest alternatives to the soil-depleted,
pesticide-laden megafarms that have become the standard-bearers
for U.S. agriculture? Specifically, what age-old wisdoms and new
innovations are reinventing the farmers' occupation and offering us
hope for a more sustainable agricultural future?

Of course the most age-old of all approaches to farming is the
organic one. As a magnet I once saw on a farmer's refrigerator
aptly stated, EAT ORGANIC FOOD. OR, AS YOUR GRANDMOTHER CALLED

IT, FOOD. This quip reminds us that the petrochemical-dependent industrial type of farming that is attracting so much negative attention lately is a relatively recent phenomenon, dating from the middle of the twentieth century. And today's sustainable food movement can trace its roots to the back-to-the-land movement of the 1960s, when writers like homesteaders Helen and Scott Nearing and agriculture and ecology poet Wendell Berry began to ask what might serve us better than this peculiarly modern food production system. Many of the newly minted small-scale farmers inspired by this historical moment devoted themselves to resurrecting the organic practices their parents' generation had abandoned.

In seeking out the alternative practitioners leading our most recent wave of sustainable food production, I wondered how many of those who had answered the call in that previous era had managed to make it work until today. Could I find an iconic sustainable small farm to showcase the best of what this decades-long movement has been fighting for? What did it take to wrest such a farm out of the untamed woods and fields and keep it going for so long?

I got my answer to both of those questions in a gorgeous, green hollow in the Berkshire Mountains, where my father's cousin Bill Stinson and his wife, Susie, have spent the last thirty-five years carving the most perfect farm I have ever seen—aptly named Peace Valley Farm—out of the emerald woods of Williamstown, Massachusetts.

Bill, a wiry sixty-year-old with white hair bristling out from beneath a green baseball cap, mud-smeared jeans, and a dingy blue shirt tinged with the acrid smell of hard work, treated me to a grand tour and an epic narrative about the harrowing toil and near-fatal mishaps that had characterized his life as a small-scale farmer.

"When you visit a farm and you see people who are doing it, they're usually possessed, kind of crazy people," he told me. He was, of course, no exception to this rule. Since purchasing his farm in 1974, he has done the work of an army all by himself: jacking up and repairing the property's dilapidated house and classic barn, installing a pond on the property, cultivating three acres of rocky soil into incredible productivity, and forging lasting ties with the community.

"I don't know how I had the resolve to do this," he told me as we stood in the front yard by his red farmhouse on a chilly, misty day, the trees rustling in an upstart breeze. "I just knew when I stepped onto this property that I loved it and that it had potential. It was run-down, completely run-down. When the banks came out they said, 'This is a negative liability. You gotta mow down the house and mow down the barn.' And I said no." His gaze swept across his lovely yard. "We built all these stone walls," he said. "We put the pond in. We cleared the land and we built the kitchen out of the trees."

He eyed the now solid-looking house and smiled affably. "That was the first time I almost killed myself," he said, describing how one of the jacks he was using to lift up the house kicked out, slammed into the wall, and then knocked him out. "Had it hit me first I would have been dead instantly," he said. "That was my first accident."

He warmed to his topic, leaning back on his heels, recounting a second accident involving "a big, big, huge tractor" that did a wheelie with him aboard and flipped over, almost slicing off his nose as he jumped off. "The third accident was the chainsaw on Halloween evening," he went on. A broken tooth in the chain caused it to kick back and chop right down his face and chest, an injury he knew was serious because the slug of Dewar's Scotch he took on the way to the emergency room tasted just like water. "I was in shock," he remembered, though the mishap miraculously left no permanent damage aside from scars on his chest. He eventually learned how to avoid such dangerous situations, only suffering one further major accident, which involved the jack he was using to fix a flat on a tractor flipping out of his hand and crushing a dent in his skull. The dent is still there.

Although Bill's obsessive determination was essential to his success, his cultivation of close ties with the larger community was what turned his venture from a small, struggling farm in the woods into a flourishing force for change in the culinary life of the local area. He developed a solid social network on which to draw for help as he taught himself the skills he would need to reinvent the old property, from putting up Sheetrock to pond building. "I would commandeer people to help me," he said. "I was kind of like a lame duck that was very persistent and wanted to succeed."

From the first, he was trying to sell to local restaurants, but for a long time he was frozen out of the business. Restaurants were used to their big distributors from Albany. "They didn't understand what we were trying to do," said Bill. Right when he was thinking of giving up altogether, his childhood friend Danny Campbell returned to town after years away in Missoula and started a restaurant called Hobson's Choice. "He said, 'I need you,'" Bill remembered. "'I need you to wait tables in the wintertime and in the summertime I need you to grow vegetables.'" This new arrangement changed everything; Bill started pushing other local restaurants to follow suit and then decided to approach Williams College, a two-thousand-student liberal arts institution in town, with the prospect of getting fresh, local foods into its dining halls.

The rest, as they say, is history. Peace Valley now supplies several high-end area restaurants, sells half of what it grows to Williams, and has recently started supplying produce to Berkshire Medical Center in nearby Pittsfield. The relationship with Williams has been particularly positive, both for Bill and for the college, which has as a result of Bill's persistence found itself unwittingly at the forefront of the institutional local-sourcing movement. For decades, Bill has engaged Williams students to work on his farm as stipended summer interns, and more recently he has partnered with the college to include a farm workday as one of the options in the freshmen's off-campus orientation program. In 2009, eighty-three Williams students worked at Peace Valley for varying lengths of time, from one day to three months. The summer interns become so attached to the place that they frequently return for working visits. On the day of my visit, three former interns in town for their class reunions arrived to spend the night in Bill and Susie's guest rooms and help out on the farm the next day.

"Isn't that the greatest thing in the world?" Bill crowed as he welcomed the arriving helpers. He used to dream of running a summer camp, and now, with all these students engaged in his work alongside him, he feels he kind of does. "So I lived my dream. I still am, doing what I want to do and no bank owns me." He smiled as he gazed around, taking in the lush yard edged with flower beds, the old white tractor parked in front of the sleeping barn, the neat row of firewood stacked beside the cozy house. "There's a little bit of an artist in me," he added. "Everything I do with this property, it's total passion. I mean, I feel like this is artwork. This is temporary art. That's the way I look at it: temporary art."

Before our pizza dinner in the farmhouse, prepared by the tireless Susie, Bill drove me and one of the visiting interns up to the vegetable fields above the house, where his crops of lettuces, fingerling potatoes, onions, chives, parsley, and basil were so closely and carefully spaced that they resembled a carpet patterned in shades of green. "We're taking the most marginal, crappy land and making a small amount of it extremely productive," Bill said, fingering a lettuce leaf tenderly. "I grow more stuff on a small amount of land than anybody's ever seen. That's what I hear from other people who have visited me and looked at it. In just three acres we produce a lot of food, *a lot* of food. It's an amazing use of a very small amount of space agriculturally."

A major reason he is able to achieve such remarkable results is that his farm is not organic in the strict sense of the word. He calls himself "pesticide-herbicide free," indicating his focus on remaining organic in what he considers the most important way while acknowledging that he uses small amounts of petrochemical fertilizer to get sufficient yield from his rocky soil.

"That is the one glitch in my armor that makes me not totally organic," he said. "But I don't mind because it's not a perfect world. I tell people, 'Look, I have a toolbox and sometimes I have to reach into this toolbox and do things to make us competitive.'" Just a tiny bit of chemical fertilizer can boost his yields tenfold. "The difference between a very small sweet Spanish onion and a big one is substantial and is also the difference between profitability and nonprofitability when you're working in a small space," he said. The way Bill sees it, his customers aren't willing to pick up the extra cost required for him to grow at the same volume without adding chemical fertilizer, so his hands are tied. He is transparent about his practices, inviting all of his customers to visit the farm and ask questions. If they were to demand vegetables grown in a fully organic way and were willing to pay the difference, he would be happy to comply.

Bill's practical, compromising approach points to the difficulty of creating a universally accepted definition of organics. Bill's "pesticide-herbicide free" method can be seen as more in keeping with the spirit of organic growing than the practices of some of the massive USDA-certified organic farms, which often have more in common with their industrial-monoculture brethren than with Peace Valley. On the other end of the spectrum from the mega-organics are many organic farms fastidious about their all-natural methods but so tiny they amount to little more than a hobby for their owners. Between these extremes is a sweet spot of viable farms that walk a balance between efficient, mechanized management and hands-on, hyperintensive nurturing of the plants, soil, and water. Such farms come in a variety of sizes and styles and use a range of practices, but all the best examples have one thing in common: they focus on the health of the plants and the soil to offer a positive alternative vision of what a more sustainable agricultural landscape might look like.

That being said, I wondered: What of the farms out there that reject the kind of shortcuts that Bill has been forced to accept? Have any of these purists been able to survive and thrive during the last several increasingly nonorganic decades of our agricultural life? I decided to look for the most purely and robustly organic farm I could come across and was soon rolling out of the wet, green hills surrounding Ghent, New York, a two-hour drive north of New York City, and shooting down a straight country road that sliced through a warren of rustic houses, buildings, and barns. This was the Hawthorne Valley community, comprising a wide range of social, educational, and artistic enterprises centered on the four-hundred-acre biodynamic Hawthorne Valley Farm.

In an office in the rambling administration building beside a huge barn, I found Martin Ping, executive director, who greeted me with a gentle but intense attention and a warm handshake. As we made our way outside and headed for the farm's organic grocery store to get something to drink, he told me how the farm was founded in 1972 by followers of Rudolf Steiner, an Austrian philosopher and founder of anthroposophy, a scientifically minded, human-centered spiritual movement. The Hawthorne Valley Association, according to its mission statement, aims for "social and cultural renewal through the integration of education, agriculture, and the arts." Steiner's legacy also includes the Waldorf educational philosophy, a whole-child-oriented humanistic approach that integrates practical, artistic, and conceptual elements, and the biodynamic method of farming, which is unique in the extent of its commitment to the integration of every aspect of a farm's life into a harmonious whole. Indeed, as Martin explained, the farm is perceived as "a living organism that has to be maintained in balance" so that the land and the people working it can produce food "in a way that is improving the situation every year, not taking away from it."

To illustrate the concept, Martin offered the example of a cow and a pasture, which, he said, "have a unique symbiotic relationship." The grass has stored energy from sunlight, so when the cow eats the grass the energy goes into the cow. What's the cow thinking as he patiently digests the grass in his four stomachs? Martin asked. "In my imagination, the cow's wondering, 'What does this pasture want from me? What does this soil require in order to grow better and better grasses for future generations of cows?' And they deliver a perfect package of fertility specified for that place. They know exactly what the land is asking for." Biodynamic agriculture is based on the idea that when all the elements of a farm are engaged in supporting one another in this way as part of a diversified living system, no chemically based enhancements or additives are needed.

In keeping with Steiner's perspective of the farm as a living organism sufficient unto itself, Hawthorne Valley's founders wanted the farm to be self-sustaining, a project that required aggressive direct marketing and development of value-added goods to sell. "We were one of the first stands at the Union Square Greenmarket in Manhattan," Martin told me. "We were one of the earliest CSAs. We started our on-site dairy processing plant, so we're making yogurt and cheese and we're selling raw milk in our store, which we can only sell on the farm. We're renowned for our raw milk." The farm also has a bakery, a kitchen for processing vegetables into pickles and sauerkrauts through lacto-fermentation, and a fourteen-acre market garden. Everything the farm produces is available at the full-line on-site organic grocery store. "For thirty-eight years, it's been a bootstrap, pay-as-you-go, blood-sweat-and-tears operation, and we're really proud of that because that means that there's relevancy to what we're doing," said Martin. "It's meaningful and it can stand on its own two feet."

The farm's first goal was to serve as an agricultural education experience for students from New York and Boston, to acquaint them with what environmentally friendly agriculture looks like. Since then, some six hundred children have visited the farm every year, totaling more than twenty thousand since its founding. Many classes come on day trips, but others, mostly third graders, participate in a weeklong summer program during which they live in the main farmhouse and experience every aspect of farm life. "When you see how enthusiastically they take up the task of mucking out a cow stall or turning a compost pile . . . they are *so* happy," noted Martin. "We just recognize the profound impact that that experience has on a young soul, especially somebody who's never had those connections, who thought that food came out of a refrigerator case or a can. And they're able to take a warm egg from a chicken's nest and bring it in and prepare breakfast."

Martin took me to the new garden across the street from the supermarket, which was at that point so new that it was just a set of bare fields, a shed, and a detailed illustration of what would soon bloom there. After a series of floods ruined a quarter of the farm's crops the year before, the farmers had decided to move a portion of the garden here and work the land without tractors using a biointensive method of farming. Biointensive cultivation allows farmers to get a lot of diverse productivity out of small pieces of land with crop-friendly, organic techniques like hand-weeding and -watering, intercropping and cover cropping, composting, and natural pest control such as the use of beneficial insects. The plans for this hands-on garden also reflected the importance of education in the life of the farm and the community. Visiting students and kids from Hawthorne Valley School, the community's Waldorf school next door to the garden, will get access to the full processes involved in bringing food to a table.

"That's winter rye over there that the students are growing. They will harvest it by hand, they'll winnow it and thresh it and grind it and they will actually bake bread for the neighboring senior center," said Martin, smiling, benevolent wrinkles appearing at the corners of his eyes. They also make pancakes, growing and harvesting the grain themselves and making all the toppings. "Right over here on the other side of the stream is our sugar bush, and they tap the maple trees and boil the sap down so they can make their maple syrup," said Martin. "They can get milk from the cows, and they shake the jar until they get butter." To finish off the meal, the students collect cattails and bark to weave place mats. "The idea is what does it really take to bring a meal to a table, lest we take things for granted," said Martin. "We begin to understand it's not just magically there; this is people's real work."

Following Hawthorne Valley Association's broad anthroposophic mission, the community is engaged in a much more wide ranging and well balanced set of activities than simply planting and sowing and eating. The Farmscape Ecology Program, headquartered in a house far across several fields from the main farmhouse, grocery, and school, employs three full-time social scientists studying the role of agriculture in the local social and environmental landscape. During my visit, the team was undertaking a community food assessment, looking at the shopping patterns in the county, where food is available, how far food is being shipped, and other related questions. At the Farmers' Research Circle, local farmers discuss topics of mutual importance, and "landing workshops" bring farmers and nonfarming landowners to talk about questions of land tenure and access to land with the goal of keeping as much land in active production as possible.

Martin ticked off a diverse laundry list of other ventures the Hawthorne Valley Association runs. The Farm Learning Center does farmer training, the Adonis Press publishes science textbooks, and the Alkion Center for Adult Education offers foundational studies in anthroposophy and Waldorf teacher training. The Center for Social and Environmental Responsibility concentrates on ways to heal and repair our economy and our society. Think OutWord is a peer-led group of young people learning how to be actively engaged citizens to bring healing and regenerative thinking into society. The Free Columbia Art Course is a yearlong arts training program, and the Art Lending Library makes original artwork available to borrowers for an annual fee so that, as Martin put it, "the paintings don't have to just live in the closets and basements and attics of the artists" and the community can "move away from commodification of culture."

As we climbed up a hill behind the gardens to a spot with a panoramic view of the entire community, Martin grew thoughtful about the bigger picture. "We're attending to our outer work and our outer landscape here," he commented. "But we have to pay equal attention to our inner landscape, cultivating our inner life and finding time to pause and reflect and take stock of what's motivating us and what are our intentions." He cast an appraising eye down on the cluster of silos, barns, and other buildings beyond the fields, then brought the conversation back to the cow in its pasture, reminding me that the idea of organic agriculture in general and Hawthorne Valley's many ventures specifically is to serve as an active caretaker of a fragile environment. "Wouldn't we all benefit from taking the cow's part and really thinking, 'How are my actions today improving the chances for future generations to have a lifestyle at least as good as the lifestyle I have?'" he asked.

CHAPTER 14

Farming In and Out of the Box

New farming technologies try to redefine sustainability

ALTHOUGH THE REALITIES OF OUR modern life make the lovely sustainability-minded farms I had seen much more the exception than the rule, their continued existence in this age of mechanization and consolidation is by itself a reason for hope. Places like Peace Valley and Hawthorne Valley remind us that farming in a way good for the earth and its people is not an unattainable ideal; it can and is being done. And while I recognize that not every farm can be a perfect patch of sculpted nature tucked into lush woods and manned by passionate farmer-philosophers, the principles on which they operate provide essential guideposts by which to measure the sanity of our agricultural universe.

Many of the standard practices of industrial agriculture, after all, likely strike farmers focused on sustainable production as quite simply insane. The massive use of nitrogen fertilizers created out of fossil fuels—which has just about quadrupled since 1960, along with the price per ton, according to the USDA—allows for large-scale, mechanized production by fewer and fewer farmers but also pollutes groundwater, acidifies soil, and threatens biodiversity. These fertilizers are used in excess, as crops only absorb about one-half of the nitrogen in the fertilizers that are applied to fields, leaving tons to run off into waterways and wreak havoc on marine ecosystems. Chemical pesticides, of which 1.1 billion pounds were used in the United States in 2007, also pollute our soil and water and are associated with cancer and endocrine disruption in farmworkers.

It seems that regardless of where you fall on the industrial-versus-sustainable-food continuum, you might well agree that many of the effects of petrochemical pesticides and fertilizers on human and environmental health are not positive. And that's leaving aside the fact that their sources are nonrenewable, which leads to inevitable questions about how we can sustain their use into the future. Indeed, it only really seems sane to strive as a society to reduce the use of chemicals—which pollute our environment and our health and limit our agricultural future—as much as we can through incentives, public policy, and other tactics. Do we as a nation prioritize reducing petrochemical inputs however we can? Or do we regard their unrestrained use as a necessary evil, or worse, the inevitable by-product of "progress" and therefore somehow positive?

Critics of increasing incentives and support for small-scale organic farming are quick to point out that the globe might hold 9 billion people by 2050, a prediction that has occasioned much hand-wringing about our ability to feed all those mouths. Supporters of industrial agricultural practices predictably say that we just need more of what they have to offer. Boosters of biological engineering, for their part, argue that genetically modified seeds will increase yields enough to meet the world's growing demand for food. The blatant profit motive of the companies controlling the seeds makes me distrust such statements immediately, but beyond that, the Union of Concerned Scientists has found that twenty years of field trials on genetically modified organism (GMO) seeds have failed to produce such results. Further ramping up of industrial agricultural practices means trashing our soil and water beyond recognition until all of us end up starving, while GMOs, the most supposedly promising technological fix to such problems, have failed to live up to their claim of salvation.

But truthfully, the question of whether industrial or genetically enhanced agriculture can grow greater and greater masses of food matters little, because feeding all the people on Earth has little to do with how much we grow. Having enough food to feed everyone, while a noble goal, doesn't mean everyone will get fed. Hunger is not a problem of supply, but one of access and distribution, a problem created almost entirely by our political limitations, not our agricultural ones. "Virtually all the authorities on world hunger agree that the problem is due not to overpopulation or lack of food availability," wrote the *New York Times* in 1981. "The cause of hunger, it is agreed, is poverty and poor income distribution." Add political instability, natural disaster, and food distribution problems to that list and you start to have an accurate picture of reality for many of the world's hungry. In the United States, the proof that hunger is unrelated to how much food we produce is provided by the glaring contrast between the massive amount of food we waste—34 million tons a year, an amount the EPA calls "staggering"—and the unacceptably high levels of hunger, malnutrition, and food insecurity that exist across our country at the same time.

Despite being misdirected, however, the agricultural community's obsession over heightening yields continues, along with a vociferous debate about whether sustainable farming, however one defines that slippery term, could indeed (theoretically, of course) fill the bellies of everyone on Earth. While skeptics say the yields from organics aren't high enough, others insist that such methods are sufficient to produce both quality and quantity. Considering that many small-scale developing-world farmers grow organically by necessity, it is worth asking whether methods of support other than a shift toward industrial production might benefit them and their societies the most. The Worldwatch Institute, an environmental organization, wisely points out that reducing waste and encouraging self-sufficiency by promoting urban agriculture, environmentally adapted species, women's rights, access to markets, and other low-tech developments would have a more profound impact on widespread food availability than increasing production. Focusing on simple, low-cost, context-appropriate technologies; info-sharing methods; and improved distribution networks for developing-world farmers would also have an enormous impact. But while the debates over the matter rage, there's no reason that we can't at least push ahead in using far more sustainable farming practices than we already are in our own country, especially because the project of reducing petrochemical pesticide and fertilizer use is no longer just the province of precious places like Hawthorne Valley.

I pulled up at the University of Arizona's Controlled Environment Agriculture Center (CEAC), situated at the corner of two busy streets just south of Tucson's Catalina Mountains, on a blindingly hot day in July—the thermometer would hit 104 that afternoon. The monsoon should have arrived a couple weeks before, and in its absence the city's beige desert landscape had become apocalyptically parched. In the gravel parking lot beside a row of large greenhouses, I felt I might burst into flames as I shook hands with Josh Hottenstein and Myles Lewis, the young founders of a fledgling company called Verdant Earth Technologies. We immediately took refuge in a cool classroom building equipped with long rows of tables, where they enlightened me about how they are combining greenhouse technology with advanced IT systems to design what basically amount to farms inside shipping containers, a project that fits into an emerging field known as "vertical farming."

Vertical farming refers to any growing method that takes advantage of vertical space, from cultivating herbs in the pockets of an over-the-door shoe organizer hanging from your backyard fence to glass-walled skyscrapers containing entire farms in densely populated urban centers. While the former can hardly be called revolutionary and the latter does not yet exist (though architects and designers around the world are actively imagining prototypes), there is a sweet spot of innovative, small-scale vertical farming projects that are immediately feasible, technically sound, and promise to revolutionize our conception of what a farm can look like in the here and now.

Verdant Earth Technologies is one of these. Their company, Josh told me, aims to harness the potential of the greenhouse technology that's been developed at the CEAC, a research and education facility dedicated to the practice of controlling every element of a plant's growing life. They aim to go well beyond greenhouses, however; by adding artificial light to their toolbox, they can grow several layers of plants in a chamber that never sees real sunlight.

"No matter what we do, we're going to have to become more efficient in how we produce food," Josh said in reference to the Earth's booming population, leaning back in his wooden chair and propping his ankle on his knee. "Greenhouses and the associated technologies are one way to do that."

Josh has a background in management information systems and looks the part—soft-edged, polo-shirted, his blondish hair fringed straight across his forehead. He moved on from the company shortly after I met them, leaving the business entirely to Myles, the greenhouse expert, who is wiry and quiet, at home in sporty sunglasses, and apt to screw his face up self-consciously when he says something funny. The pair met in the University of Arizona's McGuire Entrepreneurship Program, where their farm-in-a-box idea won the business plan competition in 2009. Their plan took aim at a limiting feature of the greenhouse industry: each greenhouse is unique, and there are only so many people out there knowledgeable enough to design and maintain them to best advantage. As Josh put it, "everything's a craft" with greenhouses. The dynamic duo set out to find a way to make such complex enclosed growing systems accessible to everyone by standardizing the environment inside 160-square-foot shipping containers. They planned how to use sensors and IT components to replace the need to have what Josh called "ridiculous amounts of chemistry knowledge." (Which, he added, "Myles has.")

The "containerized system" the company is designing will produce lettuces, herbs, and grafted seedlings for use in the greenhouse industry. Myles led me into one of the CEAC greenhouses to show me the way the plants will be grown hydroponically—that is, in water, not soil. He picked up a marshmallow-sized lump of something called rock wool with a texture like a cross between a cotton ball and cardboard. This substance functions as the "soil" in which the seed is planted. Myles pointed out how this plug of material would fit into a hole in a light blue foam bed floating atop a large tray of nutrified water; some 120 tender little plants sprouted from their holes set in even rows, their roots dangling into the water below.

The containerized system will use this technique and will also incorporate a remote-controlled camera like the one that was suspended over our heads: a white box able to turn in any direction and zoom in close enough to see the details of bugs on a leaf. Once when he was traveling away from the lab, Myles recounted, a friend back at the CEAC reported that his greenhouse wasn't looking too good, and after an online session manipulating the camera remotely, Myles could tell his friend exactly what to change to put things right. In the containerized system, the role of the friend will be played by an exterior—possibly eventually online—control panel, through which a user will be able to manipulate about fifteen variables including the pH of the nutrient solution, air temperature and flow, artificial light, and humidity, without ever opening the box.

"We can, with a ninety percent degree of satisfaction, say we know how the plant is going to grow," said Myles. "We let our automated systems go according to the set points we've set through research." Ideally, growers would not open the box or have any contact with the plants until they are ready to be harvested, a method that reduces risk of contamination. "By closing it up, it keeps the pests out, it keeps the diseases out," Myles continued. "I'm not touching the plant, so when you get it, it's had no human interaction, so your chances of *E. coli,* salmonella—all these things—are drastically reduced. Up to the point someone takes it out, I can guarantee no human's ever touched it and there's been no pathogens in there."

Josh and Myles were working up a prototype of the system in a walk-in refrigerator at the time I visited, and they generously gave me a peek, leading me through a heavy white door and into a sterile, bright space as cold and windowless as the outside world was hot and blazing with sunlight. Myles handed me a head of lettuce from a stack of shelves meant to approximate the five shelves that will divide the eventual shipping container, each of which will be able to be manipulated separately to allow the cultivation of five different crops at once. As I shivered in my T-shirt admiring the shining green leaves, the gravity of this project suddenly hit home: we were talking about growing plants in pools of water suspended in sunless boxes, a total reversal of millennia of wisdom about the requisite order of the natural world.

"We're growing plants without soil or sunlight anywhere you have power and water," said Josh matter-of-factly. "Whether you want to do it in the South Pole or whether you want to do it on the back of a loading dock in downtown Manhattan, you have the capability to grow plants in that location."

I stared at him. Pondering the idea of growing plants on the South Pole while my retinas still burned from a scorching outside world more akin to Mars than Earth made me feel like I had stumbled onto the set of some corny sci-fi movie. Later that afternoon, this feeling would be reinforced when Dr. Gene Giacomelli, director of the CEAC and one of Myles's former professors, showed me the Lunar Greenhouse, a research project involving a growing chamber capable of producing vegetables on the moon. And I learned that Dr. Giacomelli had already in fact helped design a growing chamber on the South Pole that now supplies researchers at the U.S. South Pole Station a healthy diet of leafy greens.

While these particulars made me feel that I was a forbiddingly long way from Peace Valley Farm, the more I talked to the young entrepreneurs, the more I realized that those two enterprises are not as different as one might think. One of the chief advantages of the farm-in-a-box system, after all, is massively reducing if not eliminating the amount of chemical fertilizer, pesticides, and other inputs it takes to grow vegetables. Vegetables grown this way use a tenth the amount of fertilizer of those grown in soil and require no pesticides at all. On top of that, the systems prevent soil degradation, eliminate runoff and groundwater pollution, require no oil to run tractors, produce a lot on a small footprint, reduce transportation needs, and use relatively little water. In fact, the water in the system can be reused continuously, since the plants themselves filter it; some commercial hydroponic greenhouse systems have been using the same water for ten years. "What goes into the system stays in the system and is utilized by the system," said Josh. "When you're talking about per-unit input, we're much, much more efficient [than growing in soil], which is going to make the process more sustainable."

But what about the artificial lighting and heating, I wondered? Surely that must take up so much energy as to render the other ecological advantages of the containerized system moot. Josh conceded that these systems consume more electricity than growing plants in a field. But the bigger picture is still positive: "At the end of the day you're talking about an economically productive process that uses significantly fewer resources." Plus, the lighting and other equipment produce heat as a by-product, and in many cases it will be possible to tap waste heat from nearby buildings or other installations. The needed electricity can be acquired during off-peak times, bringing down the cost as well as providing an outlet for energy the utility company can't store. But such arrangements are not the final word; Josh and Myles believe that the containerized systems can eventually be run on solar power, obviating the need for almost all external inputs. Their plans require reduction in the price of solar technologies, which is already happening at a rapid rate, and advances in LED lighting and solar panel efficiency, which they are certain will inevitably occur. "We're waiting for the technology to catch up with what we want to do," said Josh.

It all seemed too good to be true, but I was still cautious in my optimism. I could already hear the chorus of skepticism from the organic farmers of the world, the dirt under their fingernails hinting at their years of toil coaxing tender leaves from hard earth. I could see how something like the containerized growing system, when compared with the holistic vision of the farm as a vital, living organism, could seem like the advance guard of some soulless robotic dystopia. But Myles was quick to point out that the distinction such critics make is not as clear as it might seem and often centers around a romantic vision of small-scale agriculture and a sense of the moral rightness of a life of honest toil under the hot sun. "What's different about what you're doing than what I'm doing?" he asked the hypothetical organic farmer. "You have soil. I don't have soil. Does that mean mine's any less of a living, complete system? I've got insects in here that I use as beneficial insects; I've got predators, animals floating around just like they will. I've got living plants. I've got air moving around. I've got water. The only difference is I don't have soil."

Even if, as Myles contended, a farm in a box is as much a farm as any other, I could see how these systems' impact on the larger agricultural landscape could strike some as unpleasant. Who wants to live in a countryside dotted not by farms but instead by warehouses filled with shipping containers stacked to the ceiling? Josh jumped in to address this concern. "It's a balance between open space and nature and habitat and development," he said. "From a conservation standpoint we're freeing up more space. You can find new business models to preserve open space, to preserve farmland and other types of areas." He urged me to imagine a twenty-acre farm with all of the land under cultivation. Now, he said, picture placing a bunch of the containerized systems on two of the acres and making three other acres into an area for renewable energy generation to run the boxes greenly. Since one of the farm-in-a-box containers can produce ten to twenty times as much food as a field of the same dimensions and can reliably produce a specified amount every day regardless of weather, the two acres of boxes could produce as much or likely even more food than the twenty acres of soil under cultivation. With that in mind, picture setting the remaining fifteen acres of the original farm aside as forest to provide habitat for wildlife, a sink for carbon, and a pleasurable vista to the surrounding community.

Another vision to ponder is an urban landscape improved by the easy, direct, and reliable access to fresh food such containers make possible. "This is a tool that can be used to put food back where people are consuming it," said Josh. Greenhouses, of course, are already being put to work in this way; BrightFarms, the company that designed the greenhouse at P.S. 333 and the Science Barge, teamed up with a company called Gotham Greens to create commercial hydroponic farms on New York City rooftops, which are supplying local supermarkets with fresh greens. BrightFarms is also involved in building and managing greenhouses on the roofs of large supermarkets, growing fresh veggies as close to the produce section as they can get. But the containerized technology Verdant Earth is marketing could be especially helpful in overcoming the logistical hurdles greenhouses face in high-density urban areas, such as shadows from looming buildings and the complications of zoning laws. Since shipping containers would likely be considered semipermanent or temporary structures instead of permanent installations, zoning regulations for them would likely be more flexible than those applying to permanent greenhouse structures.

Indeed, the urban environment is ripe—so to speak—to take full advantage of the kinds of technology Josh and Myles are working with. The emerging field of vertical farming, if such a thing can be properly said to exist, focuses on developing building-scale farms that would use these same tools to provide high volumes of food in city centers. Dickson Despommier, the progenitor of the idea and a professor of environmental health sciences at Columbia University, says that the only way for cities to be sustainable is to become self-sufficient in respect to food production.

"Cities right now represent parasites," he told an interviewer from *The Economist.* "I'm a parasitologist; I can recognize a parasite when I see one. I can recognize a parasite when I live in one. The city is totally parasitic with regards to the environment." Ideally, he said, we could compare our cities not to bloodsucking leeches but to natural ecosystems. "Ecosystems make their own food. Ecosystems process their own water. Ecosystems live within their energy means," he said. "And they live very happily. If you go down to the tropics, you'll see how robust an ecosystem can be. A city can behave exactly the same way, but it has to start with the same premise. That is, you have to make your own food."

Despite such logical justification and a frenzy of interest in the idea in recent years, a city-center, building-scale farm has yet to be produced. With urban land at a premium, the cost of the building itself—not to mention the massive energy requirements of the lighting and heating—can be prohibitive, especially when the plans involve growing low-margin produce like the kind we eat in our salads. "If you have high-density, high-value crops such as seedlings or certain plants that are being grown for pharmaceutical reasons . . . given the current technology and prices of outputs, that's perfectly viable in and of itself," Josh told me. "When you start to get into these more encompassing visions with the lower-value crops, that's when it becomes a little bit sketchier." The first hurdle such projects face is financing. "Typically these types of projects don't get into the portfolio of traditional venture capitalists," Josh said. "You're looking at traditional banks or high net-worth individuals that are looking for a slower rate of return."

Luckily, however, as Josh and Myles demonstrated to me, vertical farming isn't a skyscraper-or-bust proposition. And whether it's in a skyscraper, a greenhouse on the grocery roof, or a shipping container in the basement below the cafeteria, growing quantities of food in close proximity to eaters does indeed have many advantages. Vertical farming methods can slash greenhouse gas emissions by reducing shipping requirements and runoff by growing hydroponically. Eaters can get the freshest food possible ("You can have a minute-old meal," chuckles Despommier).

Grocers with access to this kind of technology can improve

their margins by producing greens on demand, thereby cutting the vast amount of waste and the cost of the middleman they now have to build into their budgets. Josh believes there's a compelling business case in this technology: Considering that produce is mostly composed of water, a traditional produce supply chain means shipping "very perishable water . . . very, very long distances," he said. "Anything we can do to collapse that is very interesting from an economic standpoint and a business standpoint." With the cost savings of reducing waste, might grocers remain better able to resist the pull of consolidation and the need to move out of poor areas? Alternately, imagine if community organizations or soup kitchens with no room or time to keep a garden had control of one of Verdant Earth's containers to feed the hungry.

I was surprised by the considerable positive potential in Josh and Myles's approach to greenhouse technology. The farmers to whom I had mentioned the concept were unanimous in their disdain of such a mechanization of their livelihood, and my own initial reaction had been admittedly skeptical. But on a practical level, the farm-in-a-box concept seemed to present solutions to real and intransigent problems. I was left wondering what other emerging technologies might be able to address problems that bedevil our agriculture. What about the crops that can't be contained in a box—for example, the corn and the wheat that largely fill the vastness of our farmland? Was there any technology that could help cultivate these in more sustainable ways?

This question took me to a town called Reardan, Washington, on the outskirts of Spokane, where I met friendly sexagenarians Karl Kupers and Fred Fleming, business partners in Shepherd's Grain, a unique venture that is changing the way the area's farmers grow and sell their wheat. We sat down in an office at Fred's farm, hemmed in all around by the endless green of rolling wheat fields and across a big gravel yard from several silver silos with conical roofs that compose Fred's seed plant. Karl, an inveterate talker with a tidy cap of gray hair, a white polo shirt, and loafers, explained how, in a region where farmers have been cultivating wheat for hundreds of years—and on a farm, no less, where Fred's great-great-grandfather grew it as a homesteader in the 1880s—he and Fred have gone against the grain (so to speak) in two important ways. First, they are advocates of no-till farming, or, as they prefer to call it, direct seeding, which involves growing crops without tilling the soil, a rejection of the way farming has been practiced for hundreds of years. Further, they market this no-till wheat directly to consumers at a price they set themselves, turning away from the commodity wheat market and its requirement of accepting whatever price the market offers. Shepherd's Grain is based on these two principles, both of which fly audaciously in the face of the typical methods of growing and selling wheat in the modern United States.

In direct seeding, a farmer uses special equipment to insert seeds into the soil through the residue of the previous year's crop. The soil is not broken up by a plow, so that organic matter can collect and microbial life can flourish in the top portion of the soil, which in a tillage-based system is basically a dead medium that depends on heavy fertilization to function. "Actually tillage was intended to create a dead zone," Karl told me. "This was supposed to be fluffy, dry dirt that would prevent water from evaporating out. Based on our rainfall patterns we needed to do that because summers were hot and dry and if you let the ground kind of lay open it would just bake it off, and your water would wick up and go back into the atmosphere. So they created this dead zone. It's easy to manage."

Things aren't so straightforward with direct seeding; the work is less about controlling inputs and more about managing a complex soil environment. "The basis is soil health," said Karl. "The elevator speech is: nature doesn't till. We tilled for 140 years, so basically in the top four inches we've destroyed the habitat. As soon as you stop tilling and go to no-till, those microbes come back." After a long transition period—as many as fifteen years—crops can grow in no-tilled soil without added fertilizer. Fifteen years might sound like an eternity, but seen against the centuries of tillage-based farming, it's a short interval for complete healing of badly damaged soil.

Healthy soil, Karl said, "creates a healthier plant." But it isn't just about healthier plants, which Karl and Fred insist make more nutritious food for us eaters; it's also about creating a healthier landscape. "When you till, you break down the soil particle and it becomes real fine and so when a raindrop hits it, it splatters and compacts," Karl said. Whereas when water hits no-tilled soil, "it just comes in. It's a huge, huge difference.... These tilled soils literally seal up and won't let the water penetrate after a period of time and then it just all runs off and it carries the soil with it. That's the real devastation." A 2006 study in the *Journal of the Environment, Development, and Sustainability* found that U.S. soil is eroding ten times faster than the natural rate of replenishment, which costs an estimated $37.6 billion per year in productivity losses and of course leads to dire predictions about agricultural sustainability. The problem is in fact global; 30 percent of the Earth's arable land is now unproductive due to decades of erosion.

Fred, a slim, smiley fellow with a stubble of gray surrounding a bald pate, recalled a big rainstorm the prior year that sent water and soil rushing off tilled fields but seeping into the ground in those that had been directly seeded. It was a storm of similar intensity to one that had washed out a local road in 1972, he said, and would have certainly washed the road out again if the majority of the surrounding fields had still been tilled. "So there's a social component that cannot really be quantified," he said. "I'm here to say that road would have been washed out and the state would have been spending good money to put it back."

Later that afternoon on a tour around his own fields and the surrounding area, Fred pointed out to me exactly what he was talking about: a thick stand of green wheat in a neighbor's tilled field was cut across by jagged scars, gullies that had been carved out by rains that had hit before the field was planted. "See those nasty ditches and stuff?" he said. "That's what happens when you farm conventionally versus no-till. You have those gullies that over the winter months cut into that guy's fields and he's washed away a certain level of land now. . . . For most farmers it's like collateral damage, like generals figuring out war: 'We have to do it this way and we're going to lose X.' But over time, if we keep losing X, we don't have anything left."

It was the ability to keep his soil that had first convinced Fred that transitioning to no-till was a worthy undertaking. "I wasn't convinced on the process of no-till until I planted my first crop," he told me. "Then we had a spring rain and my neighbor next door watched most of his crop wash down the crick and mine stayed. At that point what we were talking about became real to me."

He took me to his own no-tilled field resting fallow for the season, a rolling expanse of brown stubble with brittle old stalks of grain thatched over the sleeping soil. "Feel how spongy that is?" he said, testing the ground with his foot. He scooped up a handful of earth and held it out for me to inspect. "See how the microbes and the activity in the soil has broken down more of the organic matter in this soil?" The dirt was dark and moist, made of cohesive chunks cut through with roots and organic debris. "You can smell it," he said, putting it to my nose. The aroma was rich and loamy. In a field next door farmed conventionally by Fred's neighbor, the brown earth etched with tire tracks looked shockingly bare when compared to the no-till field. We stood at its edge and Fred displayed a handful of the dry, empty soil for my inspection. It looked parched and anemic and smelled like nothing. "Once they start working it, it gets to be a powder, almost like a talcum powder," said Fred, gazing over the ground. "You get a cloudburst in here and this stuff will wash out of here lickety-split."

Fred and Karl were unlikely candidates for promoting an alternative, eco-friendly approach to farming, considering they're of a conservative bent typical of Washington wheat farmers. In 2010, they accepted the Growing Green Business Leadership Award from the Natural Resources Defense Council, a major environmental nongovernmental organization, even though, as Karl put it, "personally, professionally, I disagree with them ninety-eight percent of the time. Not a fan. And they know it." For Karl what mattered was that the organization was recognizing their success "using the marketplace to create change, rather than litigious or legislative." Karl and Fred's view of sustainability is heavily weighted toward revitalization of soil health and rural communities rather than the more common tilt toward curtailing industrial farming practices in favor of less mechanized and chemically dependent methods, or the more mainstream definition of changing one's lifestyle to conserve dwindling resources.

As we bumped over a dirt lane cutting between wheat fields, Fred turned to me with a mischievous smile. "Do you like seafood?" he asked. "Do you like to have suicide by fork?"

"What?" I said.

"Keep eating till you die!" he crowed with a delighted smile, explaining that he wanted to take me to the seafood night hosted by an all-you-can-eat buffet at a local casino that evening. "You don't *have* to eat until it hurts," he conceded. Later that day he made good on his promise, generously treating me to what can only be described as an insane gorge-fest at Rivers Edge Buffet at Northern Quest Resort and Casino, a complex owned by the Kalispel Tribe of Indians. While Fred's wife, Vicki, went to the garishly carpeted casino to gamble in the slots, Fred and I settled into a dining room edged by a series of buffet stations offering an endless parade of food—a carving station heaped with meat, a salad bar, piles of sushi, platters of shrimp and crab, a range of fish fillets, shelves of desserts. Fred ate plate after plate of king crab legs as we discussed our profound political disagreements with a surprising amount of goodwill.

Fred was right that encouraging soil health and cohesion are convincing arguments for no-till, but there is of course much more to sustainability than a healthy microbial population on one's farm. But while you're not going to win any sustainability awards for eating mountains of crab legs in Spokane, Washington, there was more ecological good news to the no-till story than I had first heard: another advantage of the system is a drastic reduction of fossil fuel inputs. The equipment used for direct seeding does fewer passes over the fields and is also able to go substantially faster: eight miles an hour, versus around five on a conventionally seeded field, allowing farmers to cover the same amount of land in a much shorter time.

"We save about thirty-eight percent or forty percent of our fuel bill," Fred had told me during our farm tour as we stood in front of his elaborate direct seeding machinery, a complicated tangle of tubes, springs, and metal shanks. "Usually it would take twelve passes and now it takes probably three to four. But two of those are usually by the sprayer." The need to do passes with a pesticide sprayer is one of the most criticized aspects of no-till farming. Tilling the soil helps keep weeds from growing, so no-tilled fields need other aggressive methods of keeping them at bay. Critics of the practice argue that no-till actually requires more pesticides than conventional farming.

Some organic advocates—notably Rodale Institute—are working to adapt the no-till system to organic growing.

Once Fred and Karl got their no-till operations up and running, they set out to market their crops to the type of customers that might appreciate the benefits of the direct seeding method. Since the nutrient needs of no-till farming require diversifying ones' plantings—in the case of eastern Washington, branching out into such things as sunflower, safflower, buckwheat, alfalfa, and other native grasses—Karl went to a health food store in Portland, Oregon, to see about selling a range of crops. The store had advertised an interest in working directly with famers, but Karl found them to be less than enthusiastic. Fred laughed at the memory of a despondent Karl returning from that first scouting expedition. "It was sort of like the kid who goes to school here in the country and he's got his little baseball and his cap and his Roy Rogers lunchbox," he said, chuckling. "First day of school, and the bus drives by, and little Karl turns around"—Fred mimicked a whimpering kid—"'Fred, they just don't want my products.'"

Karl regrouped and took to studying his potential customer base up close, hanging around at a natural food co-op in Seattle. "I'd go there and I'd watch people buy things," he remembered. "The co-op used a lot of language. They'd have two or three sentences of language above a product. One of the first things I learned is I'd look in these glass cylinders and there were these wheat kernels, but they were called 'wheatberries.' I go, 'What the heck's a wheatberry?' Well, it wasn't anything more than a wheat kernel, but they call them a berry, so you learn that. I went back a third time and the third time I got up the guts enough to ask people when they'd buy something, 'What part of that language made you buy that product?' It became very clear. I came away from that going, 'What we're doing is what they want. We just have to learn their language.'"

Next came the watershed moment when Karl and Fred decided to walk away from the commodity market. An impromptu focus group of a few bakers and a miller liked the idea of a company selling flour made from no-till wheat, but they asked how Karl and Fred planned to make it work financially. Karl started talking about wheat futures and premiums, then he suddenly changed tack. "I said, 'If you're truly going to be sustainable you've got to cover your cost of production, and the commodity market never gives you that,'" he told me. "We said, 'We're not going to take the commodity price. We're going to do a true cost of production. That's going to be our price.' We all kind of looked at each other and went, 'Why not?'" That policy has made the price higher than commodity prices generally are, but Shepherd's Grain customers are glad to pay. "The consumer appreciates the fact that they know this farmer's making a profit," said Karl. "They're tired of him being this person who can't make a profit and then he goes away and we lose our rural landscape and we lose our ability to feed ourselves locally."

Pricing was far from the most complicated thing about setting up Shepherd's Grain, however. To ensure that all of the flour that goes into Shepherd's Grain bags is in fact made from the no-till wheat grown by their contracted producers, Karl and Fred had to figure out how to keep that wheat separate from the conventional commodity wheat throughout the process. This is harder than it sounds, since in a commodity system every farmer's wheat is added to a giant pile, making it impossible to keep a particular producer's grain separate or to trace a certain farmer's wheat to a specific bag of flour. Unable to use the conventional system for processing and distribution, Karl and Fred had to figure out alternate storage (on each producer's farm), distribution (a specialized trucking company), and milling (an Archer Daniels Midland mill at which Fred had contacts agreed to mill Shepherd's Grain flour separately and package it in branded bags).

As family farmers with generational roots in the area, Fred and Karl market their flour wholesale throughout the Northwest and are intent on encouraging a revitalization of the regional farming economy. Their cost-of-production model means their wheat producers can earn a living wage, and Shepherd's Grain is encouraging a new generation of young people to stay on or return to the land by providing a sense of excitement in connecting producers directly to their product and its consumers. "We can talk about . . . all the good environmental components, but if you don't have a new young farmer coming back here, you're done," said Karl. In the commodity system, he continued, "we couldn't follow [our wheat] if we tried. We couldn't say, 'That's my wheat in that biscuit or bun.' Now we can. And that joy and that passion that's been created from that is brought back to the farm. And the sons and daughters are seeing that. There wasn't that joy and excitement before. They were fleeing. Now they're seeing their moms and dads excited about what they're doing, and they're coming back." The average age among Shepherd's Grain farmers is now forty-eight, almost ten years younger than the national average for farmers, and Karl estimated that one-third of farms that supply wheat to the company are now farmed at least in part by people under thirty-six. "That's huge," said Karl, looking from me to Fred with a smile. "That's huge."

"What Shepherd's Grain is all about is perpetuating that legacy of allowing the next generation to have an opportunity to come back," commented Fred, who lives in the house that has sheltered four generations of his farming family since his grandfather built it in 1938 to replace the hut his great-grandfather had dug out of a nearby hillside. Toward the end of our visit, standing in the midst of a gorgeous green stand of wheat across the road from his house, Fred swept his gaze across the nine hundred acres that made up the original farmstead his great-grandfather cultivated with teams of horses, now only a portion of his approximately forty-three hundred acres. "Now it's my responsibility," he said, shielding his eyes with his hand. "And over the years we have transitioned from growing crops in their style of farming to the way I farm." He brushed his open palms over the tops of the plants as they rustled in a stiff breeze. "This is truly a way to change an ecosystem."

CHAPTER 15

Surf & Turf

Aquaponics and mobile slaughter offer humane, eco-friendly proteins

THE TYPE OF TECHNOLOGIES A new generation of sustainability-minded farmers may need to master goes beyond no-till drills and greenhouses, or even black-box growing systems. Especially when it comes to raising food beyond vegetables and grains—the meats and fishes for which American taste buds seem particularly suited—things get complicated fast. For example, the same hydroponic method Myles is using in his containerized systems is being adapted for the fledgling industry of aquaponics, a combination of hydroponics and aquaculture: growing fish and plants jointly in a closed-loop, low-input system.

I had heard about this type of operation but wondered how exactly it worked. Were such arrangements effective enough to become substantial and dependable contributors to our food supply? Americans continue to eat more and more fish, but many of our planet's fish stocks are under pressure from overfishing, some of them to such an extent that they shouldn't be fished at all. Most seafood Americans consume is imported, often from countries that inadequately regulate fish farming operations and cause ecological damage to sensitive ecosystems. Aquaculture might just be the only viable and ecologically sound fish-supply method we can count on in the future, and combining fish cultivation with hydroponics only makes the system greener. Needless to say, I found the idea of a growing aquaponics industry to be uniquely good news.

I found an aquaponic farm to visit in an unexpected place: Cape Cod, where fish are abundant from saltier sources. E&T Farms in West Barnstable, an adorable village with the shingled houses and quaint general store typical of the Cape, is housed in a large wooden barn off a quiet side street behind the library. On a bright summer day, a clang of the nautical bell on the wall by the barn's front door summoned a burly guy in a gray tank top with pale, sunburned skin and a blond mullet-ponytail. This was Ed Osmun, former manager of a group of hardware stores, who started the operation six years ago and has been overseeing the row of large water tanks and the hydroponic array blooming with greens seven days a week ever since.

We strolled among the large, lined tanks, our faces moist from the continual mist rising from the water agitated and oxygenated by large, multilayered waterwheels coated with beneficial bacteria. Peering over a tank edge, I could see the shadowy forms of tilapia and koi in the depths darting, looping, and lazing. The water from the tanks is piped over to the hydroponic system in the attached greenhouse, where seeds planted in plugs of coconut husk and perlite are set into boards over which the water drips. The water is nutrified by the fishes' waste, mainly in the form of ammonia that bacteria convert into nitrate, which is nontoxic to the fish and offers plants the form of nitrogen they take up most readily. Nothing else usually need be added for the plants to grow. The plants in turn purify the water before it is pumped back into the fish tanks.

With a strong, blunt finger, Ed pointed out the way the pipes and trays of his hydroponic system take advantage of gravity in irrigating the plants, and told me how he designed and built it with the help of an expert from the University of Massachusetts. When I asked where he got the inspiration for such a project, he looked thoughtful. "People ask me that all the time," he said. "And the best answer I can come up with is my wife always tells me that on our first date I was talking about controlled environment systems. And we'll have been together thirty-eight years this December."

I poked my nose into some big plastic barrels next to one of the tanks and discovered the cache of fish food—brown pellets that looked a lot like what I used to feed my pet rabbit when I was a kid. The only regular inputs into this system are these pellets, the fish themselves as tiny newborns, beneficial insects for pest control, and electricity—which, admittedly, the system uses a lot of to power the waterwheels and air pumps that must run all the time. These relatively few inputs are enough to create both the fish and a large range of leafy greens.

The symbiosis of this system precludes the application of pesticides to the plants, which would damage the fish, as well as the use of medicines or hormones for the fish, which would impact the plants. Ed's most prominent pest-control method is releasing ladybugs and parasitic wasps. As we stood inspecting a tray of lettuces, I felt an itch on my sandaled foot and discovered a ladybug that apparently took me for a pest. Ed also on occasion uses homemade pesticides, such as a spray of cayenne pepper and garlic dispensed out of an industrial paint sprayer to control aphids.

To make sure the fish fry he has shipped in from New Mexico (tilapia) and Malaysia (koi) don't have viruses that could contaminate his whole aquaponic system, Ed maintains one quarantine tank with separate water and sterilized equipment where he can keep the fry while samples of the fish are checked by a lab. While the suppliers vouch for their fish's health, dealing with foreign imports leaves Ed feeling somewhat vulnerable. "I don't know the guy, and he's in

Malaysia," he said. "If I have a problem, I have to go to Malaysia." While such long-distance fish shipping might seem patently adverse to the sustainable ethic, transporting tiny fish is preferable to shipping full-grown creatures, which is currently how most people's tilapia and koi reach them. Ed, on the other hand, is able to sell locally. He and his wife attend four farmers' markets each week at which they sell the tilapia, as well as homegrown honey and beeswax products. The koi and the remainder of the tilapia go wholesale to area buyers.

If all the tanks were full of tilapia, Ed told me, the system could produce forty thousand pounds of fish at a time. But koi, which he sells for ornamental purposes, need a bit more space. Ed considers his farm a smallish aquaponic operation; he harvests the fish using handheld nets. Even running a "small" operation, however, makes for a very busy life; Ed and his wife haven't had a vacation in a long time.

While aquaponic businesses can survive in and benefit all manner of places, even coastal communities, these systems offer unique possibilities to urban environments, where the need for fish is most concentrated. To learn more, I arranged to meet Mike Yohay, a pioneer of urban acquaponics, for lunch at a hip San Francisco Thai restaurant. I had settled in with a tall glass of Thai iced tea when he arrived in a black jacket and cap, his serious demeanor softened by a wide, handsome smile. He proffered a bumper sticker emblazoned with the phrase FARM YOUR ROOF! and the logo of his incipient company, Cityscape Farms, which will erect aquaponic greenhouses on the tops of city buildings and in vacant lots around town. Although none of his planned greenhouses were up and running at the time of our meeting, his optimistic vision, ambitious business plan, and evident networking skill had landed him among the likes of Michael Pollan and Jamie Oliver in *Fast Company* magazine's March 2010 list of "The Ten Most Inspiring People in Sustainable Food."

Sliding onto the chair across from me, he ordered his usual, a vegan eggplant dish, and explained how he had run into more problems than he could have foreseen setting up on a rooftop, mostly because of building codes that don't take into account the possibility of such a use of the space. The difficulty, he said, was not necessarily due to obstacles purposefully thrown in his path—San Francisco is, after all, a very urban-ag-friendly city—but because his project defies usual bureaucratic descriptions, so exceptions must be made, regulations changed, or categories invented.

"There's a disadvantage to being a pioneer in this space, because we're working to set a precedent," Mike had told me in an earlier phone interview. That being said, he believes cities are rapidly working to incorporate this new movement. "Cities are catching up with regard to their building codes and zoning laws and how they can incentivize or promote or really even allow urban farming to take place."

A focus of his company is integration of the new facilities into community life, both by supplying food to those in the immediate area and by creating good local jobs. "Creating jobs is one of the best things you could do for someone," he said, spearing a piece of eggplant with his fork.

Cityscape's first greenhouse, for which he was still raising funds and doing groundwork when I met him for lunch, would be able to feed a few hundred families. But that's just a start, and Mike doesn't see any limit to possible expansion. This type of venture could, if done on a large enough scale, really change the urban food landscape, especially because his greenhouses would be able to produce fish and out-of-season foods that are usually transported long distances. "We're in many ways a food-insecure nation that depends on a very elaborate and inefficient import and export system," he had told me in our phone interview. "I'm not saying this is something that can replace conventional farming. I don't think that's possible. But I think it'll be a necessary and welcomed amendment and contribution to our local-food economy. If it means that we don't have to import strawberries from New Zealand or tomatoes from Mexico half the year, then I think everybody's better off."

We'll also be better off with companies like his around, Mike believes, because he predicts that the next generation of farmers will come disproportionately from urban environments and will be able to gain valuable experience by working with such ventures. "We need people with a diversity of backgrounds," he said as we wound down our lunch, not just farm kids who know their way around a tractor. Working with outfits like Cityscape, this diverse crew of new farmers can master not only the basic skills of growing plants, but also the ins and outs of producing protein sources in alternative ways and running a food production business, the unique complexities of growing in urban environments, and, perhaps most importantly, the special technological knowledge needed to maintain the new types of growing systems that will likely play an ever-larger role in our farming future.

Finding new and better ways to supply fish to the American people is fabulous, but let's be honest: what Americans really love is meat, seemingly as much of it as we can fit down our gullets. And meat production in this country presents particularly disturbing problems. The industry, like much else in U.S. agriculture, has consolidated at an alarming rate. According to researchers at the University of Missouri, as of 2007, 83.5 percent of U.S. beef was produced by four large companies: Tyson, Cargill, Swift & Co., and National Beef Packing Co., up from 76 percent a decade earlier.

Meanwhile, four companies—Smithfield, Tyson, Cargill, and Swift & Co.—control 66 percent of the pork industry, almost double the 34 percent of the market they controlled in 1989. Likewise, 58.5 percent of chickens and 55 percent of turkeys are produced by the top four companies in those respective markets.

As the big meat producers have gained increasing shares of the market, it has become more and more difficult for small-scale operations to stay in business. Economies of scale and the particular financial efficiency of industrial production methods—the disturbing, inhumane nature of which has been widely chronicled—mean that smaller meat producers, especially family farms, cannot compete on price with the big guys. But beyond price, the consolidation of the meat production infrastructure presents profound logistical challenges to small-scale operations. The USDA requires that any meat destined for sale be slaughtered at a USDA-inspected facility, and since the requirements of USDA inspection frequently prove prohibitively costly for small facilities, many independent slaughterhouses have been forced to close. The big companies that remain have little incentive to make their facilities available to small producers, so mom-and-pop livestock farmers are often left out in the cold. The paucity of slaughter facilities available to them has become a major bottleneck for local, small-scale meat production.

Luckily, not every small slaughterhouse has gone out of business, and some people are even thinking up new ways to make slaughter available and affordable to small farmers, not to mention more humane. On Lopez Island, a gorgeous, evergreen-covered slice of land in the cold sea off the coast of Washington State, livestock farmers faced a unique hurdle: they were a forty-five-minute ferry ride from the closest slaughterhouse on the mainland, two hundred miles from the island's farms. This meant trucking their animals across the water on the ferry and then hauling them for miles to be slaughtered, a logistically challenging proposition that distressed the livestock, was prohibitively costly for many farmers, and generally gave everybody a headache.

It just so happened that one of Lopez's farmers is a former engineer. In 2002, Bruce Dunlop, who raises apples, pigs, and lambs at Lopez Island Farm, designed a mobile slaughterhouse—the first in the nation—in cooperation with Washington State University Extension and Lopez Community Land Trust. A consortium of meat farmers in the San Jan Islands, which includes Lopez, formed the Island Grown Farmers Cooperative to organize the effort and pool resources to lease the slaughter truck from the land trust and to rent a central facility on the mainland for the final butchering and packing. The mobile slaughterhouse travels among the farms as needed, with farmers paying per animal for slaughter. A USDA inspector travels with the abattoir, which means all of the meat it processes can be sold on the open market, and the farmers of the islands can stay in business and make a living.

I couldn't even begin to imagine what a mobile slaughterhouse might look like. My imagination conjured a rectangular, concrete building hauled on a flatbed truck, a WIDE LOAD ribbon tied across its back end. But surely the facility must be clean, efficient, and modern; the USDA has specific requirements, and this slaughterhouse would be held to all of them, regardless of it being on wheels. Still I wondered, how do you slaughter and butcher an entire cow in a vehicle so slim it can drive down a highway? Clearly this was something I needed to witness for myself.

I arrived on Lopez Island on board a ponderous ferry from Anacortes. The scenery was magnificent: Mist hovered over choppy aquamarine water, obscuring sleeping pine-clad humps of land. The spire of a sailboat's mast sliced darkly through the white wisps and then was gone. As we moved farther from shore, the mists cleared off, revealing the rocky edges of the islands, slanting into the sea, evergreens holding fast to the crags.

On Lopez, I found a bucolic landscape: green fields and forests framed by blue in all directions. Bruce's little corner of this heavenly place was fronted by a charming white farmhouse bordered with flowers and hemmed in by fields where pigs rutted in the dirt and sheep clustered under trees. Beyond a clutch of apple trees behind the house lay an old wooden barn and beyond that, forest.

Bruce, a fifty-five-year-old Steve Martin look-alike with a sun-reddened face and a cheerful, laid-back manner, told me to jump in his truck so we could go look at the hay field. As we trundled down Cross Road and into a bumpy hidden drive through the woods, he punctuated his speech with an occasional chuckle as he told me that he has been raising lambs, pigs, and apples since he moved to Lopez and started farming ten years ago. This means that he spends most of his time growing grass and hay for the animals. We pulled into a wide field covered with rows of cut hay waiting to be baled, where Bruce climbed down from the truck and fingered hunks of his crop to make sure it was ready. The baling crew was lined up for six o'clock that evening.

"You want to be put to work?" he asked, and before I knew what had happened, I was recruited onto the crew as well. That evening, I met Blake and Ben, two young guys making a go of farmwork on Lopez. Bruce drove the baler while I piloted a big truck with a flat trailer onto which Blake, with a mass of blond dreadlocks, and Ben, his dark hair tucked under a green cap, loaded the bales. We made three trips between the field and the barn in the golden sunlight of late afternoon, Bruce driving the truck pulling the trailer piled high with rectangular bales and the rest of us reclining on top of the load. My muscles aching after heaving the hay from the trailer and stacking it high against the barn's back wall, I slept like the dead that night in a cozy little boardinghouse on the edge of the marsh and the sea.

The next morning, I steeled myself as I headed back to the farm to witness the slaughter, one of three Bruce had scheduled with the mobile slaughterhouse that summer. I had spent eleven years as a vegetarian, and while I had started eating meat several years before, convinced by the reasoning that supporting small, local farmers and positive production practices is a way of voting with my dollars, I was prepared to be traumatized by the sight of animals being killed in cold blood. What in the world had possessed me to sign up for this particular adventure?

It was cool and sunny as I arrived at Bruce's farm, where I found a tractor-trailer-shaped vehicle parked in front of the barn with two butchers setting up inside. USDA inspector Jim Donaldson, a friendly, portly fellow with a white beard, chatted amicably with Bruce in the yard. "How you guys coming on the house?" he asked.

I had never met a USDA inspector before, and he wasn't what I was expecting. In my imagination, they are bored, humorless bureaucrats, somehow simultaneously overly serious and appallingly negligent. But Mr. Donaldson was a jolly, relaxed bear of a man; if he were your next-door neighbor, he'd be the one to put on a cool haunted house for the local kids at Halloween. I grilled him for info, eager for a peek into the life of such a seemingly paradoxical person. He had started his career in meat as a butcher at a small plant, he told me, then applied to be an inspector to get better pay and benefits. His first inspection gigs were for big facilities, where he'd rotate from station to station—viscera, head, liver, et cetera— and be exhausted by the end of the day. Inspecting smaller facilities is a lot easier. "This is like retirement," he said, gesturing to the mobile abattoir, one of the smallest slaughterhouses anywhere, parked amid the bucolic surroundings of the farm.

The facility in question had its back doors open thanks to the lack of flies that day, revealing a sterile space outfitted with metal hooks and cradles for holding up the carcasses, sinks, and hoses. Behind the butchering area was a door leading to the interior of the truck, a refrigerated space where the hanging carcasses are stored after the initial butchering. After a day of slaughter, the truck goes back to the Island Grown Farmers Cooperative's full-time packing facility in Bow, Washington, not far from the ferry dock on the mainland, where seven employees of the co-op cut and pack and freeze the meat. The farmers who use the mobile slaughterhouse, residing in four surrounding counties, must pick up their meat from the Bow facility.

The mobile slaughterhouse's manager and head butcher, Jim Wieringa, is an employee of the co-op and spends all his time either slaughtering in the mobile facility or working in the packing plant. He stood ready in a heavy-duty rubber apron, rubber boots, and a hard hat, waiting for the first animal of the day to come his way. Before long, a truck pulling a trailer with a cow in the back arrived and backed up beside the slaughter truck. The man who emerged from the cab, who sells his full-grown cows to Bruce for slaughter, looked like he had just stepped off the range: cowboy hat and boots, a rugged, tanned face. His current specimen was starting to buck and kick inside the trailer, sensing danger as Jim raised a rifle from about ten feet away. Suddenly, the animal stopped moving, sizing up the marksman through the bars, and for a few breathless seconds the man and the beast looked each other in the eyes as Jim took his aim. Then *bam,* a bullet hit its mark right between the eyes, and the cow went down, kicking spastically by reflex, then quieted completely. The butchers opened the trailer, attached a wire to the dead cow's legs, and reeled it into the slaughter truck with a motorized winch.

Jim and his partner laid the body in a metal cradle and went to work, their motions quick and exact as they rapidly removed the feet, peeled off the hide, split open the cow, and pulled out the innards, which they shoved out the small trapdoor at the bottom of the trailer into a revolting heap on the grass. They were artists with knives, their efforts resulting surprisingly quickly in a splayed skinless carcass hanging cleanly from a special hanger at the top of the vehicle. Jim was clearly a man of experience.

"I've been watching it since I was five," he told me when I asked where he'd learned his craft. It turns out his dad was a butcher, too, and he started Jim down the same path early. Jim went to Holland, his father's homeland, when he was sixteen to do several months of training before starting his own butchering career. Being a mobile butcher, he said, was demanding work, and he was looking to hire a trained apprentice to allow him more time in the packing plant and less in the mobile facility. "When you're mobile like this, you gotta get in there, get it done, get back, and get ready for the next day," he said, pausing his cutting for a moment. The schedule is very tight, as there's a ferry to catch. Plus, he said, "We got inspection time, too, which is seven to three." He gestured to Mr. Donaldson, who stood nearby grinning in his white lab coat and hard hat. "So if we hold this guy over, we have to pay . . . what? . . . seventy dollars an hour?

"Somewhere between sixty-five and seventy, I think," said Jim. "It's a spendy idea. You get eight hours' free inspection."

Just as Jim had said, the pace never slackened. I observed for hours as Jim and his partner proceeded to slaughter and butcher four pigs and fourteen lambs, one after another. Each farm that uses the mobile facility must have a clean concrete slab that serves as the slaughter floor adjoined by a suitable pen for holding the animals and a small enclosure on the concrete in which to pin each one while it is stunned. The pigs—enormous, ugly beasts that seemed surprisingly unfazed by being herded, poked, and prodded into the wooden pen attached to the side of the barn—were first to go. Then the lambs, which to my surprise did not look like cute little fluffy babies, as I'd always imagined slaughtered lambs to (tragically) be, but like the sheep: they are dingy and skittish and a little bit ornery.

As it came time for each animal to meet its fate, Bruce pulled a wooden board up to make an opening in the pen's wall and pushed the next unlucky creature out into the enclosure, where it was caught motionless for a moment while Jim's partner pressed a specialized tool, a thick metal cylinder, against the back of its head and stunned it with a bolt to the brain. The stunned animal, rendered immediately unconscious and insensible to pain, would slump to the ground and then begin spasming—kicking and squirming and sometimes even flipping over—which is apparently a normal sign of an unconscious, dying brain. The butcher would drag the animal from the slaughter enclosure, leaving it free to convulse on the concrete, and then, as soon as he could steady it with one hand on a front leg, cleanly slit its throat so the blood could drain out. This is the action that effectively ends its life.

The spasming was the hardest part of the slaughter to watch, as the animals looked like they were writhing in pain. But Bruce insisted that they are stone-cold unconscious as soon as they are stunned, unable to feel pain. "That's all just reflex," he said as we watched an unfortunate pig kicking on the slab. The butcher noted that the spasms are useful because the heart is still pumping at this stage, and the movement helps shoot the blood out of the slit in the throat. Indeed, crimson torrents coated the concrete in a gruesome display that I became quickly used to.

I was surprised to find, in fact, that the slaughter process traumatized me far less than I had expected. It was all so routine—so organized, controlled, and exact. In my imagination, the idea of "slaughter" had conjured images of chaos, disarray, mess, and filth, but the scene on Bruce's farm was just the opposite. Even the inevitable mess was promptly and usefully dealt with. Bruce cheerfully went about loading the discarded viscera that had piled up beside the truck into his front loader and motoring it away to add to his compost heap. Using the animal parts is great for fertility, he told me as I watched him scoop the cow's stomach into the front loader with a pitchfork. Bruce pointed to the spot where blood had seeped into the grass, making a bright red swamp of a small section of the lawn.

"You're going to have a really nice patch of grass growing here in a little while," he said. "There's a lot of nitrogen in that." Bruce collected all of the animals' blood he could for the compost as well. There was a drainage grate along the side of the kill slab, but instead of washing the blood away Bruce preferred to let it coagulate on the concrete and then shovel it into a bucket, a task he completed in a no-nonsense manner over and over throughout the day. Before long, birds of prey were circling overhead, on the alert for fresh intestines. Bruce told me he has to bury the offal under several inches of old compost and leaves or else the birds dig it up and drag it away.

After the butchers had finished with each animal, they sprayed the hanging carcass with a vinegar solution to kill bacteria and then attached it to special hooks that could be dragged along a track in the ceiling into the refrigerated chamber. Slaughtering Bruce's many animals took all day, and at the end of the long slog, Jim reflected momentarily before starting the journey back to the mainland.

"We had a combo—three different animals in one day," he said. "It's unusual."

Bruce was satisfied, glad that his pigs had weighed in much higher than he expected, most at over two hundred pounds. "My customers will be happy," he said. He sells to shops, restaurants, and individuals organized into buying clubs in Seattle and Tacoma, getting lots of his business by word of mouth. Bruce appreciates that his loyal customers are willing to pay a premium for the kind of high-quality meat he produces, but he regrets that the industrialized food system makes it difficult for many to afford such products. One advantage of the mobile slaughterhouse is that it is less expensive to get up and running than a fixed abattoir would be. You can build a mobile slaughterhouse for $250,000, Bruce told me, and then rent space and buy equipment for a processing plant, which is a lot cheaper than buying an entire facility. All in all, Lopez Island's setup cost was around $350,000. But even so, the facility can process relatively few animals—ten beef per day, for instance, compared to several hundred *per hour* in an industrial facility—which hikes up the cost of each slaughter. Farmers pay a premium per animal—thirty-eight dollars per lamb, for instance—for the services.

"What bothers me is that we produce good food and we have to sell it at a price, but there's a lot of people who can't afford to buy it," said Bruce.

Despite such systematic flaws, the mobile slaughter concept is one of the few solutions to an increasingly difficult equation for small-scale meat producers, and the concept has rapidly gained traction since Bruce designed the country's first mobile facility.

"We get inquiries literally every week from people who are interested in what we're doing and who want to do it," he told me. "The bottom line is [these units] work. [Lopez Island's] has been working for quite a while now and paying all its bills and paying all its employees." He has started to sideline as "a mobile slaughter engineering consultant"—most likely the only person in history with that particular job title—working with a company called Tri-Van Truck Body to build more of these facilities. As of the summer of 2010, there were about a half-dozen mobile slaughterhouses operating in the United States.

"It's a good economic development," said Bruce. "The amount of money that went into this project to get it started—private money and some grant money to do some of the study work, the design work—has been paid back manyfold." Each of these mobile slaughter facilities enhances the local economy, bolsters the self-sufficiency and cohesion of the agricultural community, and makes higher quality, humanely raised meat more widely available.

CHAPTER 16

Going Native

Foodies, farmers, and desert dwellers
promote diverse crop species

I WAS HAPPY TO SEE an innovation that was enabling small meat producers like Bruce to get along in this consolidated food system. Not only is their success good for the local communities they live in and serve, but their meat provides a high-quality alternative to that produced by the industrial system, which relies on environmentally destructive megafarms. These are places where animals are kept in unsanitary conditions in tight confinement, requiring the application of hormones and antibiotics to promote growth and prevent illness, and where the meat comes out all too often contaminated by pathogens like *E. coli*. In addition, facilities like the one Bruce designed allow small meat farmers to raise breeds of animals that have been staples of farm life for decades but don't necessarily lend themselves to large-scale production, often referred to as heritage breeds.

Most pigs raised by industrial pork producers are Berkshire, Hampshire, Landrace, Yorkshire, and Duroc breeds, with the latter four of these making up 87 percent of the purebred pigs in the United States, according to the National Swine Registry. Advocates of increasing the species diversity in our food supply include animals in their purview, arguing for the continuing production of age-old pig breeds like Gloucestershire Old Spots, Tamworth, Red Wattle, Berkshire, and Mangalitsa ("Wooly Pig"). While Bruce is not dedicated to heritage breeding (though the cute piglets I saw rooting around in his side yard were Tamworth-Berkshires), small pig farms like his, where the animals can be raised in more natural conditions well suited to their biology, are the ones keeping these breeds from slipping toward endangerment and extinction.

Indeed, around the country, efforts are afoot to ensure the continued diversity of both animal breeds and plant species (whose traditional types are usually called "heirloom"), an effort spearheaded by dedicated small-scale producers who rely on educated consumers willing to pay extra. Some of these consumers are motivated by the prospect of creating a more diverse food system, while others are convinced that heritage plants and animals simply taste better than the species bred for the hardiness and fast growth favored by industrial production.

An uber-foodie event called Cochon 555, a touring culinary contest that has chefs in a series of cities compete to prepare family-farm-grown heritage pigs from nose to tail for a crowd of pork-loving guests, is the ultimate in heritage breed promotion. I attended the event's Washington, DC, rendition two years running and couldn't decide whether it represented the worst of American eating (considering it was a shameless gorge-fest) or the best (considering that it combined an entrepreneurial spirit and an appeal to people's taste buds to support improvements in our food system). The mission of the event is to promote the awareness and use of heritage pig breeds, and by inviting each city's elite chefs to compete and charging $125 for a ticket, Cochon 555 is helping make small-farm-raised heritage meat a stylish commodity among those with the income to afford it.

"It's really all about the pigs," Chef Scott Drewno told me at the 2011 event as he offered me a tiny Asian pork dumpling covered in pink sauce, one of the dishes that would propel him on to win the competition that afternoon. "We need to get away from mass production."

The need to get away from mass production so we can increase species diversity is perhaps even more urgent when it comes to plants. "For all life on Earth depends on plants," wrote Andrew Wood of the organization Botanic Gardens Conservation International in England's *Guardian* newspaper. Plant diversity, he stated, "is more valuable than all the money in all of our banks." It's a bold statement, but one we would be wise to heed. Thankfully, some intrepid souls are finding ways to grow, promote, and sell species not usually found on the supermarket shelves.

While I was in Tucson, I went to find Brad Lancaster, advocate for a practice called permaculture, which is focused on taking advantage of an ecosystem's natural aspects and native species adapted to the landscape to enable sustainable food production. Considering he lives in a desert, he faces some unique challenges in this regard, but that makes the organization he founded, Desert Harvesters, and his expertise on what he calls "rainwater harvesting," all the more admirable and intriguing.

At the house he shares with his brother, sister-in-law, and young nephew, Brad ushered me into a cozy living room crammed with toys and bookshelves. A gentle, red-haired guy, he greeted me warmly before popping on a straw hat and leading me out into the yard. He has made his house and its yard into an experimental expression of all the principles he teaches at various venues, including in the Middle East on educational excursions with the State Department. He has also encapsulated his ideas about desert permaculture in two volumes of a book called *Rainwater Harvesting for Drylands and Beyond*.

His passion is finding ways to grow native plants by capturing and using what he calls the desert's "native water." Tucson has rainstorms twice a year, the water from which mostly pours across roads and parking lots and is lost down sewers and into the desert sand. Brad led me into a strip of earth beside the road in front of the house and pointed out the way a wide notch cut out of the curb gave onto a stone-lined channel carved out of the ground, which led downhill to a tree planted at the lowest point. When the rains come, the water is directed off the pavement and directly into the roots of the tree.

"We planted all the vegetation within or beside sunken, water-harvesting earthworks," he told me. "It's self-maintaining because the water will fill up, the mulch will float to the top, the water will infiltrate, and the mulch settles back. We don't lose mulch, we don't lose soil, there's no erosion. Actually it's the opposite: we can really gain organic matter and soil." This method is distinctly different from the usual method of growing in Tucson and, really, everywhere else. "People plant on mounds, which drains water, topsoil, and organic matter away, and creates the need to irrigate with ever-more water," Brad said. "We pump our groundwater at a rate that exceeds natural recharge, and also it's Colorado River water. We import it at huge cost." By catching runoff, he said, "We're doubling the available rainfall—instead of twelve inches of rain we're getting twenty-four along this street because the water that hits the street comes to the plant."

When Brad and his brother Rodd started harvesting water in their yard in 1994, using a curb dip that had once been an opening for a driveway, the practice of cutting such notches into curbs to harvest rainwater was illegal in the city. He worked with the city government to overturn that rule, and the technique is now not only legal but most new development is required to incorporate it. There's now an official rainwater-harvesting guidance manual for the City of Tucson and a Commercial Rainwater Harvesting Ordinance—the nation's first—that requires all new commercial development in Tucson to provide a minimum of 50 percent of landscape irrigation from harvested rainwater. The state of Arizona even gives an income tax credit for harvesting rainwater. "It's really taken off," Brad commented.

So has his carefully landscaped yard. His eighth-acre parcel was positively lush for a desert, with a patchwork of dusty green leaves shading us from the beating sun. "The vegetation you see, ninety percent of it's native," he said, casting an appraising glance across his miniature homestead. "But we didn't just select them because they're native; we selected them for their food-producing capabilities." He broke a thin, dry pod off a branch and handed it to me. "The mesquite has edible seed pods. You can chew on that if you want." I was surprised at the smoky, nutty flavor. "We grind this up into a sweet, edible flour," he told me. He has written about that and other uses for the plant in his other book, *Eat Mesquite! A Cookbook.* We moved over to a fat, aggressively spiny cactus topped with yellow fruits. "This is barrel cactus, and you can just eat the tart yellow flesh," he said, breaking off one of the fruits and biting into it. "We make chutneys and stuff. The black seeds you can use as poppy seeds or pop them like amaranth seeds."

The tour continued through a wonderland of other edible desert vegetation: pomegranate, European olive, desert ironwood, saltbush, cholla cactus, prickly pear, creosote. He pointed to the prickly pear, its flat pads bristling with needles. "It's a great one for making juice, margaritas, jams, jellies, and whatnot." The dangerous-looking pads are, he said, "a vegetable known as nopal, which you can cook up with eggs." He plucked a fuzzy bud from the creosote bush and held it to my nose. "That's what the desert smells like when it rains."

Ten to 25 percent of Brad's family's diet comes from their own yard. "The great thing about native plants is they're already adapted to the rainfall patterns and soil," he said, which means they thrive quite easily in the environment, especially when supplied with extra water using Brad's techniques. I asked where he had learned so much about native plants. Friends among the Tohono O'odham Native Americans indigenous to the area had taught him a lot. Plus, he joined groups of primitive skills enthusiasts who get together to exchange knowledge and trade traditional foods and other goods. "I bring saguaro fruits, and they're like gold because nobody outside the Sonoran Desert can get saguaro fruit," he said. "So I can get pounds and pounds of hand-picked wild rice from Minnesota for just a little bit of this fruit. And I can get elderberry wine for mesquite flour. I can get elk jerky for cholla buds."

His expertise in water harvesting came from a surprise assignment teaching a class in the subject. When he told the instructors of a permaculture class he was taking that the water-harvesting component was lacking, they suggested he teach it himself. "I decided to take the challenge," he said. "I had a year to prepare for the next course and just went crazy pursuing it. I found that in every part of the world where there's a dry season, there's a rich culture of water harvesting, but almost all over the world that tradition largely started to get forgotten when piped-in water appeared. But now it's resurging around the world."

Brad also captures rainwater in huge enclosed earthen tubs in his side yard, directing it through gutters and pipes off the roofs of his house and shed. The tubs collect so much water that they usually still hold a supply by the time the next rains come, even though the water supports a kitchen garden that grows vegetables not particularly suited to dry environments. The garden is helped along by a primitive irrigation system that uses unglazed terra-cotta pots buried in the soil to seep water slowly into the earth. Water used in the household is also put to good use; in the other side yard, Brad showed off an orange tree and a fig tree, both hydrated at the roots by wastewater from the sink, washing machine, and shower, in which the family uses special biodegradable soap. A system of pipes leading from the house directs specific portions of the gray water strategically to the various trees and other plants that depend on it.

While it was clear that there's a lot of potential in using the desert's native water efficiently, Brad was careful to emphasize that he is not advising that everyone in Tucson should exist only on the scant water supplied by the rains. He believes importing water is necessary to support the city's booming population, but he believes a focus on native plants and proper use of rainwater to grow them should be a prominent part of the agricultural and landscape-design equation.

To encourage people to harvest their rainwater and incorporate some native foods into their diets, he started an all-volunteer nonprofit called Desert Harvesters. The organization grew out of a neighborhood tree-planting project. Volunteers harvested mesquite pods from some of the twelve hundred trees the project has planted since 1996, but then they realized they didn't have an effective way of grinding them into flour. Brad and the other native-food advocates involved in the project figured out they could get small hammer mills to transport around the city on a trailer. They applied for a grant to host an annual mesquite-pancake breakfast at which to grind people's mesquite pods for free and expose newbies to native foods. "If they tasted it and got excited, then we'd say, 'Okay, well, you can plant trees that will grow this food,'" Brad recalled. "And we'd tell them how to plant the rain before they plant the plant"—molding the landscape to channel water to the roots—"in the hopes that they would then bring back the native food-bearing vegetation to their part of the community in a way that would also recharge the groundwater table."

Only ten people attended Desert Harvesters's first event in 2003. "We had one Coleman cookstove and one table," recalled Brad, chuckling. "But every year it's grown." By 2009, they were serving more than two thousand pancakes and had three hammer mills running. The people were lined up around the block to have their mesquite pods ground into flour. Communities that participate benefit from more than just interesting foods. These plants attract birds and more than one hundred native pollinators, fix nitrogen in the soil, and have many medicinal values. "You can suck on the sap if you have a sore throat or a cough," Brad told me. The trees also offer needed shade on the streets of a hot, hot city. "We've noticed what's approaching a ten-degree Fahrenheit drop along our strip of the road compared to strips that have not been planted out with trees," Brad noted. Neighbors on their way to the bus or out walking their dogs choose to traverse this pleasant, shady strip. True to form, as Brad was giving me his tour of the barrel cactuses and prickly pears by the sidewalk, a woman greeted us as she strolled by with her dog. "We know a lot more of our neighbors," Brad said. "That then results in living in a community, which makes for a safer community and a more enjoyable one."

While Brad encourages interest in traditional food plants with an eye toward improving community life and the environment in his city, growing rarely cultivated plants can also be a passionate anti-establishment calling as well as a viable business prospect. Farmers and entrepreneurs are staking their hearts and their fortunes on traditional and heirloom species. In Oregon, a group of young farmers are busy putting heirloom and downright unusual species on the U.S. agricultural map. In a ranch house tucked between the tidy plots of well-tended Open Oak Farm in rural Sweet Home, Oregon, I met Andrew Still and Sarah Kleeger, small-scale farmers and founders of the Seed Ambassadors Project, and their friends and fellow farmers Jeff Broadie and Kasey White, who maintain Lonesome Whistle Farm down the road in Eugene. Sarah handed me a mug of coffee as I settled into one of the living room's couches.

The Seed Ambassadors Project began with a trip to Europe Sarah and Andrew took to find seeds for vegetables that people in the United States don't have access to. "The way I remember it is Andrew said, 'I love kale,'" said Sarah from her place on the couch opposite me. "'Let's go to Europe and find some more kale.' And I said, 'All right, I guess.' There's Red Russian kale—"

"Curled green Scottish kale . . . ," said Andrew.

"We were like, 'Let's go to Russia! Let's go to Scotland!'" Sarah continued. "There has to be other kinds of kale there. And we got like seventeen varieties that aren't available in this country."

They traveled for four months, hitting Russia, Lithuania, Latvia, Germany, Switzerland, Belgium, England, Ireland, and Denmark, along the way collecting eight hundred seed varieties. "We met a lot of people in a kind of semilegal underground of seeds," said Andrew. "There's a lot of people saving seeds still because there's a lot of diversity in Europe. They're not supposed to sell seeds but they do and the regulators know that it's a big farce." Andrew was referring to the European Union's laws that strictly limit seeds approved for sale on the open market to the specific varieties listed in the EU's Common Catalogue of Varieties of Vegetable Species. The policy has raised concern among many farmers, environmentalists, and advocates of limiting corporate control, as it effectively criminalizes the sale of heirloom species not recognized as legitimate by the authorities.

"We brought seeds with us," Andrew continued. "We would give seeds to people who were seed geeks and they would give us seed. You give and are generous and they run home and run back with their family heirlooms and want you to have some. It's really good."

Sarah and Andrew brought the seeds they had collected back legally through the USDA quarantine in Seattle. "They kind of laughed at us because all they care about is corn and soy palettes and tractor trailers full of weird things from China," said Andrew. Back at the farm, they started growing the new varieties of plants, swapping the seeds with other farmers and growing more of the seed to sell. They started a business, Adaptive Seeds, to market their unusual wares.

"I came to agriculture to avoid dependence on large powerful structural aspects of culture that I didn't approve of, that I wish didn't exist," said Andrew. "Being dependent on hybrid seeds is like a big slap in my face. Half the time, my least favorite corporations are producing the hybrid seeds and kind of imposing them economically on us."

The creative, exploratory, and anti-establishment nature of Andrew and Sarah's project represents what many small farmers value most about their occupation. "That's what I think attracts people to farming," said Sarah, of the continual problem solving that the job requires. "It's always something new. You always have to be on your toes."

For Andrew, that intense engagement with the craft, a sense of "having a relationship with the crops that I grow," is the essence of his love for the work. "You can also improve it over the years if you have that stewardship relationship where you're saving seeds, choosing the better individuals," he said. "It's kind of like bringing back an ecological co-evolutionary element where we're now again evolving in our ecosystem as opposed to being a genetic dead end in a hybrid. Without the constant co-evolution within an agro-ecosystem I think our agriculture's doomed to failure. If you have a more wild population that is more diverse and more flexible ecologically speaking, it can adapt."

Along with seeds for all sorts of kale, Sarah and Andrew had collected seeds for a wide variety of other plants, from arugula to Brussels sprouts to parsnips. But the unassuming beans they brought back have become some of their most prized possessions.

"We're all just total geeks about dry beans," said Kasey. "We'll be sitting around having beers and just talking about beans, staring at bags of beans. Basically we just have the buckets of beans and are talking about how cool they are and sticking our hands in them—"

"And finding the ones that might have gotten cross-pollinated—," said Jeff.

"And eating beans together," resumed Kasey. "We're all obsessed with beans now. It's food security. We eat them every day. They store. And they're a good protein source. They're high in fiber, high in calcium. It's a great food to have around. It's like we just got all into beans."

But not just any beans. These are, of course, heirloom varieties, with names like Soldier and Hutterite. Sarah and Andrew had collected a couple hundred varieties on their European tour. "They taste so much better than the regular old beans," said Andrew from behind his shaggy beard.

"Some of them, it's turning out, are not only incredibly beautiful but do very well here," Sarah commented. And growing any beans at all on their farm, heirloom or not, increases the area's agricultural diversity, Sarah pointed out, "because people just don't grow dried beans."

Still, Andrew commented, "I would like to end up seeing rare heirloom dried beans in a bulk bin at a food store."

Our visit ended, appropriately, with a delicious lunch of beans and salad after a tour of the charming farm, and I went away with my mind yet again focused on the unique, flavorful mystery of heirloom beans.

I had one last stop to make.

Conclusion: Room for Everything

I TRAVELED TO THE TIDY little wine-country town of Napa, California, so I could end where my journey through the hopeful side of American food began. In a humble plate-glass-fronted shop on a quiet side street, I found the heirloom bean mothership: Rancho Gordo New World Specialty Food. When I arrived in Steve Sando's little office off the sales floor, decorated with colorful Mexican movie posters, he was busy piling everything on his desk—papers, coffee mugs, bags of heirloom corn from Mexico—in a heap to one side.

"There, I'm organized," he said, chuckling as he added a final handful of papers to the teetering stack. He leaned back in his chair and peered at me through rectangular glasses, offering a friendly smile.

When I first learned about Rancho Gordo, I had framed Steve Sando in my mind as an avenging angel of a morally superior, more biologically diverse—and frankly saner—U.S. food system. But the portly man in the brown polo T-shirt behind the desk turned out to be anything but the spokesperson I had imagined. For a guy who's built an improbable company—beans? really?—into a successful venture that counts the astronomically high-end restaurant the French Laundry among its clients and who's actually spoken, for goodness' sake, to Oprah, Steve is refreshingly humble and notably wary of making grand political statements. His attitude seemed to say that he's just a guy who really likes good beans and thinks you would, too, if you ever tried them.

When I harangued him to confess his role as a grand pooh-bah in the growing sustainable food movement, he demurred, insisting again and again that he's "not qualified" for much besides eating and selling beans. "There is a food movement, but I don't know if I'm part of it," he said. "I don't know."

This was not the answer I was hoping for. Surely, I plowed on, he must know a thing or two about the politics of the situation. Isn't upping the country's crop diversity a noble goal? Surely he could recognize his role as a pioneer in this effort.

"I don't see myself as a pioneer at all, because I'm not qualified," he obstinately stated. I wasn't sure what exactly does qualify one for such a title. Surely managing to sell what Steve himself called "the most lowly, Depression-era, poor people's food" to a place like the French Laundry had to count for something.

"Our goal is to make money and I want to help people work and provide jobs," Steve said. "But I think it's a great by-product that we're saving all these varieties."

He's indeed concerned with changing things for the better, but for him this means improving the lives of the Mexicans whose beans he's selling. Rancho Gordo is instrumental not only in feeding people and increasing agricultural diversity, but also in bolstering the economic fortunes of some of the world's most needy. With a smile, he launched into an animated explanation of his new Xoxoc project, which is engaging Mexican farmers to grow the heirloom beans and corn themselves instead of having the farmers

Rancho Gordo employs grow them all in California. When we met, he was considering opening a tortilla factory in Napa using the corn, but he later ended up engaging a shop called La Palma in San Francisco's Mission District to make them for him instead. He fished a bag of the corn out of the pile on his desk—a pound of beautiful purplish red kernels—noting with amusement that it makes milky pink tortillas.

"What's great is men are working in Mexico because of this, as opposed to coming up here," he told me. With NAFTA in place, the Mexican farmers were told that if they abandoned the bean varieties they had been growing for generations and instead cultivated Michigan black beans—which Steve calls "a boring hybrid"—they could sell them on the international market. Just as all the farmers had given up their traditional bean varieties, the Chinese swept in and undercut the price of Michigan black, leaving the farmers with beans nobody wanted. Rancho Gordo rode into the breach, suggesting the farmers revert to what they knew best. "By telling them to grow the beans they've grown for thousands of years and that we'll buy them, we're creating a market for them," Steve said. "Even if the market isn't there, it's here."

His comments reflected an idea I heard over and over in my trip around the country's food universe: the good he's doing is all about jobs. The issues surrounding food, it became clear to me over my months of travel, are as much about the health of economies and the vibrancy of communities as they are about filling people's bellies. And the sustainability of our food system is about much more than the environment.

But you won't find the idea of "making a difference" anywhere on Rancho Gordo's website or on any of its other materials. The idea is that the people who buy these beans are buying them because they like his beans, period. Which is, of course, why I buy them.

"People hate moral food." Steve smiled again, a thing he was doing more or less the entire time we talked. "So we don't market any of this that way. The main thing is they taste great. And my whole thing is New World food. So these are foods from the Americas. We've been really bad neighbors. Here's a great way to think about ourselves as on the same page as the rest of Latin America."

As he led me on a tour of the facility—the sparse storefront and a large warehouselike back room where young Hispanic women were hand packing bags of beans and loading boxes for shipping—I was left to wonder how a business like this might fit in to the larger landscape of a sustainable food system. Steve didn't embrace any of the common tropes I had heard over and over and had myself rehashed in my time as a food writer: local food is the answer, organicness is next to godliness, moral food is where it's at.

In the shadow of giant shelves loaded with massive bags of beans, the employees looked relaxed and happy. The one packing customers' orders was bopping to a song on her headphones. "Faster!" Steve joked, and she turned and smirked at him. The box she was packing of these almost-extinct beans resurrected by this unassuming savior would wing somewhere far away, most likely, clocking those dreaded "food miles" that are the bane of every sustainable food maven's existence.

I could see that the complicated operations of our food economy—the interplay between crop diversity, production efficiency, long-distance shipping, economic viability, trade relations, and myriad other factors—were a whit more complicated than the strident voices on the food blogs are often willing or able to account for.

What about local food, I asked Steve, the pet issue of food activists? If we are all to eat local, as the popular line of reasoning prescribes, only those in the Bay Area would have the benefit of eating these delicious beans unless people all over the country start cultivating them, an approach that might not work in places where they don't grow well. Does it make sense for East Coasters to forgo these tasty, saved-from-extinction, fairly traded beans, all in the interest of keeping close to home? What if there were no locally grown beans available? Should they then eat no beans at all? Or, improbably, only eat beans they grow themselves? And if that's not the solution, what would a sustainable food system look like, anyway?

It dawned on me that the answer to this final question that I had been turning over and over in my mind during my many miles in my many rental cars was a system designed to bring people and their food into a closer relationship, but not just in terms of geography. Such a system would also shrink the distance between farmers and eaters in other ways, for instance in the areas of knowledge, finance, and labor. American eaters suffer acutely from an estrangement from those who grow our food, the places where it is grown, and even the food itself. If we know more about how our food is produced and who produces it, give more of our food dollars directly to those who create it, and commit to doing more of the hard work of building a quality food system—from growing tomatoes to teaching our children—we will be closer to our food in many ways and more apt to demand changes that benefit everyone. For an East Coaster, ordering a shipment of Rancho Gordo's beans is a much different action from buying a can of plywood-tasting, industrially produced canned beans grown by impoverished migrant workers, even though both options would run afoul of the eat-local paradigm.

What we need is not an entirely localized food system, but a more human-sized one. The problems we experience—obesity, dependence on petroleum-based fertilizers and pesticides, unregulated genetic engineering, loss of farmland and genetic diversity, decline of rural communities, inner-city neighborhoods with no food stores, water shortages, labor problems, and on and on—all arise from the system's overgrowth. It has, to use an apt agricultural metaphor, gone to seed.

In the United States, we live in an agricultural universe designed perfectly for the purposes it serves: creating low-quality, low-priced food and large profits for a handful of big corporations. The businesses that grow the food have consolidated until they have overgrown appropriate boundaries. They are no longer of an appropriate scale, no longer able to focus on and respond to the human needs of the communities they serve. They produce massive quantities of food on huge farms, mountains and mountains of corn and soy that go to run the motor of an industrial system that has overgrown its regulatory constraints. This food is transported enormous distances, processed in huge batches, and served in jumbo helpings and at breakneck speed, which contributes toward making many of us ourselves overgrown, as we become obese at alarming rates.

We need to shrink all the aspects of this system back down to a size that fits our lives. We need a lot of small to medium-sized enterprises working together, as well as competing, at short and middle distances from the communities they serve. Regional-food economies can most effectively do the heavy lifting in such a system, with local foods taking a prominent role and national and international sources represented where and when it makes most sense. Some big corporations will surely be a part of such a system, but we need to move away from a setup that makes them the prominent—and in many cases the only—players.

My mind was straining under this complicated calculus while Steve answered my question with simple logic: "My wisdom says that vegetables on the whole should be local, that dairy and meat regional, and that grains should grow where they grow best," he said, with none of the angst most people—including me, apparently—seem to attach to the subject. "It's not the same thing for everything."

This matter-of-fact sentiment, it occurred to me, had been a major theme running through my journey: one simple solution is not our answer. What we need, in fact, is more and increasingly diverse farmers, types of farms, ways of farming, uses for urban space in food production, options for food processing and distribution, methods for connecting producers with consumers, approaches to supplying institutions, kinds of food under cultivation, and avenues for engaging young people in the process of growing, processing, and preparing food.

And I had seen firsthand that this is exactly what we are little by little getting. All over this wide country, inspiring people are hard at work innovating on all these aspects of the new food economy. That economy and its appeal to the general public are quickly growing; many of these visionaries are feverishly working to keep pace with exploding interest in their enterprises and projects. If we could support them, fund them, buy from them, visit them, get to know them, lobby on their behalf, work for policies that help them, talk about them, replicate them, and, most important, eat the good food they provide, we will be on track to building a better food system. We must start by engaging a vision of our farms, kitchens, and communities as diverse and flexible institutions that can make room for a whole range of enterprises—humble and grand, traditional and experimental—as long as everybody, particularly the powerful corporations, vows to play fair. Even-handed government regulation will be essential. The problems with our food system, after all, are more about fairness and democracy than they are about food.

Standing in his shop next to a table displaying bags of *de arbol* chiles like red witchy fingers, "mouse ear" oregano cultivated in

Mexico for centuries, and smooth, mottled beans like river pebbles, Steve expressed it best. "We tend to be all or nothing," he said. "We only want horrible hybrids or we only want heirlooms." He looked at me with his habitual smile. "In fact, there's room for everything."

ACKNOWLEDGMENTS

I owe a debt of gratitude to my friend Caroline Walker, who first saw promise in my idea, and to Adam Korn, my former agent at DeFiore and Company, whose faith in me and steadfast support through the proposal process made this book a reality. Thanks to Nichole Argyres, my editor at St. Martin's Press, who understood that revolutions happen, to Laura Chasen, her indispensable editorial assistant, and to Adam Schear, my new agent at DeFiore, who worked so tirelessly to support me. I offer my sincere appreciation to all those who appear in these pages for giving me their time, attention, and expertise, and I am also grateful to a variety of other individuals and organizations that I did not write about but that generously shared their knowledge, perspectives, and connections with me. That includes most especially my great advocate Jennifer Buffett, along with a host of others: Pamela McVeagh-Lally; Tim Crosby; the Sustainable Agriculture & Food Systems Funders; Lisa Chen of Urban Sprouts; Pat Hardage of Foothills Connect Business and Technology Center; Rich Pirog of the Leopold Center for Sustainable Agriculture; Marianne Ali of DC Central Kitchen; Jason Ingle of Greener Partners and the staff of Hillside Farm at Elwyn;

Michelle Long and Michael Shuman of Business Alliance for Local Living Economies (BALLE); Bob Dandrew; John Bloom; Anthony Flaccavento; Michael Roberts of First Nations Development Institute; Jerusha Klemperer of Slow Food USA; Destin Joy Lane, Regina Weiss, and Scott Cullen of GRACE; Steph Larsen and Wyatt Fraas of the Center for Rural Affairs; Paul Lightfoot of Better Food Solutions; and Sarah Nelson of Pacific Coast Farmers' Market Association. My heartfelt gratitude to friends who offered vital advice, perspective, and lodging throughout my publishing journey: Lauren Groff, Cathleen Sullivan, Beth and Kevin Rodin, Emily Greene, Lori Guerra, Deirdre McCarthy, Leslie Corless, David Owen, and Leo Francis. Finally, I am thankful for the moral support and encouragement of my family and my wonderful husband, Aaron, who always knew I could do it.

BIBLIOGRAPHY

Introduction

Miguel A. Altieri, "Modern Agriculture: Ecological Impacts and the Possibilities for Truly Sustainable Farming," Agroecology in Action website, University of California, Berkeley. Accessed August 24, 2011 at http://nature.berkeley.edu/~agroeco3/modern _agriculture.html

U.S. Environmental Protection Agency, "Major Crops Grown in the United States," last updated September 10, 2009. Accessed August 24, 2011 at http://www.epa.gov/agriculture/ag101/cropmajor.html

Convention on Biological Diversity, "What's the Problem?" Accessed September 29, 2011 at http://www.cbd.int/agro/whatsthep roblem.shtml

International Development Research Center, "Facts and Figures on Food and Biodiversity." Accessed September 29, 2011 at http://www.idrc.ca/en/ev-31631-201-1-DO_TOPIC.html

David Pimentel and Marcia Pimentel, *Food, Energy, and Society* (Boca Raton, FL: Taylor and Francis Group, 2008), 99.

Food and Agriculture Organization of the United Nations, Office of Director-General, "Harvesting Nature's Diversity: Crop Plants and Their Relatives," 1993. Accessed September 29, 2011 at http://www.fao.org/DOCREP/004/V1430E/V1430E04.htm#ch3.1

Food and Agriculture Organization of the United Nations, "Human Nature: Agricultural Biodiversity and Farm-based Food Security," by Hope Shand, Rural Advancement Foundation International, December 1997. Accessed September 29, 2011 at http://www.fao.org/sd/EPdirect/EPre0040.htm

U.S. Department of Agriculture, Economic Research Service, "The 20th Century Transformation of U.S. Agriculture and Farm Policy," by Carolyn Dimitri, Anne Effland, and Neilson Conklin, *Electronic Information Bulletin,* no. 3 (June 2005). Accessed September 29, 2011 at http://www.ers.usda.gov/publications/EIB3/EIB3.htm

Gretchen Metz, "Study: Farm Resources Slipping Away from Area," *The Times Herald,* April 6, 2010. Accessed September 29, 2011 at http://www.timesherald.com/articles/2010/04/06/business/doc4bba9df3d0a3d156961066.txt

U.S. Environmental Protection Agency, Ag Center, "Ag 101: Demographics," last updated September 10, 2009. Accessed September 29, 2011 at http://www.epa.gov/agriculture/ag101/demogrphics.html

U.S. Department of Agriculture, *2007 Census of Agriculture,* 2009.

Accessed September 29, 2011 at http://www.agcensus.usda.gov/ Publications/2007/Full_Report/index.asp

Pesticide Action Network North America, "What's on My Food?" Accessed September 29, 2011 at http://www.whatsonmyfood.org/ howmuch.jsp#1

Edie Lau, "Grocery Quandary: For U.S. Shoppers, a Lack of La- bels Limits Choice on Biotech Products," *The Sacramento Bee,* June 10, 2004. Accessed September 29, 2011 at http://www.sacbee .com/static/live/news/projects/biotech/c5_1.html

The Organic Center, Critical Issue Report, "Impacts of Genetically Engineered Crops on Pesticide Use in the United States: The First Thirteen Years," by Charles Benbrook, November 2009. Accessed September 29, 2011 at http://www.organic-center.org/reportfiles/ 13Years20091126_FullReport.pdf

U.S. Department of Agriculture, Food Safety and Inspection Ser- vice (FSIS), FSIS Recalls, Recall Case Archive 2009, last modified April 27, 2011. Accessed September 29, 2011 at http://www.fsis .uda.gov/fsis_recalls/Recall_Case_Archive_2009/index.asp

Shelley A. Hearne, "Save Lives, Save Animals by Saving Antibiot- ics," *The Huffington Post,* March 23, 2010. Accessed September 29, 2011 at http://www.huffingtonpost.com/shelley-a-hearne/save -lives-save-animals-b_b_508847.html

U.S. Department of Agriculture, Economic Research Service, "Antimicrobial Drug Use and Veterinary Costs in U.S. Livestock

Production," by Kenneth H. Mathews, Jr., *Electronic Agriculture Information Bulletin,* no. (AIB766), May 2001. Accessed September 29, 2011 at http://www.ers.usda.gov/publications/aib766/

Food and Agriculture Organization of the United Nations, Agriculture and Consumer Protection, "Livestock's Long Shadow," 2006. Accessed September 29, 2011 at http://www.fao.org/docrep/010/a0701e/a0701e00.HTM

Centers for Disease Control and Prevention, "U.S. Obesity Trends," last updated July 21, 2011. Accessed September 29, 2011 at http://www.cdc.gov/obestiy/data/trends.html

Chapter 1: School Bus Farm Market

Jane Black, "What's in a Number? How the Press Got the Idea That Food Travels 1,500 Miles from Farm to Plate," *Slate,* September 17, 2008. Accessed September 29, 2011 at http://www.slate.com/id/2200202/

U.S. Food and Drug Administration (FDA), "NY Gourmet Salads Inc. Recalls Chick Pea Salad Because of Possible Health Risk," last updated April 22, 2010. Accessed September 29, 2011 at http://www.fda.gov/Safety/Recalls/ucm207340.htm

U.S. Food and Drug Administration, "My-A & Co. Recalls Ground Black Pepper Double Golden Fish 3.5 oz Jars Due to Salmonella Contamination," last updated April 22, 2010. Accessed September 29, 2011 at http://www.fda.gov/Safety/Recalls/ucm208587.htm

U.S. Food and Drug Administration, "Freshway Foods Voluntarily Recalls Products Containing Romaine Lettuce Because of Possible Health Risk," last updated May 6, 2010. Accessed September 29, 2011 at http://www.fda.gov/Safety/Recalls/ucm211131.htm

U.S. Food and Drug Administration, "Caldwell Fresh Foods Recalls Alfalfa Sprouts Because of Possible Health Risks," last updated May 26, 2010. Accessed September 29, 2011 at http://www.fda.gov/Safety/Recalls/ucm213119.htm

U.S. Food and Drug Administration, "Portland Shellfish Company Recalls Cooked, Frozen Claw Island Brand, Craig's All Natural Brand and Inland Ocean Brand Lobster Claw and Knuckle Meat Because of Possible Health Risk," last updated June 16, 2010. Accessed September 29, 2011 at http://www.fda.gov/Safety/Recalls/ucm215524.htm

U.S. Food and Drug Administration, "Lancaster Foods, LLC Voluntarily Recalls Fresh Spinach with Best Enjoyed By Dates of June 19 to June 27, 2010 Due to Possible Health Risk," last updated June 24, 2010. Accessed September 29, 2011 at http://www.fda.gov/Safety/Recalls/ucm217207.htm

U.S. Food and Drug Administration, "Feline's Pride Issues Nationwide Recall of Its Natural Chicken Formula Cat Food Due to Salmonella Contamination," last updated July 1, 2010. Accessed September 29, 2011 at http://www.fda.gov/Safety/Recalls/ucm217826.htm

Chapter 5: Advocating for Agriculture

U.S. Environmental Protection Agency, Ag Center, "Ag 101: Demographics," last updated September 22, 2011. Accessed September 29, 2011 at http://www.epa.gov/agriculture/ag101/demographics.html

U.S. Department of Agriculture, National Institute of Food and Agriculture, "Beginning Farmer and Rancher Development Program." Accessed September 29, 2011 at http://www.csrees.usda.gov/fo/beginningfarmerandrancher.cfm

U.S. Department of Agriculture, *2007 Census of Agriculture,* 2009. Accessed September 29, 2011 at http://www.agcensus.usda.gov/Publications/2007/Full_Report/index.asp

U.S. Department of Agriculture, Economic Research Service, "Structure and Finances of U.S. Farms: Family Farm Report, 2007 Edition," by Robert A. Hoppe, Penni Korb, Erik J. O'Donoghue, and David E. Banker, *Economic Information Bulletin,* no. (EIB-24), June 2007. Accessed September 29, 2011 at http://www.ers.usda.gov/Publications/EIB24/

National Gardening Association, "The Impact of Home and Community Gardening in America," 2009. Accessed September 29, 2011 at http://www.gardenresearch.com/files/2009-Impact-of-Gardening-in-America-White-Paper.pdf

U.S. Department of Agriculture, "2007 Census of Agriculture: Farmers by Age," fact sheet, 2009. Accessed September 29, 2011 at http://www.agcensus.usda.gov/Publications/2007/Online_Highlights/Fact_Sheets/farmer_age.pdf

The Greenhorns, About website page. Accessed September 29, 2011 at http://www.thegreenhorns.net/about.html

International Farm Transition Network Website. Accessed September 29, 2011 at http://www.farmtransition.org/

Iowa State University Extension Service, "Iowa Farmers Business and Transfer Plans," by Michael Duffy, May 2009. Accessed September 29, 2011 at http://www.extension.iastate.edu/bfc/pubs/IA%20Farm%20Business%20survey%20results.pdf

U.S. Department of Agriculture, "2007 Census of Agriculture: Demographics," fact sheet, 2009. Accessed September 29, 2011 at http://www.agcensus.usda.gov/Publications/2007/Online_High lights/Fact_Sheets/demographics.pdf

Sam Roberts, "In a Generation, Minorities May Be the U.S. Majority," *The New York Times,* August 13, 2008. Accessed September 29, 2011 at http://www.nytimes.com./2008/08/14/washington/14census .html?pagewanted=all

Susan Crowell, "2007 Census of Agriculture: Agriculture's 'Middle' Slipping Away," *Farm and Dairy,* February 9, 2009. Accessed September 29, 2011 at http://www.farmanddairy.com/uncategorized/2007-census-of-agriculture-agricultures-middle-slipping-away/11165.html

Chapter 6: New Farmers in the Dell

Iowa State University Extension, "Farmland Ownership and Tenure in Iowa 2007," by Michael Duffy and Darnell Smith, November

2008. Accessed September 29, 2011 at http://www.extension.iastate
.edu/Publications/PM1983.pdf

Mark Clayton, "Women Lead a Farming Revolution in Iowa," *The Christian Science Monitor,* February 25, 2009. Accessed September 29, 2011 at http://www.csmonitor.com/Environment/Living-Green/2009/0225/women-lead-a-farming-revolution-in-iowa

Mike Duffy, "Farmland Ownership," *Ag Decision Maker* 13, no. 2 (December 2008). Accessed September 29, 2011 at http://www.extension.iastate.edu/agdm/newsletters/nl2008/nldec08.pdf

Untied Nations, Women, "Facts & Figures on Gender & Climate Change: Agriculture & Food Insecurity." Accessed September 29, 2011 at http://www.unifem.org/partnerships/climate_change/facts_figures.php

Marshall County Iowa, Official General Election Results November 7, 2006. Accessed September 29, 2011 at http://www.co.marshall.ia.us/departments/auditor/election/archivedresults/election-news/u/

Chapter 7: Seeds of Learning

Andrea Griffith Cash, "Town Treasures 2011," Chapel Hill magazine blog, October 20, 2011. Accessed November 14, 2011 at http://www.chapelhillmagazine.com/blogs/chapel-hill-magazine-blog/town-treasures-2011

Joe Schwartz, "A Rural Row Over Maple View Farm," *Indy Week,* July 7, 2010. Accessed September 29, 2011 at http://www.indy

week.com/indyweek/a-rural-row-over-maple-view-farm/Content
?oid=1520104

U.S. Department of Agriculture, *2007 Census of Agriculture,*
"Table 6. Income from Farm-Related Sources: 2007 and 2002,"
2009. Accessed September 29, 2011 at http://www.agcensus.usda
.gov/Publications/2007/Full_Report/Volume_1,_Chapter_2_US
_State_Level/st99_2_006_006.pdf

Kerri Macdonald, "On a School Rooftop, Hydroponic Greens for
Little Gardeners," *The New York Times,* November 22, 2010. Accessed September 29, 2011 at http://cityroom.blogs.nytimes.com/
2010/11/22/on-a-school-rooftop-hydroponic-greens-for-little
-gardeners/#more-246271

Chapter 8: Farming Their Futures

University of California Santa Cruz, Public Information Office,
"Graduates of UCSC's Apprenticeship in Ecological Horticulture,"
May 31, 2007. Accessed September 29, 2011 at http://news.ucsc
.edu/2007/05/1330.html

Chapter 9: Cultivating the Urban Jungle

Alameda County Public Health Department, "West Oakland Community Information Book Update," October 2005. Accessed September 29, 2011 at http://www.acphd.org/media/53477/woakland05
.pdf

Brahm Ahmadi, "Learning to Grow Community Leadership: Why
Leaving Is My Greatest Accomplishment," *Grassroots Economic*

Organizing (GEO) Newsletter, II, issue 5 (2010). Accessed September 29, 2011 at http://www.geo.coop/node/431

David Runk, "Detroit Leads the Way in Urban Farming," *The Christian Science Monitor,* April 28, 2010. Accessed August 18, 2011 at http://www.csmonitor.com/The-Culture/Gardening/2010/0428/Detroit-leads-the-way-in-urban-farming

David Whitford, "Can Farming Save Detroit?" *Fortune,* December 29, 2009. Accessed August 18, 2011 at http://money.cnn.com/2009/12/29/news/economy/farming_detroit.fortune/

Hantz Farms, "Michael Score Named President of Hantz Farms L.L.C.," December 15, 2009. Accessed August 18, 2011 at http://www.hantzfarmsdetroit.com/press.html

Chapter 10: To Market, to Market

ScienceDaily, "Lower-Income Neighborhoods Associated with Higher Obesity Rates," February 10, 2008. Accessed September 29, 2011 at http://www.sciencedaily.com/release/2008/02/080207163807.htm

ScienceDaily, "Neighborhood Socioeconomic Status and Diabetes," February 15, 2010. Accessed September 29, 2011 at http://www.sciencedaily.com/releases/2010/02/100209152227.htm

Population Reference Bureau, "For Women in the U.S., Obesity Links to Socioeconomic Status and Poor Diet," by Eric Zuehlke, April 2010. Accessed September 29, 2011 at http://www.prb.org/Articles/2010/usobesity.aspx

Annenberg Public Policy Center, "Farm Bill Funds Distribution," *FactCheck.org,* May 23, 2008. Accessed September 29, 2011 at http://www.factcheck.org/askfactcheck/in_the_farm_bill_how _much_money.html

U.S. Department of Agriculture, Economic Research Service, "Farm Income and Costs: Farms Receiving Government Payments," last updated February 14, 2011. Accessed August 22, 2011 at http://www .ers.usda.gov/briefing/farmincome/govtpaybyfarmtype.htm

Emily Farris, "Kansas City Farming for Cash," *Urban Farm Online,* June 22, 2010. Accessed September 29, 2011 at http://www .urbanfarmonline.com/urban-farm-news/2010/06/22/kansas-city -urban-farming.aspx

Chapter 13: Organic Idyll

Michael Pollan, "The Food Movement, Rising," *The New York Review of Books,* June 10, 2010. Accessed September 29, 2011 at http://www.nybooks.com/articles/archives/2010/jun/10/food -movement-rising/

Elizabeth Rosenthal, "Organic Agriculture May Be Outgrowing Its Ideals," *The New York Times,* December 30, 2011. Accessed January 3, 2012 at http://www.nytimes.com/2011/12/31/science/earth/ questions-about-organic-produce-and-sustainability.html

Gail Feenstra, Chuck Ingels, and David Campbell, "What Is Sustainable Agriculture?" University of California, Sustainable Agriculture Research and Education Program website. Accessed August 24, 2011 at http://www.sarep.ucdavis.edu/concept.htm

Robert Mays and Sune Nordwall, "What Is Anthroposophy?" *Waldorf Answers*. Accessed September 29, 2011 at http://www.waldorf answers.com/Anthroposophy.htm

Geotheanum, "Rudolf Steiner 1861–1925." Accessed September 30, 2011 at http://www.goetheanum.org/rudolfsteiner.html?&L=1

Agroecology Research Group at University of California Santa Cruz, "Case Study: Small-Scale Farming with Enormous Rewards: Biointensive Agroecology on a Community Farm in California, USA," *Agroecology* website. Accessed September 29, 2011 at http://www.agroecology.org/Case%20Studies/biointensive.html

Chapter 14: Farming In and Out of the Box

Leo Horrigan, Robert S. Lawrence, and Polly Walker, "How Sustainable Agriculture Can Address the Environmental and Human Health Harms of Industrial Agriculture," *Environmental Health Perspectives* 110, no. 5 (May 2002).

USDA Economic Research Service, "Fertilizer Consumption and Use—by Year: U.S. Consumption of Nitrogen, Phosphate, and Potash, 1960–2009" and "Fertilizer Prices: Fertilizer Price Indexes, 1960–2010." Accessed August 22, 2011 at http://www.ers.usda .gov/Data/FertilizerUse/

Nancy M. Trautmann, Keith S. Porter, and Robert J. Wagenet, "Nitrogen: The Essential Element," Cornell Cooperative Extension Pesticide Safety Education Program Factsheets. Accessed August 22, 2011 at http://psep.cce.cornell.edu/facts-slides-self/facts/nit-el-grw89.aspx

Environmental Protection Agency, "2006–2007 Pesticide Market Estimates: Usage—Section 3.1: 3.1 World and U.S. Pesticide Amount Used," last updated on March 29, 2011. Accessed August 22, 2011 at http://www.epa.gov/opp00001/pestsales/07pestsales/usage2007.htm#3_1

Population Reference Bureau, "World Population Growth, 1950–2050." Accessed September 29, 2011 at http://www.prb.org/Educators/TeachersGuides/HumanPopulation/PopulationGrowth.aspx

Union of Concerned Scientists, "Genetic Engineering Has Failed to Significantly Boost U.S. Crop Yields Despite Biotech Industry Claims," April 14, 2009. Accessed September 29, 2011 at http://www.ucsusa.org/news/press_release/ge-fails-to-increase-yields-0219.html

Gar Lipow, "Feeding the World Sustainably," *Grist,* April 24, 2007. Accessed September 29, 2011 at http://www.grist.org/article/feeding-the-world-sustainably/

Worldwatch Institute, "Worldwatch Institute's State of the World 2011 Shows Agriculture Innovation Is Key to Reducing Poverty, Stabilizing Climate," 2011. Accessed September 29, 2011 at http://www.worldwatch.org/sow11/press-release

The Economist, "Does It Really Stack Up?" December 9, 2010. Accessed October 24, 2011 at http://www.economist.com/node/17647627 (including embedded video)

BrightFarms Website, "Gotham Greens Putting Roots on the Roof to Better Serve Restaurants and Retailers," July 15, 2011. Accessed Oct 24, 2011 at http://blog.brightfarms.com/GothamGreensputtin grootsontherooftobetterserverestaurantsandretailers

The Economist multimedia blog, "The Father of Vertical Farming: Toward the one-minute meal" video. Accessed November 9, 2011 at http://www.economist.com/blogs/multimedia/2010/12/father _vertical_farming

Susan S. Lang, " 'Slow, Insidious' Soil Erosion Threatens Human Health and Welfare as Well as the Environment, Cornell Study Asserts," *Cornell University Chronicle Online,* March 20, 2006. Accessed September 29, 2011 at http://www.news.cornell.edu/ stories/march06/soil.erosion.threat.ssl.html

Environmental Protection Agency, "Basic Information about Food Waste," last updated on July 26, 2011. Accessed August 30, 2011 at http://www.epa.gov/osw/conserve/materials/organics/food/fd -basic.htm

J. Craig Jenkins and Stephen J. Scanlan, "Food Security in Less Developed Countries, 1970–1990," *American Sociological Review* 66 (2001): 718–44.

Ann Crittenden, "World Hunger Is Exacting High Human Toll," *The New York Times,* August 17, 1981. Accessed August 30, 2011 at http://www.nytimes.com/1981/08/17/us/world-hunger-is-exact ing-high-human-toll.html

Chapter 15: Surf & Turf

Mary Hendrickson and William Heffernan, "Concentration of Agricultural Markets," University of Missouri Extension Food Circles Networking Project, April 2007. Accessed September 29, 2011 at www.foodcircles.missouri.edu/07contable.pdf

Chapter 16: Going Native

National Swine Registry, "NSR Breeds." Accessed September 29, 2011 at http://www.nationalswine.com/Home_pages/NSR_Breeds.html

Andrew Wood, "Plant Diversity: The Key to Life on Earth," *The Guardian,* October 28, 2010. Accessed September 29, 2011 at http://www.guardian.co.uk/commentisfree/2010/oct/18/plant-diversity-needs-protecting

City of Tucson Government Website, "Rain Water Harvesting." Accessed September 29, 2011 at http://cms3.tucsonaz.gov/water/harvesting

City of Tucson, "Water Harvesting Guidance Manual," October 2005, Ordinance Number 10210. Accessed August 30, 2011 at http://www.dot.tucsonaz.gov/stormwater/downloads/2006WaterHarvesting.pdf

City of Tucson, "Development Standard No. 10-03.0: Commercial Rainwater Harvesting," June 2, 1010. Accessed August 30, 2011 at http://cms3.tucsonaz.gov/files/dsd/DS_10-03_Commerical_Water_Harvesting_04-27-09.pdf

Arthur H. Rotstein, "Tucson Rainwater Harvesting Law Drawing Interest," *Arizona Daily Sun,* July 5, 2009. Accessed August 30, 2011 at http://azdailysun.com/news/article_falc307a-4148-5852-93d5-f7cbe29a0a6e.html

State of Arizona Department of Revenue, "Water Conservation Systems (Individual Income Tax Credit) and Plumbing Stub Outs (Corporate Income Tax Credit)." Accessed August 30, 2011 at http://www.azdor.gov/TaxCredits/WaterConservationSystems.aspx

GRAIN, "EU Seed Laws (Official Consultation)," May 19, 2011. Accessed September 30, 2011 at http://www.grain.org/bulletin_board/entries/4235-eu-seed-laws-official-consultation

Guy Kastler, "Seed Laws in Europe: Locking Farmers Out," *Grain Seedling,* July 22, 2005. Accessed August 22, 2011 at http://www.grain.org/article/entries/541-seed-laws-in-europe-locking-farmers-out

European Commission Common Catalogs—Legislation Webpage, last updated October 10, 2009. Accessed August 22, 2011 at http://ec.europa.eu/food/plant/propagation/catalogues/catalogues_leg_en.htm

European Commission, "Council Directive 2002/55/EC of 13 June 2002 on the Marketing of Vegetable Seed," *Official Journal of the European Union L 193* (July 20, 2002). Accessed August 22, 2011 at http://eur-lex.europa.eu/LexUriServ/LexUriServ.do?uri=CELEX:32002L0055:EN:HTML

European Commission, "Commission Directive 2008/62/EC of 20 June 2008 Providing for Certain Derogations for Acceptance of Agricultural Landraces and Varieties Which Are Naturally Adapted to the Local and Regional Conditions and Threatened by Genetic Erosion and for Marketing of Seed and Seed Potatoes of Those Landraces and Varieties," *Official Journal of the European Union L 162* (June 21, 2008). Accessed August 22, 2011 at http://eur-lex .europa.eu/LexUriServ/LexUriServ.do?uri=OJ:L:2008:162:0013: 01:EN:HTML

FIAN, "FIAN Calls for Seed Trade Regulations to Respect Right to Food," April 15, 2011. Accessed August 22, 2011 at http://www .fian.org/news/press-releases/respect-right-to-food-regulate-seed -trade

DISCUSSION QUESTIONS

1. Which person or enterprise discussed in the book did you find most interesting or exciting? Why?

2. Did reading this book change your thoughts about what a more sustainable food system might look like? In what way? What similar enterprises or efforts, if any, are at work in your own community?

3. What do you think are the greatest challenges we face in improving our food system? What challenges do we face in improving what and how we eat?

4. Katherine Gustafson writes that Cheetos are an "irredeemable love" for her. How did the food traditions (or lack of traditions) you grew up with influence your own approach to food?

5. What inspiring food-oriented projects could you create or contribute to in your own community? This could be anything from volunteering at the soup kitchen to planting an empty lot to setting up a new farmers' market where there's a need.

6. How do you balance the philosophy behind sustainable food with your budget? What quality is most important to you about your food: local, organic, affordable, sustainable?

7. In what ways did *Change Comes to Dinner* help you feel hopeful or discouraged about the quality of the American food system?